A JOHN CATT PUBLICATION

Global Perspectives in Positive Education

D1715931

Edited by Rob Stokoe

First Published 2018

by John Catt Educational Ltd,
12 Deben Mill Business Centre, Old Maltings Approach,
Melton, Woodbridge IP12 1BL

Tel: +44 (0) 1394 389850 Fax: +44 (0) 1394 386893
Email: enquiries@johncatt.com
Website: www.johncatt.com

ISBN: 978 1 911382 78 2

Set and designed by John Catt Educational Limited

About the Contributors

Adrian Bethune is a teacher and Healthy Body & Mind Leader at a primary school in Hertfordshire. He was awarded a 'Happy Hero' medal by Lord Richard Layard at the House of Lords in 2012 for his work on developing wellbeing in schools. He has worked closely with the charity Action for Happiness on their 'Wellbeing in Schools' program. In 2015 he was invited to speak at their event on stage with the Dalai Lama. Adrian is author of *Wellbeing in The Primary Classroom: A practical guide to teaching happiness* and founder of www.teachappy.co.uk Twitter: @AdrianBethune

Roy Blatchford CBE is founder of www.blinks.education, working with schools, colleges and universities in the UK and internationally. He has spent the past two years implementing education system reform in the Middle East. Roy was also Founding Director (2006-2016) of the National Education Trust, an independent foundation that leads excellent practice and innovation in education. Previously he served as one of Her Majesty's Inspectors of Schools (HMI) in England, with national responsibilities for school improvement and for the inspection of outstanding schools. He has extensive experience of writing inspection frameworks, nationally and internationally, and has reviewed over 1000 schools and colleges in Europe, USA, Middle East and India. He is the author and editor of over 150 books, including *Sparkling Classrooms, The Restless School* and *Success is a Journey*.

Emma Burns, Andrew Martin and Rebecca Collie are members of the Educational Psychology Research Group in the School of Education at the University of New South Wales, Australia. Emma is a postdoctoral research officer in educational psychology whose research focuses on student motivational attitudes and self-beliefs, self-regulation, goal setting, engagement, and growth approaches to education. Andrew is Scientia Professor, Professor of Educational Psychology, and Co-Chair of the Educational Psychology Research Group specializing in motivation, engagement, achievement, and quantitative research methods. Rebecca is a Scientia Fellow and senior lecturer in educational psychology whose research focuses on motivation and wellbeing among students and teachers.

Amba Brown is an Australian positive psychology author, and the creator of the *Finding Your Path* books, a happiness series to support and inspire youth through their major life transitions: starting school, starting high school and finishing school. Her work has been featured in Readers Digest, ABC National Radio, The Huff Post, and The Positive Psychology Blog, to name a few. She has also delivered her message on the TEDx Stage. Amba holds a psychological science degree with honors, majoring in positive psychology. Originally from Sydney, Amba has also lived in California and now resides in Singapore where she writes and works at the Australian High Commission. Being the eldest of six siblings, Amba is passionate about alleviating youth anxieties. Her goal is to share these positive transitioning tools as far and wide as possible.

Sam Burrows is a New Zealander who currently teaches at Stamford American International School in Singapore where he is the Head of Grade 8, a secondary math teacher and varsity rugby coach. He is currently helping update and improve the Middle School advisory program. Prior to teaching at SAIS, he was the inaugural Positive Education Coordinator at Avondale Grammar School in Singapore where he led the school in developing a whole school curriculum map for the implementation of positive education. He has led workshops in Singapore and Australia about the process of creating and implementing the curriculum map across the whole school.

Matthew Easterman is an award-winning teacher from Sydney, Australia, with over 15 years experience working in schools. He holds two Master's degrees: one in history and another in learning science & technology. Matt has experience working with colleagues and students in all Australian school sectors and has engaged with educators, networks and experts from every continent. Matt has a keen interest in the future of teacher professional learning and growth, the future of schools and the ways we can redesign both to build an outstanding learning experience for students, teachers and parents. He has contributed articles and chapters to various publications; he has run dozens of workshops, seminars, and committees on a range of topics in Australia, Asia, the UK, and the USA. He is a founding member of the TeachMeet community in Australia.

Katy Granville-Chapman is a Deputy Head at Wellington College. She has co-founded an international leadership program, Global Social Leaders, focused on developing positive leadership and social action. Katy has also advised 10 Downing Street and the Cabinet Office on leadership and character development. Before Wellington, Katy served in the British Army as a Troop Commander and then trained soldiers and young officers in leadership serving in Iraq, Nepal, USA, and across Europe. Katy is currently reading for a DPhil (PhD, part-time) at Oxford University asking, 'how could school leaders improve the flourishing of teachers?'

Dr. Abdulla Al Karam is the Director General and Chairman of the Board of Directors at KHDA. He is an engineer by trade, a leader by profession, and an educator at heart. He believes a better name for the organization would be the Knowledge and Happiness Development Authority. KHDA is the regulatory authority responsible for the growth and direction of private education in Dubai, which includes nearly 300,000 students in 194 schools, 26 branch campuses of international universities, and hundreds of training institutes. Since he helped to establish KHDA in 2007, private education in Dubai – including early learning centers, schools, universities and training institutes – has not only improved, but thrived. Through the lens of happiness and positivity,

Dr. Al Karam has applied a strengths-based and collaboration-driven strategy to Dubai's private schools sector. 'Our role as a government regulator is to bring out the best from within community and focus on what's working,' he says. 'We all have something to contribute to education, and the more we give, the happier we are.'

Professor of Pedagogy **Leonid Ilyushin** and Doctor in Educational Psychology **Anastasia Azbel** both work in St. Petersburg State University, Russia. Being initially qualified as school teachers they have developed their joint research ideas in the field of new values and meanings for effective, positive dialogue within the flow of school education. They do a lot consultancy for schools aimed to help them in establishing and introduction classroom practices, such as informal assessment, heuristic approach in extra-curriculum activities, school-walls design, etc. Their critical thinking style, together with openness in articulating ideas and working-out projects, help them to work successfully with adolescents, teachers and school administrators.

Virginia Millar is a lifelong learner and educator. She is a veteran teacher of special education in Atlantic City, New Jersey. Inspired by her many students who thrive in the midst of seemingly overwhelming challenges, Virginia embraces the science of positive education as the means to elevate and empower human strengths in all learners. She graduated from MAPP in 2008 and since then has incorporated the lessons and interventions of positive psychology into both her 8th grade curriculum and after-school Girl Power Club, for which she designed the curriculum. She is currently measuring the club's impact on students' self-reported wellbeing and correlations with growth on standardized test scores toward strengthening the case for wellbeing as an explicit goal in public schools. Virginia has stayed connected with the MAPP program as an assistant instructor for the past six years. She is also a global representative for IPEN and recently instructed in a US pioneering school district-wide training at the Shawnee Institute.

Ian Morris is Head of Wellbeing at Wellington College, UK. Ian has taught in independent and state schools since 2000. Originally trained as a philosophy and religion teacher, Ian began the teaching of wellbeing at

Wellington in September 2006. Since then, Ian has written two editions of Learning to Ride Elephants and was a contributing author to *Teaching Character in the Primary Classroom.*

Rob Stokoe OBE is Director of the Al-Futtaim Education Foundation, having recently led Avondale Grammar School in Singapore following 16 years as Director of JESS, Dubai. With 30 years leadership experience, including primary, secondary and a five-year spell with the University of Sunderland, it's fair to say that his career has been varied. He is passionate about great learning and views positive education as an essential ingredient for effective learning and future schools.

Rob is still listening, learning, sharing, and continually striving to stimulate debate and growth for the most valuable of professions. He continues to value the privilege of working with and alongside many gifted and dedicated educationalists that continue to inspire him.

Dr. Helen Street founded the Positive Schools movement in 2008 with Neil Porter. Helen is viewed as a visionary leader in the support of youth wellbeing, motivation, and engagement in learning. The incredible success of Positive Schools is a satisfying reflection of her passion to establish a more supportive and equitable approach to education across the developed world.

Helen is an education consultant with a background in social psychology and mental health. When not at the helm of Positive Schools, she presents her research and ideas in schools, colleges, and at educational events on a global stage. Helen is an honorary fellow at The University of Western Australia and a research consultant for the WA Healthy Department's Centre for Clinical Interventions. She also writes regularly for educational magazines and has authored three books on mental health and wellbeing, in addition to many academic chapters and papers.

Mick Walsh has been a leading and innovative positive education author, educator and speaker across Australasia and internationally for many years. As a highly experienced former college leader and an avid researcher of positive psychology, he created and authored the evidence-based Learning Curve Positive Education and Wellbeing program used in numerous schools worldwide. Many schools are keen to introduce positive education but have little practical knowledge of how to do it. Mick knows schools and understands how to effectively coach them on how to implement a robust Positive Education and Wellbeing program.

Yukun Zhao is a PhD candidate of social psychology at Tsinghua University, focusing in positive psychology. His main research interests are positive education, big data and wellbeing, self-determination. He also serves as the Administrative Director of the Positive Psychology Research Center at Tsinghua University, China. In this role, he organizes events like China International Positive Psychology Conferences and Chinese delegations to the International Positive Psychology Association (IPPA) World Congresses. He develops programs like Positive Education curriculum and Positive Enterprise solutions and disseminates positive psychology in various sectors and channels. He is IPPA's Special Representative to China, and co-founded Beijing Positive Psychology Association. He received the Master of Applied Positive Psychology degree from University of Pennsylvania in 2010. He also holds Master's degrees in computer science and chemistry from Rutgers University. Yukun has published five books in China and translated two books, including Flourish by Martin Seligman.

Foreword
Rob Stoke OBE

Having had the opportunity to experience positive education in The Middle East, The United Kingdom, Singapore and Australia, working with talented and passionate advocates of positive education from around the world, I conclude that we need to get connected. The purpose of this publication is to embrace and share some of the great things that are happening around the world, to bring the positive education community a little closer together.

Why is positive education so important to us? My thoughts on this are not complicated, nor are they new as well over a century ago John Dewey proposed a philosophy of education addressing the needs of the whole student. Today his words still hold true. He held that the purpose of formal education was not to prepare children for any fixed goal, but rather that schools should be devoted to encouraging children to grow and to prepare them to continue to grow and develop as adults in the uncertain future that they would face. As we come to the end of the second decade of the 21st century these words are surprisingly familiar. Put simply, we need to put the 'whole child' and happiness first, always taking the individuals wellbeing seriously. Good schools have great teachers and offer an exciting curriculum and the students come into contact with lively adults and mature minds. Very good schools add to this an ability to understand learning and grow the learning potential of each and every student as collaborative and independent thinkers. The best schools add in an understanding of the individual, accepting, nurturing and growing robust, self-aware and highly-valued young people. Warm, aware and understanding relations abound, built upon mutual respect and trust. Understand that all students know the educators that truly care for their wellbeing.

Given the uncertainties of today's world, more than ever before, we need to let our young people know that we care for them, and we are committed to helping them to create a brighter future. That, through our meaningful and exciting classrooms, we are intent upon giving flight to thousands of butterflies, each of whom has the potential to create a better future for themselves and us all. One size fits all was never enough because when students are at the center of the education system we are capable of achieving so much more.

Dr. Abdulla Al Karam, who heads the Knowledge and Human Development Authority (KHDA) in Dubai, is a valued colleague and a visionary leader. He states, 'We all have something to contribute to education, and the more we give, the happier we are.' Giving is what great educators do best and I am indebted to all of my co-writers who have contributed so freely and positively to this publication. All of the royalties from this book will go to the International Positive Education Network (IPEN). The IPEN is an organization dedicated to informing a better future for all as they strive to encourage practitioners to educate for character and wellbeing alongside delivering rigorous and stretching academic study based on the best evidence-based research. To give every student the opportunity for a rich intellectual life and rewarding human relationships, a life filled with happiness, purpose and joy.

I hope you enjoy reading this book and what you find is insightful, motivational and, on occasion, inspirational.

Contents

Chapter 1:
Positive Education in the UAE

Dr. Abdullah Al Karam

'What is the purpose of government if it does not work toward the happiness of the people? It's the duty and role of the government to create the right conditions for people to choose to be happy.'[1]

This quote from the UAE's Minister of State for Happiness, Her Excellency Ohood bint Khalfan Al Roumi, encapsulates the drive of the leadership of the United Arab Emirates (UAE) towards broader goals than simply economic growth and community engagement. Her main responsibility is to harmonise all government plans, programmes and policies to achieve a happier society through the 'National Programme for Happiness and Positivity'. The programme includes the establishment of the Emirates Center for Happiness Research that is designed to conduct specialised scientific studies related to the science of happiness and measuring and assessing happiness indices.[2]

The UAE's National Agenda aims to position the UAE as one of the top five happiest countries in the world by 2021. In the 2017 version of the

1   Simmons, A. (2017): *UAE's minister of happiness insists her job is no laughing matter.* Los Angeles, CA: Los Angeles Times. Available at: www.latimes.com/world/middleeast/la-fg-global-uae-happiness-2017-story.html
2   UAE Ministry of Cabinet Affairs and the Future. (2017): Happiness Research Institute to be set up soon. Abu Dhabi, UAE: Ministry of Cabinet Affairs and the Future. Available at: www. mocaf.gov.ae/en/media/news/happiness-research-institute-to-be-set-up-soon (Accessed: 2 October 2017)

World Happiness Report, which ranks 155 countries by their happiness levels, the UAE ranked 21st in the world and was the happiest country in the Arab region.[3] By encouraging the wellbeing of students at schools and helping children develop positive character attributes, parents will feel more at ease and happier in the knowledge that their children are being well cared for. Positive education in schools throughout the UAE will play a critical role in helping to improve the nation's happiness.

As Dubai's regulator of private schools in Dubai, the Knowledge and Human Development Authority (KHDA) oversees the growth of quality education for more than 90% of Dubai's school students. The World Bank in its 2014 report 'The Road Traveled' identified that KHDA has used a mixture of accountability through information and incentives to engender growth in the quality of schools in Dubai.[4] 'The KHDA approach is entirely transparent, openly accountable, and has strong stakeholder participation – all hallmarks of good governance.'[5] Through increasing the supply of schools, competition for school places is viewed as a driving force for change.

The World Bank report also noted the development of collaboration in Dubai, both within schools through teacher peer review and between schools. Inter-school collaboration has been fostered by the What Works Dubai series of workshops over the past five years. These events, based on the Appreciative Inquiry approach of focusing on identifying and doing more of what is working, have had almost 20,000 attendees at about 700 workshops.[6] KHDA provides the platform for the events that are run by teachers, for teachers, to promote collaboration and sharing of best practices in Dubai. The strengths-based collaborative approach of What Works Dubai has further helped to redirect the focus of KHDA and the schools beyond academic progress to also highlight the development of character strengths and wellbeing of students. The value

3   Helliwell, J., Layard, R. & Sachs, J. (2017): *World Happiness Report 2017.* New York, NY: Sustainable Development Solutions Network.
4   Cuadra, P. & Thacker, S. (2014): *The road travelled: Dubai's journey towards improving private education – a World Bank review.* MENA development report. Washington, DC: World Bank Group.
5   Ibid, page 49
6   Cooperrider, D. & Srivastva, S. (2008): Appreciative Inquiry in Organizational Life. *Research in Organizational Change and Development,* 1, pp. 129-169.

of positivity – of concentrating on what's working – has strengthened the working practices of educators across Dubai and the learning outcomes of students. What Works Dubai has created a compassionate ecosystem of schools, teachers, parents and students that recognises and values the role each plays in improving education in Dubai.

KHDA has developed a number of projects to support student happiness and positive education. One of the first initiatives was the collaboration with WestEd in 2015 and 2016 to initiate the School of Hearts and Minds survey, a tailored version of the California Healthy Kids Survey. This survey for late primary and middle years students was an opt-in survey for schools to assess student wellbeing. With the wellbeing questions that formed part of existing surveys for parents, teachers and older students, a comprehensive overview of the extent of satisfaction with schools was obtained. In total, 69,000 survey responses were received from 98 schools with 96% of parents commenting that their child enjoys school and 95% of teachers stating that they enjoy working at their school.[7]

Expanding on the success of this survey, the KHDA commenced a long-term partnership with the Government of South Australia's Department of Education and Childhood Development to further develop the assessment and analysis of student wellbeing in all private schools in Dubai. The Dubai Student Wellbeing Census commenced in November 2017 and covered all children in Grades 6 to 9 at private schools in Dubai – about 70,000 students altogether. The results of the census aims to help schools understand how their students feel and think about their own wellbeing, happiness and quality of life. Every Dubai private school received a report that enabled the community – as policy-makers and educators – to put together more targeted, evidence-driven policies to improve student wellbeing and facilitate schools to act to further improve student wellbeing. Future plans include the analysis of teacher wellbeing and correlating that with the wellbeing of students, as well as providing schools with an interactive website to conduct further analysis of their students' responses.

---

7   KHDA. (2017): *Nurturing Hearts and Minds: The Happiness Journey of Dubai's Private Schools.* Available at: www.khda.gov.ae/en/publications/article?id=10230 (Accessed: 3 October 2017).

While surveys provide an understanding of the wellbeing of students at schools, teachers and administrators at schools require resources and support to develop activities to promote student wellbeing. To assist, a 'memorandum of friendship' was signed in February 2017 between KHDA and the International Positive Education Network (IPEN) to establish IPEN's first regional branch. The IPEN representatives based in Dubai work to expand and support its local and regional members in addition to helping raise awareness of the benefits of positive education throughout the Middle East region. The UAE has the largest number of members registered on the IPEN network, with just over 100 UAE-based educators registered and sharing content online.

One specific example is of a new Dubai private school that has established itself on the tenants of positive education. Every single teacher at the school received rigorous training in positive education. A wellbeing department was established with three counselors in addition to an in-house positive education team. Explicit positive education classes are taught as part of the school curriculum and parents are invited to attend regular positive education sessions. Their KHDA inspection results reported that: 'across the school students have positive attitudes. They are responding well to the Growth Mindset initiative, which is allowing them to develop their confidence, resilience and self-reliance.'

Many other Dubai's private schools already have well-developed programs in place to support student wellbeing. These programs fit across the Institute of Positive Education model (learn it, live it, teach it, embed) that brings positive education to life in school and places wellbeing at the heart of education.[8]

Learn it

Several workshops by members of IPEN, such as the Institute of Positive Education in Australia and Action for Happiness in the UK, have been delivered for parents and schools in Dubai to outline the benefits of

---

8   Hoare, E., Bott, D., Robinson, J. (2017): *Learn it, Live it, Teach it, Embed it: implementing a whole school approach to foster positive mental health and wellbeing through Positive Education*. Manuscript submitted for publication. Available at: www.ggs.vic.edu.au/Institute/About-Us/Our-Model

positive education, as well as intensive positive education training to over 500 teachers. Dubai has also seen a significant increase in the number of training institutes setting up to deliver positive education content.

Live it

Schools have introduced deliberate and personal cultural practices to improve student and staff wellbeing. For example, one school has developed a mindfulness and wellbeing room to help students mentally and emotionally by focusing on positivity. The room has smart tablets loaded with guided meditation routines, a gratitude tree for students to display what they are thankful for, a sensory room with a range of stimuli and a positive affirmation room. Over 30% of private schools now have urban gardens that promote positive relationships towards vegetables and healthy food. Some schools have started making their own compost and using the produce in the canteen or for dedicated cooking activities linked to the curriculum, inspired by Stephen Ritz at the Green Bronx Machine[9] and the Ground Up Initiative.[10] Finally, the #100DaysOfPositivity initiative, designed by the National Programme for Happiness and Positivity in collaboration with KHDA encouraged schools to do something positive every day for 100 days and share it on Twitter and Instagram.

Teach it

Several schools where positive education is taught explicitly throughout the school and have appointed non-teaching Heads of Positive Education in Primary and Secondary fully devoted to developing the curriculum and supporting student and teacher wellbeing. Approximately 30% of Dubai private schools now have allocated full time staff to focus on student and teacher wellbeing.

Embed

A Mindfulness Collective convenes at least 15 schools on a regular basis to collaborate and share existing programs in schools, collect evidence

---

9   Ritz, S. (2017): *The Power of a Plant: A Teacher's Odyssey to Grow Healthy Minds and Schools.* Emmaus, PA: Rodale Books, Inc.

10   www.groundupinitiative.org/#/ms-3433/1

to demonstrate best practice, and provide support for schools that would like to implement mindfulness programs in the future. A number of Dubai schools have incorporated mindfulness sessions within the school curriculum and have changed student discipline policies to ones based on empathy and kindness.

At the national level, the government of the UAE launched in September 2017 a pilot in positive education, where teachers and leaders from a sample of ten public schools received positive education training. An 18-month quantitative and qualitative evaluation will measure the impact of the positive education program on student wellbeing and academic outcomes, as well as teachers' perspectives on positive education. Results will be compared with those of students from a control set of ten schools that are not participating in similar wellbeing training. Based on the results, the government may choose to rollout the program to cover all public schools across the UAE. This program is being implemented in partnership with Institute of Positive Education at Geelong Grammar in Australia, United Arab Emirates University, and the University of Melbourne, with support from the UAE's Minister of Happiness.

Furthermore, the UAE has recently launched the UAE Moral Education Program across all government and private schools.[11] This is a mandatory curriculum covering the four pillars of Character and Morality, the Individual and Community, Civic Studies, and Cultural Studies. All curriculum content must be taught from Grades 1-9 by every school and this will impact more than 800,000 students across the UAE. Each school will allocate at least 60 minutes per week to the programme and they can integrate the content into their existing curriculum framework.

Positive education in the UAE is viewed as an important contributor to the overall happiness of the nation. With a large diversity of schools across the public and for-profit sectors and a diversity of nationalities and curricula at these schools, wellbeing initiatives need to be crafted that suit the context of each school community. What has been learnt

---

11   UAE Cabinet. (2017): Crown Prince of Abu Dhabi launches 'Moral Education' to promote tolerance. Available at: www.uaecabinet.ae/en/details/news/crown-prince-of-abu-dhabi-launches-moral-education-to-promote-tolerance (Accessed: 4 October 2017).

is there does not need to be a prescribed central directive in place to implement positive education. A one-size-fits-all approach will not work. Instead, an organic approach that combines wellbeing measurements, school collaboration, national marketing and evidence-based resources will help to harness the motivation of parents, student and educators to embed happiness and wellbeing throughout schools in the UAE. Such a differentiated approach will help to fulfil the remarks made by His Highness Sheikh Mohammed bin Rashid al Maktoum that: 'Yes, we seek to make people happy, and making people happy will be our objective and mission until it becomes a permanent and deep-rooted reality.'[12]

---

12   al Maktoum, M. B. R. (2017): *Reflections on Happiness & Positivity*. Dubai, UAE: Explorer Publishing.

Chapter 2:
Practical Positive Education Strategies and Activities

Mick Walsh

What is positive education?

Over the last decade, there has been an incredible increase in the number of conferences, seminars and books written about positive psychology, leading to the advent of the term 'positive education'. Consider the term for a moment; it is comprised of two words:

Positive: Relating to the relatively new science of positive psychology. Becoming your best possible self to live a life that matters and doing good to feel good.

Education: Relating to what schools' core business is, learning and teaching, developing your growth-orientated mindset and thinking abilities to possess a competent skill set to contribute meaningfully to society.

There has been a real shortfall with this plethora of conferences, seminars and books, which schools have found increasingly mystifying and frustrating. They have been nearly all exclusively focused on the first word of the term, 'positive'. There has been very little time, nor opportunity, given to the second word of the term, 'education'. Schools screaming out for help on how to actually implement it. This is what this chapter is about.

After positive education conferences teachers return to their schools very excited about the inspiring things they heard about. When asked by staff and leadership teams to explain what they propose to do to implement the principles of positive education, how it could be infused into the curriculum and possible timetabling arrangements, the process grinds to a halt; it's too hard to challenge the status quo.

Well let's challenge it right now.

Strategies and activities

There is no silver bullet to building wellbeing. To build student and teacher wellbeing, there are two key pieces of evidence-based research that clearly explain what works:

1. 'It is the frequency of positive emotion, not its intensity that builds wellbeing.' – Barbara Fredrickson

2. 'The greatest effect size in improving students' learning outcomes is self-assessing, self-reporting and setting self-expectations.' – John Hattie

As a consequence of these two pieces of authoritative research, all the following positive education strategies and activities are largely student-driven for them to experience frequent positive emotions and involves them writing down (journaling) their thoughts to connect with themselves and the moment.

Elements of wellbeing

For students and teachers to understand what elements comprise their wellbeing, it is important to have a model that describes them. Then, you can focus on building a different element each week and they will be able to focus their energies and effort on it. There are quite a number of very good evidence-based models of wellbeing for you to choose from. The following are five high quality ones:

PERMA[1]

The elements of wellbeing are:

- Positive emotions – feeling good.
- Engagement – being completely absorbed in activities.
- Relationships – being authentically connected to others
- Meaning – purposeful existence.
- Achievement – a sense of accomplishment and success.

Five Ways to Wellbeing[2]

The elements of wellbeing are to:

- connect,
- be active,
- take notice,
- keep learning,
- and give.

Positive Education[3]

The elements of wellbeing includes:

- positive emotions,
- positive engagement,
- positive accomplishment,
- positive purpose,
- positive relationships,
- and positive health.

1   Seligman, M. E. P. (2011): *Flourish*. Boston, MA: Nicholas Brealey Publishing.
2   Government Office for Science. (2008): *Five ways to mental wellbeing*. London, UK: The Stationery Office.
3   Norrish, J. (2015): *Positive Education: The Geelong Grammar School Journey*. Oxford, UK: Oxford University Press.

UESCO's Foundations of Wellbeing

The elements of wellbeing are:

- Cognitive
- Emotional
- Physical
- Social
- Spiritual

My Model of Wellbeing

The elements of wellbeing in my own model includes:

- strengths and emotions.
- skills and achievement.
- exercise and health.
- positive engagement.
- relationships and optimism.
- meaning and purpose.
- learning and giving.

Activity

Each week one of the equally important elements of wellbeing is explored, with students and teachers journaling two positive things they will start doing to develop that element. Developing this growth-orientated activity as a habit or ritual, progressively builds students' and teachers' state of wellbeing.

Example

For the element positive relationships, individually students should journal acts of kindness they have done for others, or received from others, and the emotions they felt and strengths they used. Extend the activity to students in groups of four, sharing what they wrote in their journals, and each group reporting to the class what they discussed. Finish with students individually journaling two things they will start doing for acts of kindness.

Wellbeing fitness challenges

The purpose of these weekly wellbeing fitness challenges is to build students' and teachers' self-awareness, self-regulation and empathy. Experiencing daily positive emotions doing the challenges each week will build both individual wellbeing and that of those around them (mirror neurons at work).

Thinking of others: Positive vibes – sending someone a text praising or thanking them or asking how they are travelling.

Tell me more: Interested listening – when listening to others, before I speak, I will ask them to tell me more about what they are talking about at least three times.

Others matter: Acts of kindness – looking for at least two opportunities to give of myself to make others' lives better and recognising when others do kind things for me by thanking them.

Feel good menu: Delicious feelings – choosing from my ten best feel good activities to brighten me up.

Move more: Actively active – making a focused effort to be more active at home, at school and in my community by trying different leisure and exercise activities for at least one hour.

Aimless writing: Opening floodgates – writing anything that comes into my head for ten minutes every morning.

Gratitude letter: Being thankful – writing a letter thanking someone from my heart who really helped me and give it to them.

Photo 7: Gratitude pictures – taking a photo on my mobile of something I am grateful for to create an album this week

Looking forward: Positively focused – starting each day by thinking of the three things I am looking forward to most.

Matter videos: Sharing happiness – daily, make a one or two-minute video of something that matters to me and show them to my family and friends.

Thinking spotting: Habits of Mind – being on the lookout for when I, or others, think using a different habit of mind.

Adventure eat: Variety tasting – leaving my comfort zone and doing my body a favour by having a junk food free week and trying new tastes, fruits and vegetables; I might be surprised.

Brain stretch: Improving thinking – improving the way I am thinking by intentionally using Habits of Mind and a variety of thinking tools in my learning to grow my brain's abilities.

Hidden people: Invisible champions – making a list of people who selflessly give of themselves to support me to have a good life and then thanking them.

Bright and light: Being happy – looking for at least two opportunities to lighten up, smile, laugh, have fun to experience positive emotions and feel good brain chemicals.

Emotions spotting: Mindful feelings – being mindful of positive, negative and mixed emotions I feel and notice others feeling and watching for the intensity of emotions rising in myself and others.

What went well: Being grateful – looking for three good things that happened that I am grateful for, why they happened and putting them on a gratitude board on my bedroom wall.

Discovery learning: Being curious – mindfully focusing my attention and energies on discovering one new thing about me, my friends, my family, my school, or my community.

Values living – Standing tall: choosing three 'positive personal descriptors' to live by and showing them in my thinking, words and body language.

Strengths spotting – In the moment: being on the lookout for others and myself using this week's and other character strengths to achieve what they set out to do and learning from them.

Even better – Positive stretching: when reflecting on good things that happened, I will stretch my thinking to describe how they could have been even better.

Forgiveness letter – Saying sorry: writing a letter to someone I have upset saying sorry and asking what I can do to make it right for them and giving it to them.

Courage journal – Brave acts: writing down two things I did that I believe were courageous and why I think so.

Step it up – Moving myself: building up to meeting the daily 10,000 step challenge and journal the number of steps I take each day.

Activity

Each day for a week, students and teachers focus their energies to meet the nominated challenge and journal the good things they did, no matter how small they thought they were.

Example

For the wellbeing fitness challenge, 'looking forward', every morning for a week, while having breakfast, think about and journal the three things you are most looking forward to for the day. Doing this is a fabulous positive primer for students and teachers for the day ahead.

What went well this week and why boards?

WWWWW – in staffrooms and a number of classrooms for each year level, put up WWWWW white boards for staff and students to jot down good things that have happened this week and what they have enjoyed when meeting the wellbeing fitness challenges.[4]

Activities

A. At the end of each week, a staff member takes a photo on their phone of what has been shared on the boards. At the end of term, they compile a student booklet and a staff booklet of the weekly collection of good things that happened at the school and distribute the booklets on the last day of term to staff; it is an amazing morale and wellbeing building exercise. For students, a booklet could be made up for each year level.

---

4   Seligman, M. E. P. (2011): *Flourish*. Boston, MA: Nicholas Brealey Publishing.

B. Every Friday ask students and teachers to journal the three things they thought were really good for the week.

C. Encourage students and teachers to share good things with their families at home each evening.

Example

Good things that happened that students in Year 9 were grateful for this week, included:

- having a young relief teacher who shared what she learned while travelling for a year overseas.
- being on time to every lesson (and so were our teachers).
- the weather stayed lovely every lunchtime so we could play sport and games.
- my mum cooked two of my favourite meals.
- my friends had a fun time at the movies.

Character strengths[5]

Each week one of the 24 Values in Action Institute's Character Strengths is introduced for students and teachers to explore. There are a number of suggested activities, which follow to choose from, to encourage them to use as the lens they look at life through; things are much more positive and hopeful when viewed from positions of strength. The 24 Character Strengths follow in the table below.[6]

Creativity: Being original, novel and innovative in your thoughts, words and actions.	Curiosity: Being interested in exploring and seeking new experiences and things to discover more.	Judgement: Being able to consider other views and willing to change your mind because of the evidence.	Love of learning: Thriving on learning and mastering new skills and concepts in a variety of environments.

5   Seligman, M. E. P. & Peterson, C. (2004): Strengths of Character and Wellbeing. *Journal of Social and Clinical Psychology*. 23(5), pp. 603-619.

6   VIA Institute on Character. (2018): *Character Strengths*. Available at: www.viacharacter.org/www/Character-Strengths

Perspective: Being able to make sense of what's happening to and around you and sharing this with others.	**Bravery:** Speaking up and sticking to what you believe is right, even though it may be unpopular.	**Perseverance:** Following through to complete what you set out to do by overcoming obstacles and setbacks.	**Honesty:** Being genuine, true to yourself and taking responsibility for your thoughts, words and actions.
Zest: Being full of enthusiasm, energy and excitement by living your life as an adventure.	**Love:** Caring for, sharing with and valuing others and those you have close relationships with.	**Kindness:** Doing selfless acts of kindness for others to make their lives better; living by giving.	**Social intelligence:** Being aware of your and others' feelings and motives.
Teamwork: Doing your share to assist the positive working of the group and being loyal to it.	**Fairness:** Treating all people fairly and justly, giving them a chance and being unbiased.	**Leadership:** Valuing and encouraging others to achieve the desired outcome.	**Forgiveness:** Forgiving others for their wrongs, not holding a grudge and accepting them for them.
Humility: Wanting others to accept you for what you achieve and not big noting.	**Prudence:** Making responsible choices to reduce risk and regrettable outcomes.	**Self-regulation:** Being in charge of your emotions and to control your impulses.	**Appreciation of beauty and excellence:** Valuing excellent efforts and beautiful things.
Gratitude: Saying thank you to others who have done acts of kindness for you.	**Hope:** Looking to the future positively, having self-belief and having a course to follow.	**Humour:** Seeing the light and bright side of life, laughing, having fun and smiling with others.	**Spirituality:** Having a higher purpose to make a positive difference to others' lives.

Activities

A. Show the following inspiring eight-minute video clip on Character Strengths to all students and staff to ensure everyone is on the same page with their understanding of strengths. www.youtube.com/watch?v=U3nT2KDAGOc

B. To become a school of strengths, arrange for all staff, both teaching and non-teaching, to complete the free VIA Character Strengths Survey at www.viacharacter.org. Everyone will receive a printout of their individual strengths, which they really enjoy learning more about themselves. An important point to make is that there are no bad strengths, and everyone's personal mix of strengths makes them a star in their own right.

C. Arrange for all classes to complete the youth version of the survey for all students to learn about their individual mix of strengths.

D. Arrange for all students and staff to complete their individual list of top strengths and look at it often to reinforce a strengths-based approach.

E. Each week nominate a Character Strength for students and teachers to search in the media for events where they can see the particular strengths being used.

F. Brainstorm, as a class, people they know who uses this strength well. During the week students and staff can be strengths spotting to journal when they see someone else or themselves using the strength.

G. The shadow side of a strength is when it is underused, overused or misused. For this week's strength, break up the class into three groups to brainstorm what behaviours they could show for each of the shadow sides of the strength. Then share their thoughts with the class.

H. Encourage students and staff to invite their families to do the VIA Character Strengths Survey and as a family, discuss how well they currently combine their strengths to do good things, and how they could use them even better.

I.   Ask students who have this week's strengths as one of their top ones, to discuss together how they use the strength in their everyday life. Then ask them to share what they do with the rest of the class.

J.   Once or twice each week in different subjects, have Character Strengths spotting in class. Students should journal when they see others or themselves using one of the Character Strengths. Building their self-awareness of their own and other strengths will develop their abilities to confidently use their top strengths.

Examples

A.   On class rolls leave a space next to students' names to write in three of their top strengths. Then in class, encourage individual students to use their own strengths; this is a great relationship builder.

B.   Finding examples of what is occurring in the world pertaining to the nominated weekly strength enables students and teachers to see strengths in action. An example follows.

Strength of the week is bravery.

This week we are strength spotting Invictus Games: watch Prince Harry's speech and spot the strengths that he refers to about the Servicemen and women.

- Why were the Invictus Games developed?
- Why is bravery important for our servicemen and women?
- What other strengths would be needed in time of deployment?
- What does bravery look like, feel like and sound like?
- Do you think that these people get nervous and scared? If so what do they do about it to get through?
- Why does the Invictus Games logo highlight the words 'I am'?
- Prince Harry mentions the words resilience, optimism, inspiration and courage, but why?
- When have you been brave and how did that feel?
- What were the strengths that you pulled from to help you?

www.youtube.com/watch?v=5zFoMqsvXvk – Prince Harry's opening speech Invictus Games 2017.

www.youtube.com/watch?v=15aA8VZbVAo – Prince Harry's closing speech 2017.

www.youtube.com/watch?v=pIWH3PoV0hU – Toronto Invictus Games 2017, Brian Williams interviews Prince Harry and Mike Trauner.

   C. Writing a poem or literary piece about Character Strengths is another practical exercise. Following is one June Rousso penned:

WISDOM

Creativity is shaping your thoughts into something that you have never seen or heard before.

It is letting your imagination go and start to soar.

Curiosity is having an open mind and wanting to experience something new every day.

Asking questions to learn more than you do

And in this way, bring the world closer to you.

Judgment is thinking things through

Never rushing in what you set out to do.

Changing your mind when new facts come your way

And truly listening to what others have to say.

Love of Learning is mastering skills and being in the know.

Learning something new wherever you go.

Some from what you read and others from the people you meet.

Always learning, what a treat!

Perspective is using your intelligence and common sense in deciding what to do.

It's not being foolish but taking time to think things through.

Learning not to always ask others for advice.

Believing that our own good judgment can suffice.

COURAGE

Bravery is trying new things and taking risks

Even when you feel afraid and may start to shake.

It's moving forward

Without thinking much about making a mistake.

Perseverance is working hard to complete what we start

And not getting so upset that we fall apart.

It's taking things step-by-step, that's for sure.

In this way, we can always achieve more.

Honesty is being true to ourselves.

Taking responsibility for our actions and not looking to blame,

Not trying to give anyone a bad name.

Nor looking at fibbing and telling tales as just a fun game.

Zest is feeling excited about life as much as you can.

Seeing the sunny side rather than looking for all that is wrong.

Viewing life as a beautiful song.

While there may be some dark clouds along the way,

Always believing that tomorrow is a new day.

HUMANITY

Love is feeling close to people and wanting to show that you care.

Always missing them when they are not there.

Love is not focusing just on you.

Rather than one, you now think about two.

Kindness is going out of our way.

Saying good morning and have a great day.

It's holding a door for a person you don't know.

Cheering someone up when they feel low.

Social intelligence is being aware of what others may think and feel.

And counting these thoughts and feelings as all very real.

It's making decisions taking in another's point of view.

And not just counting the view of you.

JUSTICE

Teamwork is being part of a group and doing your share.

Treating members equally because that's what's fair.

You are not the one who always must stand out.

This is true beyond a doubt.

Fairness is doing what's right for everyone and not just you.

Or for that matter just a select few.

It is trying to make what's wrong right and not just let wrong be.

This is true for you as well as for me.

Leadership is encouraging others to get things done.

Taking charge without taking over, I would say.

Leading them toward a goal.

Helping them find their way.

TEMPERANCE

Forgiveness is giving others a second chance

And not holding a grudge.

It is having an open mind and not one that won't budge.

Forgiveness can sometimes bring people closer than before.

With so many good times in store.

Humility is not seeing yourself as special or better than anyone you know.

It is being who you are

And not putting on a show.

It is not bragging or boasting to make yourself feel good.

It's about being you, just as you should.

Prudence is being careful about what you do and say,

So, when all is done you do not feel sorry in any way.

It's not saying things meant to hurt or tease people you know.

It is being thoughtful wherever you go.

Self-regulation is controlling your actions and learning to wait your turn as much as you can.

It's learning to take a breath and count to ten.

It's not pushing ahead of the line and blurting out what we have to say.

It is practicing self-control every day.

TRANSCENDENCE

Appreciation of beauty and excellence is seeing the world with wonder and awe.

The flowers, trees, rivers, oceans, watching a bird soar.

The silvery moon, the sparkling stars, the snow-capped mountains and much, much more.

Gratitude is being thankful for what we have and who we are.

Taking time to express thanks for everything and everyone, near and far.

It is reminding ourselves of all that we have when we think we have none.

That behind every cloud, there is a golden sun.

Hope is looking to a future that is bright

Where things are not dark as the black of night.

Looking to a guiding star,

Wherever we find ourselves, wherever we are.

Knowing that with hope we can travel so far.

Humor is seeing the funny side of life where others may see none.

It is knowing how to laugh and to have fun.

But, is not making fun of, that's for sure.

Humor helps people not to feel less, but rather to feel more.

Spirituality is looking for meaning in life, things that make everything seem worthwhile.

Reading a good book, gazing up at the stars, chatting with a friend.

Helping people out, writing a story, taking a hike in the woods, the possibilities never end.

Thinking traps

Building self-awareness is about providing frequent opportunities for students and teachers to look at what their perspectives are about situations, and ask themselves, if their views are reasonable or affected by their emotions or previous patterns of thought. These can trap them into thinking only in black or white, jumping to conclusions or looking at situations without objective reasoning.

Adolescence is a time in students' lives in which their minds are a turbulent place, for many reasons, including puberty, rampant hormones and emotional hijacking. Exploring thinking traps is an effective way of moderating these reasons.

No evidence, then true? Because there is no evidence or points against something, then it must be true, e.g. I'll eat more ice cream because no one has proved it's not good for me.

It is deserved? Because a person needs a boost, then something is given to them, e.g. John is struggling at home, so we'll give him an award at school to brighten up his life.

Is it based on fact? An idea is accepted because another view suggests it is true without any supporting evidence, e.g. takeaway food is not good for you, so sushi is not good for you.

Who said it? Decisions are made not on the points for or against, but because of who says it, e.g. the gym coach said that low intensity training is good for runners so we all should do it.

Fortune telling. The future is suggested even though there is no evidence for or against it, e.g. this team looks ok, so I think that they will win the premiership.

Did I say that? A question is asked in such a way that no matter the answer, it can't be answered properly, e.g. how can our society move forward with or without a plan?

Everyone thinks this? Because there is popular support for an idea, despite a lack of evidence to support it, it is accepted anyway, e.g. Toyota cars are the best cars because most people drive them.

Minimising the positives is not appreciating the achievements of others and valuing them as ordinary, e.g. what's so special about that, it's what everyone does.

True all together? Several things or people have similar qualities, so it is assumed they will be good together, e.g. they are a talented group of players, so their team will be fantastic.

Bending reasons? Someone does something for a worthy reason and others think he wanted to make a gain out of it, e.g. he mowed his next-door neighbors' lawn, he must want money from him.

What ifs is when someone continually focuses on the 'what ifs' that can happen rather than what is happening, e.g. 'what will happen if I forget my lines?'

Focusing on negatives is when someone only focuses on the negatives and what can go wrong, e.g. everything always goes wrong for me and there is nothing I can do about it.

Is it both ways? Despite points for or against either way for two ideas, because one is believed to be true, then the other one must be true and vice-versa, e.g. wearing bright colours makes people feel good, therefore to feel good you must wear bright colours.

Should happen is when someone focuses on something they believe should happen rather than what is happening, e.g. Bill should be in the team even though he is playing poorly.

Feelings thinking is when someone lets their negative emotions hijack their thinking, e.g. I feel anxious, so I'll fail this test.

The way it is is when someone presents points for an idea and ignores any points against it, e.g. it is totally safe to swim between the flags at the beach; no one ever gets into trouble.

Pig headed thinking is when someone ignores any evidence for or against an idea and sticks with their beliefs, e.g. I don't care what the studies show, the real problem is not speed.

Stretching it is when someone says that an approach works well for a simple situation, then goes on to say it will work in more complex cases, e.g. eating oranges for junior sport is good for their energy, then professional sports people should eat oranges.

Believing the worst is thinking that what may happen will be so bad that it will be unbearable, e.g. I won't be able to stand it if I don't get picked in the team.

True because of that? Thinking that because something is may be true then something else is true, and not considering other reasons, e.g. eating too much pasta might not be good for us, so we should eat more dairy and meat.

Get it done is when someone just wants a decision made and won't accept any points for or against it, e.g. it's time we made our minds up, what's our decision.

Slippery slides is when someone discussing an issue using certain points, continues them on to other issues, e.g. the authorities have banned drugs in society, so let's also ban alcohol, which leads to banning fast food and more.

Nasty naming is using over the top nasty labelling of yourself or others for no reason, e.g. you are a dangerous person.

All or nothing is when someone believes that either all or nothing of something is true or false; all black or white, e.g. all people who play chess are very smart.

Are all the pieces OK? Thinking that because something is working ok, then all its parts are also working ok, e.g., the soccer team won the game well, so every player played well.

Focusing on the past is when someone continues to regret what has gone wrong in the past, rather than focusing on what is happening now, e.g. if I would have tried harder that wouldn't have happened.

Personalising is when someone thinks something happens just because of them, e.g. my team lost just because of me.

Red herring is when someone raises an issue to take attention away from what the discussion is about, e.g. when discussing students being punctual to class, someone raises the issue that students aren't engaged in class.

Generalising too much is when someone assumes most things are bad because one thing that happened was bad, e.g. I didn't get picked for the team, so I'm not good at anything.

True, False or Other Alternatives? Providing a very limited number of decision choices for others when there are others worth considering, e.g. for lunch the only food worth eating are rolls or pies.

Blaming is when someone blames others for what has happened and takes no responsibility for their own action, e.g. I failed that test because my teachers didn't help me.

Non-parallels is when someone compares themselves to others who are either much better or much worse than themselves and thinks they are better or worse than they are, e.g. I am as good as he is, and I should be captain.

Statistics is when someone thinks the statistics of something that has happened affects the chance of something else happening, e.g. three heads have come up on three tosses of a coin, therefore there is a big chance the next toss will be a head.

In the family is when someone thinks that because one member of the family was good at something, then other members will also be good at it, e.g. Janine is a good runner, so her brothers run well.

Dominos is when someone thinks that because some event follows another then the first event caused the following event, e.g. after I visited a hospital I became ill; therefore, hospitals make me ill.

Doesn't follow is when two events happen together, and someone thinks that because one happened it caused the other one to happen, e.g. the game was played in the rain and we lost; therefore, the rain caused us to lose.

Mind reading is when someone thinks they know how someone else is thinking, without any evidence, e.g. he didn't say hello to me, so he doesn't like me.

This has always worked is when someone thinks that because something has always worked in the past that it will work again, e.g. this chemical has always cleaned everything, so it will work on this new material.

Family and friends think this is when just because your family or friends make up their mind about an issue you think that it is true, e.g. my friends said he is the best singer in the band, so I think he must be.

The commentator is when someone believes everything a popular commentator says, e.g. the only possible outcome for the game will be a win because Bill the expert said that.

First impressions is when someone introduces an idea with a heavy bias in a certain direction that influences any further thinking about it, e.g. over 90% of people believe that it should happen this way.

Being a puppet is when someone who has little or no understanding about an issue blindly accepts ideas from others around them, e.g. Jane and Harry said that it should happen this way.

Iceberg thinking is when someone only considers the first things they see about an issue, without looking below the surface for stronger reasoning, e.g. that's not fair that Ally isn't allowed to be in the team.

Keep on keeping on is when someone automatically accepts a certain way of thinking about an issue because they have always thought about it that way, e.g. John always chooses the same two meals from the menu, even though others could be great.

Spent the money is when someone has spent money to do something, but more important things crop up and they feel lousy for not doing it, e.g. Oscar bought tickets to a concert, but his Mum is sick, and he feels he shouldn't go.

Find a friend is when someone really wants to think in a certain way about an idea and seeks support for their stance from a friend who they know will agree, e.g. Joey passionately wants to develop a project and asks Tasha for her thoughts, already knowing she will say yes.

That's what they are like is when someone makes up their mind about another person because of their occupations and activities they are involved in, e.g. Elijah is quite intelligent because he plays chess.

Everyone else believes this is when someone justifies what they do because they want to believe everyone else also thinks like them and does the same, e.g. it's ok for me to try these things because Issy and Jett do them.

Activity

These thinking traps can occur in all subjects across the curriculum. As such, good practice is for all teachers to weave them into their everyday teaching. Look at the thinking traps when there seems to be illogical thinking occurring, identify which one and ask students to journal their thoughts about each of the following questions:

Describe a time when you may have thought this way.

- Why do you believe that thinking this way may have caused you to arrive at decisions that really were not logical?

- Which of your top strengths could you use to overcome this thinking trap and how?

- What is one thing you could start doing to avoid thinking this way?

Example

A. Choose a story or an interview from a magazine, book, YouTube or the news, and in groups of three, students look for errors in logic and identify which thinking trap they fell into.

B. Students in pairs choose three thinking traps and write three stories that could happen for each trap. They then read each story to the class, who then must identify which thinking traps the story is about.

Becoming your best possible self?[7]

To move students and teachers along the mindset continuum towards a more growth orientated mindset, they need to understand and accept that by lifting their efforts to learn and try new approaches, that they can grow their brains' abilities in all areas of their lives. One of these approaches is to create a vision of what their best possible self looks like, and then striving to become that person.

It is important for them to believe that 'being' comes after 'doing', and that their personal growth comes from 'doing' difficult things outside of their comfort zones.[8]

Activity

Asking students and staff to complete the following activity will go a long way towards them becoming their best possible selves.

One of the most powerful growth mindsets you can have is to believe in the 'power of yet'.

---

7   Lyubormirsky, S. (2007): *The How of Happiness: A Practical Guide to Getting The Life You Want*. London, UK: Little, Brown Book Group.

8   Anderson, J. (2017): The Agile Learner: Where Growth Mindset, Habits of Mind and Practice Unite. Victoria, Australia: Hawker Brownlow Education Ltd.

You may not have become the person you wish to become **yet**, but by lifting your efforts every day you can become that person to live a more meaningful and happy life.

What do you think about this?

```
┌─────────────────────────────────────────────────────┐
│                                                       │
│                                                       │
│                                                       │
│                                                       │
└─────────────────────────────────────────────────────┘
```

Describe your 'best possible you' that you want to become. Read this often.

```
┌─────────────────────────────────────────────────────┐
│                                                       │
│                                                       │
│                                                       │
│                                                       │
└─────────────────────────────────────────────────────┘
```

TIP: Look at selecting five qualities that you want to possess for your 'best possible you'. Then pick five positive emotions that you want to experience regularly.

Which of your top strengths do you rely on most?

```
┌─────────────────────────────────────────────────────┐
│                                                       │
│                                                       │
│                                                       │
│                                                       │
└─────────────────────────────────────────────────────┘
```

How do you know you are using them?

```
┌─────────────────────────────────────────────────────┐
│                                                       │
│                                                       │
│                                                       │
│                                                       │
└─────────────────────────────────────────────────────┘
```

TIP: At the beginning of every week write down an action you will do for each of your top strengths. Then when you spot yourself doing them, jot it down.

Describe an achievement that you are very proud of, strengths you used and the positive emotions you felt.

[ ]

TIP: Read this often to relive the uplifting feelings you experienced.

Describe the qualities and strengths you like in yourself, your friends and in other people.

[ ]

TIP: Neuroscience has shown that we all have mirror neurons, which copy the expressions, moods and behaviours of those around us. Often, qualities and strengths you like in other people are those you like in yourself. The opposite is also true. Always look for qualities and strengths you like in others, no matter how few they may be. Then work on building relationships with them through these positive qualities and strengths and push the negatives out of your mind.

Write yourself a short letter on what you want to achieve and become this year through 'doing' difficult things.

[ ]

TIP: Read this often to remind you to maintain your growth-orientated mindsets.

Example

Once students have established what they want their best possible self to look like, their self-awareness of it needs to be raised further to move them along the mindset continuum. Creating realistic scenarios that could occur in their lives and asking them to journal what their best possible self would do for each of them and why, is an effective means to raising their self-awareness. Students have five minutes to journal on each scenario. Select several students to report back to the class for each scenario.

Consider these scenarios or make up your own:

- Your parents go out to the movies, and your friends come around to your place. Some of them want to start drinking your parents' alcohol.

- You are walking done the street and a person comes up and asks you if you want to buy some drugs off of him.

- You told your parents that you were going to the skate park with your friends, but some of your friends decided they would go to mess around at an empty building.

- You are sitting next to your friend in class, and he won't stop talking and mucking around, preventing you from concentrating and getting your work done.

- Your friend's older brother has just got his driving licence and asked you and your friends to go for a ride with him.

- You are at a party and your friends are jumping off the roof into the pool. They put pressure on you to also jump.

- At a party you have a disagreement with another person. Your friends start egging you on to a fight with him.

Mind and heart calmers

Classrooms are emotional places and, in many of them, this emotional perspective is not being considered nor catered for. The consequence is that two things often occur:

- Students arrive in class not ready to learn.
- Halfway through lessons, teachers 'lose' their students' minds and hearts.

Yet many teachers continue to teach on regardless; the reality is that their words are just bouncing off students' foreheads with little learning happening. Mind and heart calmers address this issue by activating students' and teachers' empathetic brain networks, thus enabling them to be emotionally prepared to learn and teach.

Several mind and heart calmers include:

What kind things have you done for other people this week?

What are times you have shown that you are fair?

What are things you find awesome at home, at school and in the community?

Who are people who make a positive difference at school and why?

What are times you were creative in what you did?

How would ask for help if you lost your phone and who would you ask?

Who is good at building relationships and what do they do?

When are times you have shown yourself to be honest?

What are things that have gone well this week and how can you make them happen again?

What are things that you have not done well this week and what can you do to do them better?

Which times were you open minded in what you listened to?

What kind things have other people done for you this week?

What is something you have loved learning about?

When are times you have forgiven other people for doing the wrong thing by you?

What are times you have felt the emotions gratitude and joy and what happened?

What is something you want to do but fear failing?

When is a time you have tried hard to be picked for something but missed out?

What are times you were impressed with someone else's perspective on an issue?

What is something you do to show you believe in yourself?

What strengths do you think bullies overuse, misuse or under use?

What are times you were nearly beaten by a challenge but persevered to overcome it?

What are things in your life you are enthusiastic about?

What are times others have forgiven you for doing the wrong thing by them?

What do you believe are things you should do to live a good life?

What are times others have shown empathy for your needs and feelings?

What are times you have shown grit and determination?

What would you say to your friends if you didn't want to do what they wanted to do?

Who is someone you admire and what are their strengths?

What are times you have shown empathy for others' needs and feelings?

What are times when you have forgiven others who did the wrong thing by you?

What are times you have shown self-regulation to not join in something risky?

What could you say to a student you didn't know to start a conversation?

What are times you have been prudent and careful in what you were doing?

What are things you can do to make a positive difference at home?

What are things you do to build relationships with others?

Who are three people you have said thank you to this week?

Who is someone who shows courage in their life and how do they show it?

What is an exercise or leisure activity that you would like to try and why?

What are things you could do to sleep better?

What things can you do to show empathy for the needs and feelings of others?

What are things you can do to build relationships with other people?

What are things you are curious to learn more about?

What is something you do to calm yourself when you feel tense?

What is something bigger than yourself that gives you meaning and purpose?

What are times you felt valued and appreciated?

Who is someone you upset that you should apologise to?

What are four strengths you look for in people when making friends?

What are times you have been humble for something you achieved?

Activity

Either at the beginning of a class or halfway through, the above questions are fabulous five-minute activities that work like this. Pose one of the questions above with students and ask them to journal their thoughts and feelings about it for two minutes. Then as a class, brainstorm for three minutes about their reflections. Students are then ready to learn, and teachers are then ready to teach.

Example

The following mind and heart calmer was asked by the teacher, halfway through a class, 'what are things you can do to build relationships with other people?' Students stopped what they were doing and started to journal what they did to build relationships. Then the class had a sharing of their ideas, which included: making eye contact, smiling, asking how others feel, complimenting others on what they are wearing, asking about others' families and their hobbies, using open and welcoming body language, having a happy and enthusiastic tone in their voice, asking others to tell them more.

Mindfulness activities

Mindfulness is a form of self-awareness where students and teachers purposely, connect with themselves, pay attention to the present moment, watch their thoughts coming and going and calm their minds and hearts. There are much more involved forms of mindfulness, which you may wish to explore later.

The mindfulness activities below are very useful when students become emotionally hijacked in class. They distract students' amygdala and enable their prefrontal cortex to regain control of their thinking.

Five senses: Think of two of your greatest achievements and describe what you experienced for each of your five senses.

Life's backpack: Think of all the people, places, pets and things that are important to you and why. Then pack your imaginary life backpack and carry it around with you everywhere you go.

Going home: Close your eyes and pretend you are travelling home from school. Focus on every turn, every time you must stop and start for to whole way home.

Favourite song: In your mind, mentally sing your favourite song while at the same time writing out all the words and describe what they mean to you and how they make you feel.

Sounds: Go outside, close your eyes and listen to the sounds around you for one minute. Then write down all the sounds you heard and what made them.

Animals: If you could be any animal, what would you choose to be and why is this animal your choice for you? What characteristics do you relate to?

Favourite meal: Think of your favourite home-cooked meal. What does it taste like? What does it smell like? What does it look like? How do feel when you eat it?

Dream holiday: If you could go anywhere for the holiday of your dreams, where would it be, why would it be so special, what things would you do and how would you feel?

Picture stories: Look at a magazine and find a picture that appeals to you. Without reading about the picture, make up a story about what you see in the picture and what it means for you.

Adapting: Think of an everyday object such as a fork, tennis racquet, or cup. Be creative and think of all the things this object could be adapted to do.

Tangled whispers: In a group, ask one of the members of the group to whisper a message to another student, who then passes it on. When it has been passed on to the whole group, how different is the message?

Opposite hands: Try colouring a picture in or writing the alphabet with your non-dominant hand. How did it feel? How were you challenged?

Tongue tingling: Place a sultana, a mint, or piece of fruit in your mouth for one minute without chewing it. Describe the sensations you tasted. Now you can eat it.

Name game: Write down all the songs you know that have the word happy in their title or their lyrics. Which are your favourite ones and why?

Describing pictures: You and a friend each draw a picture and not show each other. Then describe to each other to what the picture looks like and means to each of you.

Building empathy: In a group each of you write down on a poster note what worries and troubles you and place them in a bowl. Each person randomly picks one out and reads it to the group. What feelings do you experience?

Food names: Write down as many foods as you can. Begin with the ones that start with either the letters 'b' or 'm'. Which of these do you like and why? What dishes are they used in?

Heart feelings: Reflect on the feelings your heart has right now and describe them. Draw a picture of your heart and write your feelings on it.

Story meanings: Read or write a short story or poem and describe what it means to you and the emotions you feel.

Lucky dip: Ask a friend to put a variety of different things in a bag, such as keys, coins, pieces of fruit, paper, pens, cords and so on. Dip your hand in and describe what you are feeling. Put a glove on and do it again. Is the sensation any different?

Cloud pictures: Go outside and lie on a towel or blanket looking at the sky for three minutes. Look for and describe the different pictures of things you can see in the clouds.

Jelly beans: Close your eyes and ask a friend, who has a packet of jelly beans, to put one at a time in your mouth. Guess what the flavour of each one is. It's not a good idea to eat them all.

Ice feelings: Hold a piece of ice or put it in your mouth. Describe the feelings your hand, fingers, mouth and tongue have. Is it melting?

Winning lotto: Imagine you have just won a million pounds in the national lottery. Describe your feelings, what you would do and how it would change your life?

Gratitude thoughts: Think of a person who has done something special for you. What would you say to thank them, how would it make them feel and how would you feel?

Letter to me: Write yourself a 100-word letter describing what you are going to become as a person this year and how you are going to achieve it. Read it in a month; how have you started to do this?

The good stuff: Describe times in your life when you felt great joy, real pride and total fulfilment in what you did.

Changing names: If you were to change your first and surnames, describe what your new names would be, why you chose them and how you would act and feel.

Self-hugging: Give yourself a self-hug by wrapping your arms around yourself for one minute or longer if you like. Describe the positive emotions and feelings you experienced.

Swapping hands: Use your non-dominant hand to hold the spoon when having your breakfast cereal. When eating dinner swap the knife and fork between your hands. Describe how much do you have to concentrate?

Song words: Carefully listen to the words of a song you like and write down five emotions and feelings you have while listening to it.

Name game: Write down all the objects you know that begin with the letter 'c' and what they are used for.

Sudoku: From a newspaper, magazine or Sudoku book try do a Sudoku grid. Go back for the next three days to solve it or do a more difficult one. Describe how you felt.

Name game: Write as many books, movies or TV shows with characters whose first name begins with 'c' or 'm'.

Character imaginations: If you had a choice of any character you could be in a book, movie or TV show, who would you be and why?

Crossword magic: From a book of crosswords, do as much of a crossword that you can. Tomorrow, go back to it and push hard to do more. Repeat for two more days. Persist and you'll feel fulfilled.

Character strengths charade: Describe or role-play two things you could do for each of these character strengths: zest, curiosity and leadership.

Leaf feelings: Pick up a small piece of a plant that has fallen on the ground and remove the leaves one by one. What does their texture feel like and how many are there?

Press positives: Go through a newspaper or magazine to find three good news stories and describe why they make you feel good and the positive emotions you experience.

Character strengths collage: For each of your top five strengths describe two things you could do to make the world a better place.

Colour connections: Name as many objects, things, places, animals or people that are coloured green.

Tongue hold: Close your mouth and for two minutes hold your tongue so that it doesn't touch any part of your mouth. Describe the strengths you used and the emotions you experienced.

Character strengths charade: Describe or role-play two things you could do for each of these character strengths: hope, forgiveness and creativity.

Top five strengths scenario: Describe how you would use your signature strengths if you lost the key to your house and your parents would not be home from work for four hours.

Peeling petals: Peel the petals off a rose flower one by one, feel their texture and count them. Describe how they felt to touch and how many were there?

Character strengths search: Reflect on what you think are the top five strengths of your best friend or your mum or your dad and describe what they do to make you think that.

Flying paper: With a friend, design and make planes from sheets of A4 paper to fly as far as possible. Whose plane flew further?

Word creation: From the word 'determination', create as many words as you can from the letters.

Body focusing: Concentrate for ten seconds on doing each of following: wiggling your nose, tightening your stomach, rotating your shoulders, stretching your neck, squeezing your hands and screwing up your toes.

Activities

A. Optimal learning occurs when students and teachers feel calm and focused on the present moment. At the beginning of a class or a staff meeting, students and teachers spend between three and five minutes totally focused on a mindfulness activity. Students then journal what emotions they felt and whether they found the experience enjoyable.

B. If students are losing focus and attention during class, 'waste' five minutes doing a mindfulness activity, as this will enable them to refocus and re-enter the learning zone.

C. To become your best possible self, having three, four or five-minute timeouts every day doing any of the above mindfulness activities will benefit your progress towards becoming that person.

Example

As teachers arrive for a staff meeting after a full day of teaching, they are running on 'automatic'; there is little capacity available for executive level thinking, what you want at such meetings. To address this mindfulness works well. Staff can take their own pulse and note it down. Then, introduce the mindfulness activity: going home – close your eyes and pretend you are travelling home from school. Focus on every turn, every time you must stop and start for to whole way home. They spend four or five minutes doing the activity. At the end of it, they take their pulse again, and in most cases, it has dropped by at least ten.

Staff also say they enjoyed the experience and feel refocused on what was ahead in the meeting. A similar situation exists when students arrive for class or halfway through a lesson. Select any of the above mindfulness activities and do it with the class. You will be pleasantly surprised the way students respond so positively.

Habits of Mind

Personal growth occurs when students and teachers tackle more 'difficult' tasks, requiring them to learn new approaches to gain mastery, rather than doing the same level of things they find easy. Many students do the right thing by studying hard, but don't do the thing right because they are merely repeating more of the same comfortable tasks. Also, many students are uncomfortable doing 'difficult' tasks because their performance drops; but the reality is that this stretching promotes brain growth.

To master more 'difficult' tasks students need to be taught to learn to think in more intelligent ways. Habits of Mind are 16 ways successful people think when they are confronted with problems. Tapping into them will enable students and teachers to be in a cycle of continuous improvement. The 16 Habits of Mind are:

Persisting: Sticking to a task until it is completed. If your first approach doesn't work, being able to try other ways to solve the problem. Being able to see when something doesn't work and why it doesn't work.

Managing impulsivity: Thinking before you answer a question with the first thing that comes into your mind. Considering and understanding ideas before your make a judgement. Planning ways to solve a problem before you start.

Listening with understanding and empathy: Understanding what others are saying and reading what messages their body language is sending to you. Being able to say what another person is saying in your own words. 55% of your life is spent listening but often you don't 'tune in' to what is really being said. Listen with your ears, your eyes and your heart.

Thinking flexibly: Being able to change your mind when you receive new information. Sometimes the information may cause you to contradict your opinions and consider other viewpoints. Being able to shift in your thinking from your way when perhaps another way is better.

Thinking about thinking (metacognition): Being able to know what we know and what we don't know. Being able to plan, reflect on and assess your own thinking skills and strategies. Taking time to think why you are doing what you are doing.

Striving for accuracy: Being able to take time to check the accuracy of what you do. Taking pride in lifting the quality of your actions to the highest level you are capable of. Not being prepared to settle for second best to get tasks out of the way.

Questioning and posing problems: Being able to ask the right questions to fill in the gaps of what you don't know. Asking questions that begin with 'what if', 'why do' and 'how'. Being able to recognise the reasons behind why and how questions are asked.

Applying past knowledge to new situations: Being able to apply experience and knowledge to new problems. Being able to adapt what you have learned from a previous experience to a new situation and make connections. Being willing to apply yourself to use experience in your thinking.

Thinking and communicating with clarity and precision: Being able to communicate your thoughts with accurate and clear language, both written and verbal. Being able to explain, compare and give evidence using correct names and labels. Avoiding vague and generalising language such as 'you know', 'it's weird', 'everyone says' and 'stuff like'.

Gathering data through all senses: Being able to gain a feeling for a situation through taking in messages from all your senses. Being able to form mental images through what your senses experience. Being able to feel and communicate by considering aspects such as colours, sounds, patterns, tastes, textures, rhythms and temperature; living is not just describing it.

Creating, imagining, and innovating: Being able and prepared to look at problems and situations from many different angles. Being willing to take risks with your thinking and avoiding statements such as 'I can't', 'I'm not' and 'I wish'. Being open to advice and seeking feedback to improve your approach and thinking.

Responding with wonderment and awe: Having a 'can do', 'what to' and 'I enjoy' attitude to the challenge of solving problems. Enjoying figuring out things for yourself and avoiding statements such as 'I was never good at', 'it's boring', 'ask someone else', 'when will I use this' and 'who cares'. Being curious, enthusiastic and passionate about learning, thinking and solving problems.

Taking responsible risks: Being prepared to leave your comfort zone to adopt an attitude of welcoming a challenge and exploring the unknown. Realising that not taking the risk of a challenge is missing an opportunity to improve yourself. Being more afraid of a lack of success than a fear of failure and avoiding statements such as 'I'll look stupid' and 'I don't want to be wrong'.

Finding humour: Having a sense of humour and laughing increases your oxygen intake and lowers your pulse rate; it's good for you. Being able to laugh at yourself rather than zeroing in on the wrong places such as others' weaknesses and differences. Being able to appreciate other peoples' humour helps you to be more creative and think at a higher level.

Thinking interdependently: Accepting that, as human beings, we seek to be part of groups and teams and drawing energy and feedback from each other. Realising that us together has much more thinking power than you alone and welcoming it. Being able to accept openness and feedback from others and avoiding statements such as 'leave me alone'. 'I'll do it by myself', 'they don't like me' or 'I want to be alone'.

Remaining open to continuous learning: Being prepared to realise that there could be a better way and searching for it. Seeing problems and challenges as opportunities to develop and improve your thinking and you. Accepting that if you don't know then not being afraid to find out. It's better to ask dumb questions than to get dumb answers.[9]

Activities

A. First individually, and then in small groups, for each Habit of Mind, students are to reflect on and self-assess their thinking to answer the following questions. In the small groups they share their thoughts:

   • When is a time you thought using this way of thinking?

   • Why did you choose to think in this way?

   • Who has impressed you with their ability to think in this way?

   • For which Character Strengths could you think in this way?

B. Once or twice each week in different subjects across the curriculum, include Habits of Mind spotting in class. Students journal when they see others or themselves using one the Habits. Building their self-awareness of their own and others thinking will develop their abilities to confidently use Habits of Mind, which in turn will enable them to think more intelligently to master more 'difficult' tasks, thus promoting personal growth.

---

9   Costa, A. & Kallick, B. (2000): *Discovering and Exploring Habits of Mind.* Alexandria, VA: Association for Supervision and Curriculum Development.

C. When looking at events and analysing book they are reading, ask students to identify what Habits of Mind the characters are using in their thinking.

Example

Considering different scenarios are ideal activities for students to have to think about their thinking – metacognition. Students are to select five of the following realistic scenarios that could occur in their lives. Then individually they are to explore which Habits of Mind would be the most intelligent ways to think for each of the scenarios they selected.

The in groups of three share their thoughts on why they chose the Habits of Mind for each scenario. Then have three or four groups report back to the class. This exercise is an effective thinking self-awareness strategy.

- You are installing a new printer for your computer.
- You are talking with your parents about which subjects to select to study next semester.
- You and your friends are doing risky behaviours that could be dangerous.
- You are listening to a war veteran describe what happened while he was at war.
- You are looking after your younger brother who is being naughty.
- You are helping your grandparents prepare lunch for Christmas Day.
- You are watching the 100m Olympic sprint final.
- You are helping a friend who has lost their phone to calm down.
- You have been asked to speak at a school assembly that you haven't done before.
- You have been asked to help make up a menu for your camping trip.
- You are learning to play the guitar, but you are getting nowhere.
- You are working with friends to build a jumping castle for the school fete.
- You trip over in front of other students.

Resilience builders[10]

The term resilience is often used in conversations as if it is some type of super power you use to bounce back or forward from adversity, setbacks and challenges. The reality is that when people are asked what skills underpin this super power, they have little idea. This section is about learning how to cultivate the seven skills of resilience in students and teachers.

Also, a lack of autonomous supportive parenting and teaching, where young people are prevented from making mistakes and potential challenges removed from their paths, have contributed them being short on self-regulation and self-awareness. This makes for them being quite brittle when they come to negotiating life's inevitable challenges. The seven evidence-based skills of resilience follow:

- Optimism and hope for the future
- Regulating emotions
- Impulse control
- Flexibility of thinking
- Empathy
- Self-belief
- Building social-connectedness[11] [12]

Activities

For each of the seven skills of resilience, follows a short description of activities that will assist in cultivating them in students and teachers:

A. **Optimism and hope for the future:** Encouraging and teaching students how to set achievable goals, create short-term targets along the way to tick off and celebrate and develop process self-expectations to focus their efforts and attention on, will inspire growth orientated mindsets in them. They come to understand through doing these things that they have huge opportunities for

---

10   Shatte, A. & Reivich K. (2002): *The Resilience Factor: 7 Keys to Finding Your Inner Strength and Overcoming Life's Hurdles.* New York, NY: Broadway Books.
11   Lyubormirsky, S. (2007): *The How of Happiness: A Practical Guide to Getting The Life You Want.* London, UK: Little, Brown Book Group.
12   Fredrickson, B. (2009): *Positivity.* London, UK: Oneworld Publications.

personal growth; this, in turn, creates motivating upward spirals of positive emotions in them.

B. **Regulating emotions:** Teach students about how the part of their brain, the amygdala, creates emotions and causes the fight, flight or freeze reaction. Then, teach how the intensity of these emotions is controlled by another part of their brain, the prefrontal cortex. And how their eyes send messages directly to the amygdala, with a time delay before the prefrontal cortex receives them. Then how looking at things through their top strengths will slow down their reactions.

C. **Impulse control:** Teach students how to self-calm by providing them with frequent opportunities to experience mindfulness activities. Read a mind and heart calmer often to students and ask them to stop and think about how reasonable and logical the first thought that came into their brain was. Understanding how their amygdala and prefrontal cortex run the emotional process and then deliberating practicing the above activities and meeting the wellbeing fitness challenges each week will build impulse control.

D. **Flexibility of thinking:** To achieve personal growth, students and teachers need to engage in more 'difficult' tasks that cause them to make 'stretch' mistakes. Then, to correct these mistakes, they need to learn and try new approaches, which requires them to think in more intelligent ways. Deliberately using Habits of Mind in their thinking will achieve this. Higher order thinking routines, such as: Six Thinking Hats, Five E's of Learning, Connect, Extend, Challenge and Know, What, How, Learnt.

E. **Empathy:** Many young people in the 21st century, prefer to communicate electronically rather than have face to face in person conversations. The ability to read and use body language to communicate needs and feelings can only be learnt through doing it. Use a mind and heart calmer to engage the empathetic brain network so that students can practice listening to others' thoughts about how they feel.

F. **Self-belief:** Teach students that self-acceptance is an important prerequisite for having a healthy sense of self-belief. Encourage them to accept both the things they like about themselves and those they don't like. Becoming their best possible selves is essentially about using the other six skills of resilience well. Teach them to adopt the mindset that their top strength are vehicles to achieve continuous personal growth in all areas of their lives.

G. Building social-connectedness

Ask students to prepare a three-minute talk on:

- something that has just happened in their life.
- something they really want to do.
- something they have achieved that they are very proud of.

In threes, one student shares their stories for three minutes, and then the other two ask questions about what they heard for three minutes to learn more. Every student shares their stories. You see students socially connecting.

Example

Watch a short video with students where characters experience and overcome hardship, setbacks or challenges. Students are to identify at what stage in the video the characters used or didn't each of the skills of resilience. Such an activity raises their self-awareness of the skills of resilience and when to use each of them.

Further activities

Passion, effort and grit, staff-student relationships with class photos, thriving and flourishing, vision of students, vision of staff, glitter jar, brain hat, refocusing the reticular activating system, active constructive responding, text a friend/ family, fabulous first five minutes, help and support seeking, life's roles, silent buddy, parent letter about their child, savouring to relive the best, self-calming strategies, acts of kindness, flow and engagement, key life competencies, healthy body, healthy mind, iceberg thinking, disaster chart, mirror neurons at work, positive memory habits, reading and using body language, assertive language, worst case, best case scenario, breathing and swaying, growth mindsets, positive daily expectations, positive self-talk, feelings and emotions, personal qualities.

Positive education reading

The expression **positive education** contains two key perspective: positive – about positive psychology, becoming your best possible self to live a life that matters – and education – about learning and teaching, developing your mindset and thinking to possess a competent life skill set to contribute to society.

Following are several books that will enhance your understanding of both perspectives; they are all great reads.

Further reading

Achor, S. (2010): *The Happiness Advantage*: The Seven Principles that Fuel Success and Performance at Work. London, UK: Virgin Books.

Anderson, J. (2010): *Succeeding with Habits of Mind*. Victoria, Australia: Hawker Brownlow Education.

Anderson, J. (2017): The Agile Learner: Where Growth Mindset, Habits of Mind and Practice Unite. Victoria, Australia: Hawker Brownlow Education Ltd.

Ben-Shahar, T. (2009): *The Pursuit of Perfect*. Maidenhead, UK: McGraw-Hill Education.

Bloom, B. S. (1985): *Developing Talent in Young People*. New York, NY: Ballantine Books.

Cacioppo, J. T. (2008): *Loneliness: Human Nature and the Need for Social Connection*. London, UK: W. W. Norton & Company Ltd.

Christakis, N. A. & Fowler, J. (2009): *Connected*. Boston, MA: Little, Brown and Company.

Costa, A. & Kallick, B. (2000): *Discovering and Exploring Habits of Mind*. Alexandria, VA: Association for Supervision and Curriculum Development.

Costa, A. & Kallick, B. (2014): *Dispositions: Reframing Teaching and Learning*. Thousand Oaks, CA: Corwin, A SAGE Company.

Coyle, D. (2009): *The Talent Code: Greatness isn't born. It's grown.* New York, NY: Random House.

Csikszentmihalyi, M. (1997): *Finding Flow: The Psychology of Engagement in Everyday Life.* New York, NY: Basic Books.

Diener, E. & Biswas-Diener, R. (2008): *Happiness: Unlocking the Mystery of Psychological Wealth.* Hoboken, NJ: Wiley.

Doidge, N. (2007): *The Brain That Changes Itself.* London, UK: Penguin Books.

Dweck, C. S. (2006): *Mindset: The New Psychology of Success.* New York, NY: Random House.

Emmons, R. A. (2007): *Thanks! How the New Science of Gratitude Can Make You Happier.* Boston, MA: Houghton Mifflin Harcourt.

Ericsson, A. K. (2016): *Peak: Secrets from the New Science of Expertise.* New York, NY: Houghton Miller Harcourt.

Foer, J. (2011): *Moonwalking with Einstein.* New York, NY: Random House.

Fredrickson, B. (2009): *Positivity.* London, UK: Oneworld Publications.

Gardner, H. (1988): *Frames of Mind: The Theory of Multiple Intelligences.* New York, NY: Perseus Book Group.

Gardner, H. (2007): *Five Minds for the Future.* Boston, MA: Harvard Business Review Press.

Gladwell, M. (2000): *The Tipping Point.* London, UK: Little, Brown Book Group.

Gladwell, M. (2008): *Outliers: The Story of Success.* Boston, MA: Little, Brown and Company.

Goleman, D. (2007): *Social Intelligence: The New Science of Human Relationships.* London, UK: Arrow Publishing.

Iacoboni, M. (2009): *Mirroring People: The Science of Empathy and How We Connect with Others.* London, UK: Picador.

Kaufman, S. B. (2013): *Ungifted: Intelligence Redefined*. New York, NY: Perseus Book Group.

Lundin, C. S., Paul, H. & Christensen, J. (2002): *Fish! A remarkable way to boost morale and improve results*. London, UK: Hodder & Stoughton.

Lyubormirsky, S. (2007): *The How of Happiness: A Practical Guide to Getting The Life You Want*. London, UK: Little, Brown Book Group.

Norrish, J. (2015): *Positive Education: The Geelong Grammar School Journey*. Oxford, UK: Oxford University Press.

Peterson, C. (2006): *A Primer in Positive Psychology*. Oxford, UK: Oxford University Press.

Pink, D. (2009): *Drive: The Surprising Truth About What Motivates Us*. New York, NY: Canongate Books Ltd.

Rath, T. (2007): *StrengthsFinder 2.0*. London, UK: Gallup Press.

Robinson, P. (2016): *Practising Positive Education: A Guide to Improve Wellbeing Literacy in Schools*. Sydney, Australia: Sydney Positive Psychology Institute.

Rosenthal, R. & Jacobson, L. (1968): Pygmalion in the classroom. *The Urban Review*, 3(1), pp. 16-20.

Seligman, M. E. P. (2011): *Flourish*. Boston, MA: Nicholas Brealey Publishing.

Syed, M. (2011): *Bounce: Mozart, Federer, Picasso, Beckham, and the Science of Success*. London, UK: HarperCollins.

Yeager, J. M., Fisher, S. W. & Shearon, D. N. (2011): *SMART Strengths*. Putnam Valley, NY: Kravis Publishing.

Chapter 3:
A Lone (Wellbeing) Ranger in an American Public School

Virginia Millar

If you are reading this, you probably already have a sense of the value in targeting wellbeing and resiliency in the school setting. We know that a growing body of research shows that targeting wellbeing also significantly supports academic growth, and certainly when the National Institute of Mental Health reports ever-increasing levels of depression and suicide within adolescent and teen populations,[1] wellbeing in and of itself is a necessary initiative. Despite these facts, American public education programs, and others around the world remain eclipsed by standardized testing that guides curriculum, professional development, and school values. Sadly, it often takes a student suicide or other tragedy to shift the focus to what, in the end, we probably value most for our children – wellbeing.

I write from the perspective of an American junior high teacher in a diverse, low-income public school where no systemic or curricular approach to wellbeing is employed – as is probably the case for many reading this. This condition is especially frustrating to a graduate of the

---

1   National Institute of Mental Health. (2016): Prevalence of Major Depressive Episode Among Adolescents. Available at: www.nimh.nih.gov/health/statistics/major-depression.shtml

Penn MAPP program, whose founder, Martin Seligman believes that '51% (of the world should be) flourishing by 2051'. Lest the story become too depressing, my purpose in sharing this chapter with you is to say that, even within such barren terrain, it is possible to sew resilient seeds of wellbeing that take root, grow, flourish and spread.

During the past seven years of developing and running my own after school wellbeing program for adolescent girls known as 'Girl Power', I have learned some valuable insights about what makes such programs work. My approaches are not costly, nor highly time-intensive, but simply rely on well-established frameworks of wellbeing and resilience, clearly operationalized within core activities that I will share here. Such frameworks also provide the means to easily track quantitative outcomes and provide criteria for selection of activities. In the remainder of this chapter, I will explicate two relevant frameworks; describe how they may be used to select and create a collection of core activities; provide a sampling of activities that may be adapted for various levels and groups, and my own application and outcomes with a relatively simple measurement plan.

Frameworks of wellbeing

If we agree that it is valuable to purposefully target student wellbeing, then it is helpful that this target be clearly defined. Here I will provide a brief overview of the frameworks I have found useful toward guiding my own targeted program (If you are already quite familiar with such frameworks and simply seek useful activities, skip to the section 'Putting Theory into Practice'). From Aristotle to Maslow, Bandura and beyond, learned minds across centuries and continents have suggested a variety of consensual components. One of the more recent models that encompasses these components is Seligman's PERMA Model of Wellbeing, in which the letters represent: positive emotion, engagement, relationships, meaning, and accomplishment respectively. PERMA's scientifically-derived pillars, coupled with its simplicity, make it especially valuable for selecting curricular components, as well as provide the areas to measure when assessing outcomes. Indeed, Butler and Kern (2013) have developed the 23-item PERMA profiler for this purpose. This model was intended to describe adult wellbeing and is thus likely appropriate for developing content and measuring outcomes with high school students. However, PERMA's meaning component is developmentally too advanced for children and adolescents.[2]

Accordingly, psychologists Kern et al (2016) developed a companion adolescent model of wellbeing, the EPOCH, composed of: engagement, perseverance, optimism, connectedness, and happiness; it is also supported with a 20-item questionnaire for measurement purposes. The reader will notice that the core components of the adult and adolescent models roughly align, with the exception of the meaning component of PERMA, which is replaced with optimism in the adolescent model. This important distinction and the relationship between the two is teased out further in the 'Case for Optimism' section, which follows the description of the wellbeing and resilience frameworks.

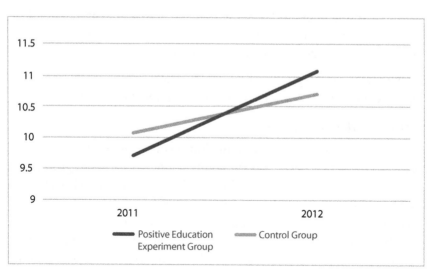

Figure 1: A comparison of the PERMA and EPOCH wellbeing models

---

2   Kern, M., Benson, L., Steinberg, E. & Steinberg, L. (2016): The EPPOCH Measure of Adolescent Well-being. *Psychological Assessment*, 28(5), pp. 586-597.

Components of the EPOCH Framework

Kern and colleagues (2016) define the components of the EPOCH Model as follows:[3]

Engagement is the capacity to become absorbed in and focused on what one is doing, as well as involvement and interest in life activities and tasks. Very high levels of engagement have been referred to as 'flow'.[4]

Perseverance refers to the ability to pursue one's goals to completion, even in the face of obstacles. It further comprises the drive component of 'grit' (that includes both perseverance and passion for long-term goals.[5]

Optimism is characterized by hopefulness and confidence about the future, a tendency to take a favorable view of things, and an explanatory style marked by evaluating negative events as temporary, external, and specific to the situation.

Connectedness refers to the sense that one has satisfying relationships with others, believing that one is cared for, loved, esteemed, and valued, and providing friendship or support to others.

Happiness is conceptualized as steady states of positive mood and feeling content with one's life, rather than momentary emotion.[6]

A framework of resilience

In addition to wellbeing, many institutions are interested in building students' resilience, defined as the ability to bounce back and grow in the face of significant challenge during an MAPP lecture in February 2018 by Karen Reivich. The need for which is critically evident in the noted increasing rates of depression and suicides within the adolescent and teen populations. As is the case with models of wellbeing, the components of resilience have also been researched by many over decades, including

---

3   Ibid

4   Csikszentmihalyi, M. (1997): *Finding flow: The psychology of engagement with everyday life.* New York, NY: Basic Books.

5   Duckworth, A., Peterson, C., Matthews, M. D. & Kelly, D. R. (2007): Grit: Perseverance and Passion for Long-Term Goals. *Journal of Personality and Social Psychology,* 92(6), pp. 1087-1101.

6   Kern, M., Benson, L., Steinberg, E. & Steinberg, L. (2016): The EPPOCH Measure of Adolescent Well-being. *Psychological Assessment,* 28(5), p. 587.

Masten & Tellegen (2012) and Werner (2005), with a general consensus across evidence-based models that suggest the following as key protective factors toward human resilience: biology (what we are born with), positive institutions (such as schools), connection, self-efficacy/mastery, optimism, mental agility, self-regulation, and self-awareness. In fact, such a model is being used by the US military to train soldiers in comprehensive soldier fitness, in part to prevent PTSD.[7]

Resilience-building: The Protective Factors

Based on Reivich (2018)

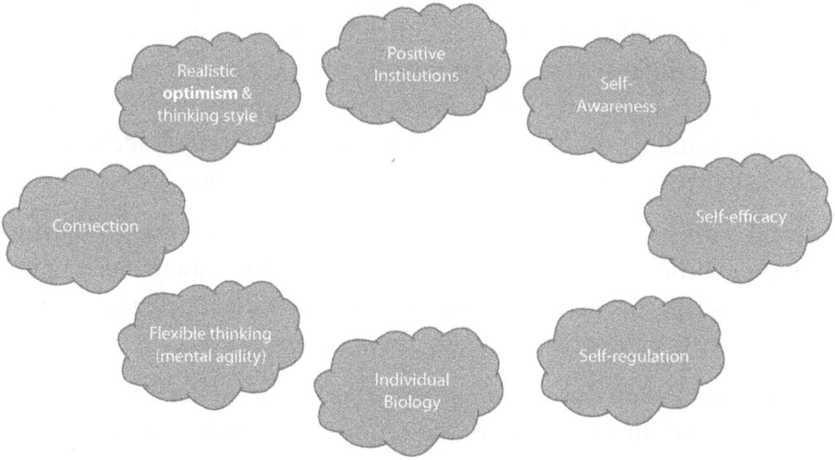

Figure 2: Resilience-building: The Protective Factors[8]

Defining the resilience framework protective factors

Self-awareness refers to an accurate assessment of personal feelings, preferences, resources, and intuitions.[9] Such awareness has relevance in building relationships with others and is considered a core capacity of

---

7   Seligman, M. E. P. & Fowler, R. (2011): Comprehensive Soldier Fitness and the future of Psychology. *American Psychologist*, pp. 82-86. Available at: www.pdfs.semanticscholar.org/4 f9d/8c2faf266ca05893555006aabd8813cc6c09.pdf

8   Reivich, K. (11 February 2018): 'Protective Factors of Resilience.' *Positive Psychology and the Individual*. Pennsylvania, PA: University of Philadelphia. Presentation.

9   Conoley, C. W. & Conoley, J. (2009): *Positive psychology and family therapy: Creative techniques and practical tools for guiding change and enhancing growth*. Hoboken, NJ: Wiley.

emotional intelligence.[10] Self-awareness has been targeted through the practice of mindfulness, which supports awareness through the practice of paying attention on purpose, to the present moment,[11] and is included in the 'core activities' section here.

Self-regulation is the uniquely human ability to intercept and direct thoughts, feelings, impulses, and behavior.[12] Self-regulation is utilized in conforming to social norms as well as in regulating personal activities such as dieting and finances. Importantly, practicing self-regulation in one realm has been shown to translate to other areas in a person's life.[13]

Self-efficacy is the belief of being able to achieve goals with one's current set of skills.[14] Positive self-efficacy within adolescents is one of the most predictive factors of future academic and personal success. Building self-efficacy within students can be implemented in a variety of ways including: skill development, positive validation, leadership and responsibility opportunities, and relationship cultivation.[15]

Mental agility or flexible thinking is shown in one's ability to adjust to change; to bend as necessary to positively cope with situations. Such agility relies on perspective-taking, another hallmark of social intelligence as well as creativity to appropriately modify thoughts and actions.[16]

Connection within this model is the connection of human relationships. Social support in the form of one-on-one relationships is one of the

10   Caruso, D., Salovey, P., Brackett, M. & Mayer, J. D. (2015): The ability model of emotional intelligence. In S. Joseph (Ed.), *Positive psychology in practice*, Hoboken, NJ: Wiley.
11   Coholic, D. A. (2011): Exploring the feasibility and benefits of arts-based mindfulness-based practices with young people in need: Aiming to improve aspects of self-awareness and resilience. *Child Youth Care Forum*, 40(4), pp. 303-317.
12   Baumeister, R. F., Gailliot, M., DeWall, C. N. & Oaten, M. (2006): Self-regulation and personality: How interventions increase regulatory success, and how depletion moderates the effects of traits on behavior. *Journal of Personality*, 74(6), pp. 1773-1801.
13   Reivich, K. (11 February 2018): 'Protective Factors of Resilience'. Positive Psychology and the Individual. Philadelphia, PA: University of Pennsylvania. Presentation.
14   Maddux, J. E. (2009): Self-efficacy: The power of believing that you can. In C. R. Snyder & S. J. Lopez (Eds.), *Oxford handbook of positive psychology* (2nd ed.) (pp. 335-343). New York, NY: Oxford University Press.
15   Tsang, S. K., Hui, E. K. & Law, B. C. (2013): Self-efficacy as a positive youth development construct: a conceptual review. *The Scientific World Journal*.
16   Caruso, D., Salovey, P., Brackett, M. & Mayer, J. D. (2015): The ability model of emotional intelligence. In S. Joseph (Ed.), *Positive psychology in practice*, Hoboken, NJ: Wiley.

biggest environmental contributors to wellbeing.[17] Although connecting students to school is important at all grade levels, it's especially crucial during the adolescent years. In the last decade, educators and school health professionals have increasingly pointed to school connectedness as an important factor in reducing the likelihood that adolescents will engage in health-compromising behaviors. A connected school environment also increases the likelihood of academic success.[18]

Optimism is characterized by hopefulness and confidence about the future, a tendency to take a favorable view of things, and an explanatory style marked by evaluating negative events as temporary, external, and specific to situation, as opposed to permanent, personal, and pervasive to all situations.[19] While hopefulness certainly has a biological component, within Hope Theory, Mayger-Moe & Lopez (2015) operationalized hope as having three actionable parts: goals, developing pathways or plans to achieve them, and the sense of agency over one's capabilities to do so. Hope considered in this manner is malleable and buildable. Further, viewing hope, or optimism in this malleable capacity in part explains the developmental growth from the optimism of EPOCH to the meaning component of PERMA and is further discussed below.

17   Meyers, D. G. (2000): The funds, friends, and faith of happy people. *American Psychologist*, 55, pp. 56-67.
18   Blum, R. W. & Libbey, H. P. (2004): School connectedness – Strengthening the health and education outcomes for teenagers. *Journal of School Health*, 74(4), pp. 229-299.
19   Kern, M., Benson, L., Steinberg, E. & Steinberg, L. (2016): The EPPOCH Measure of Adolescent Well-being. *Psychological Assessment*, 28(5), pp. 586-597.

A Comparison EPOCH (Well-being) and Resilience Frameworks

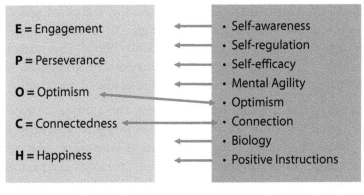

The Adolescent EPOCH Model **Proctective Factors of Resiliency**

Figure 3: A comparison EPOCH (wellbeing) and resilience frameworks

Relationships within the models

The reader will note that the resilience components of connection and optimism exactly match two components of the EPOCH wellbeing model, making them especially rich targets for supporting human flourishing. Further, the individual resilience capacities of self-awareness, self-regulation, self-efficacy, and mental agility can be viewed as support systems for connection and optimism, as well as the remaining core wellbeing components of engagement, perseverance, and happiness. In fact, when we purposefully target the wellbeing components, we are tapping into the core protective factors of resilience.

While biology may be less within our abilities to target, certainly the protective factor 'positive institutions' would be one that purposefully supports the remaining resiliency and wellbeing components. Once we are aware of the capacities that support resilience and wellbeing, we can then develop activities and programs to purposefully build these capacities. Many evidence-based programs and activities have been and continue to be developed around the world, and certainly hold value. I would suggest, however, that a more useful approach is to begin with a clear understanding of that which supports resilience and wellbeing, and use those frameworks to build your own program, whether as an individual teacher or entire system, in the manner that is most appropriate for your target population.

For example, my target population is adolescent girls, accordingly we include a module on self-image that utilizes material from the Dove Real Beauty campaign. I also do a session on choice-making (see the core activities section) given the intense peer pressure of the age and frequent failure to consider consequences. Yet, in delving into such topics, one may note that we are also targeting the resilience capacities of self-awareness, self-regulation toward future outcomes and thus supporting the wellbeing components of perseverance toward goals and happiness as positive emotions.

Furthermore, in considering the needs of one's unique population, I note that my adolescent students are on the cusp of the teenage years where finding purpose and meaning-making can have a huge impact on wellbeing.[20] Adolescence is also unfortunately a time at which depression may surface (NIMH, 2016), thus making it a critically important age to support wellbeing. Given that the differences in the wellbeing models from adolescence to adulthood includes the replacement of the optimism category with meaning, I find it especially important to examine this connection and find that wellbeing components as defined within the models provide the connective tissue, and better yet can inform the activities I include within my program. The following section makes a case for optimism, describes how it may be targeted, and connects it to the meaning piece of adulthood.

A case for optimism

On the surface, optimism may appear a very squidgy capacity that folks are either born with or not; however, as defined within these frameworks, it becomes not only less nebulous but, more importantly, buildable! Both the wellbeing and resilience models describe optimism in terms of explanatory style and hopeful thinking. The explanatory style view

---

20 Damon, W., Menon, J. & Bronk, K. C. (2003): The development of purpose during adolescence. *Applied Developmental Science*, 7(3), pp. 119-128.

of optimism is the habitual way we have of explaining the problems we experience.[21] We use three dimensions to explain why a particular good or bad event happens: *permanence* (sometimes vs always/never), *pervasiveness* (specific vs global) and *personalization* (internal vs external).[22] For example, if a student did poorly on a test, the more optimistic view would be that she did poorly on just this test – perhaps due to lack of preparation or other factors – and that she can do better next time. This is opposed to considering herself permanently idiotic and doomed to fail all such tests. Students can be taught to be aware of their own styles as well as to dispute and change them (see the core activities section).

Hopeful thinking, too, can be considered in a way that makes it buildable, as noted in the definition above. Mayger-Moe & Lopez (2016) operationalized hope into three components: goals, pathways (plans), and agency to carry them out. Considered in this manner, goal-setting activities (also included in the core activities section) can be utilized to increase optimism. One further notes that in pursuing self-concordant goals, one is also building the resilience capacities of self-regulation, self-efficacy, mental agility, and targeting the wellbeing capacity of perseverance. WOOP goals and SMART goal models have been especially valuable to support optimism in this way and are included in the collection of activities.

Considering optimism in these buildable forms allows us not only to intentionally support that capacity, but for me, as an educator, it offers a glimpse at the tangible lifelines that connect adolescent optimism to adult meaning. Volumes have been produced over centuries on the innately human capacity to make meaning, yet contemporary research into the construct offers some insight on the relationship between optimism and meaning, and how we as educators can then support that relationship. Damon, Menon, and Bronk (2003) designate purpose as one element within meaning, an intention to accomplish something that is meaningful to the self and of consequence to the world beyond the self. In his work on researching the human constituents of meaning, Baumeister (1991) found that four patterns of motivation contribute to

---

21   Reivich, K. & Shatte, A. (2002): *The resilience factor: 7 Essential skills for overcoming life's inevitable obstacles.* New York, NY: Broadway Books.
22   Seligman, M. E. P. (1990): *Learned optimism.* New York, NY: Knopf.

one's sense of meaning: purpose, values, self-efficacy, and self-worth.[23] Furthermore, all these researchers also cite relationships as a factor in finding purpose.[24] When optimism or hope is considered as described above as 'goals, pathways, and agency', the connection to Baumeister's meaning constituents (purpose, self-efficacy, and self-worth) becomes apparent. As an educator, I am struck by the future value to be gained from building optimism in this very intentional and direct manner to not only bolster the capacity of adolescent resilience and wellbeing, but also toward building a foundation for the adult capacity to make meaning.

Proposed Relationship Between Adolescent Optimism and Adult Meaning

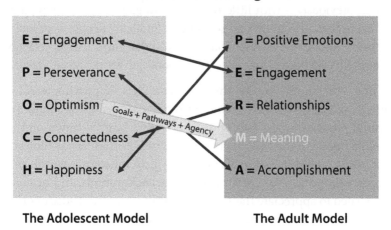

The Adolescent Model   The Adult Model

Note: This diagram represents the author's interpretation based on Kern et al's 2016 wellbeing model, Reivich's 2018 proposed Protective Factors of Resilience and Mayger-Moe & Lopez's Hope Theory.

Figure 4: Proposed relationship between adolescent optimism and adult meaning. Note: The diagram represents the author's interpretation based on Kern et al's 2016 Wellbeing Model, Reivich's 2018 proposed Protective Factors of Resilience and Mayger-Moe & Lopez's Hope Theory

23   Baumeister, R. F. & Vohs, K. D. (2002): The pursuit of meaningfulness in life. In C. R. Snyder & S. J. Lopez (Eds.), *Handbook of positive psychology* (pp. 608-618). New York, NY: Oxford University Press.
24   Damon, W., Menon, J. & Bronk, K. C. (2003): The development of purpose during adolescence. *Applied Developmental Science*, 7(3), p. 125.

Putting theory into practice

Getting started

Like too many wellbeing initiatives, my own program began in reaction to a near tragic situation. Late on a Friday afternoon, in my entirely low SES, extremely diverse school, student note-passing revealed that three of my students (all special needs classified) had made arrangements online to be picked up after school by unknown adult men to 'go for pizza'. Just a few minutes away from tragedy, parents, teachers, and administrators were all understandably shaken deeply that these three 8th Grade girls thought so little of themselves that they, without regard for consequence, sought validation from predatory strangers. As a recent graduate of the MAPP program, I had tried previously – with little response – to gain support for wellbeing additions to the curriculum and school day. Suddenly people were looking for answers, and it was then in March of 2010 that three female colleagues and I started 'Girl Power', a weekly after school club for the 8th Grade girls.

That first year about 70% of the 8th Grade girls (approximately 25 of them) showed up and stuck around for the remainder of the school year. My initial program was a collection of activities largely drawn on those that we had done in the MAPP program, as well as traditional adolescent female needs. The shift in the participating girls, indeed across the entire 8th Grade was pervasive. Girls of different backgrounds and academic levels learned to appreciate their own strengths, as well as those of others. They worked together to think about the future, set personal goals, and counsel and support each other to achieve the goals, which ranged from physical exercise, to improved academics and beyond (examples of the core positive activities are provided below). The effect, although not then formally measured, was powerful. Girl Power has continued in our school ever since, beginning in December and running through June. I, as well as my colleagues (both from junior high and MAPP), have asked what it is that generates such positive outcomes that, as noted above, spread across the whole 8th Grade and into the academic realm. Here is where I have found great value in the use of wellbeing and resiliency frames to dig into the engine of my program – to explore what makes it tick, and further to assess, augment, and improve the program.

Core activities

As noted above, the frameworks offer guidance in constructing one's own program in attunement to the needs of the target population and use of guiding frameworks may offer greater flexibility than specific programs. As McLaughlin (1994) notes in her study of effective inner-city youth organizations, while the structure and diversity of such programs is endless, what they shared was an emphasis on meeting the needs of the youth – a belief in the potential of each child. Accordingly, while researchers seek to broadly define factors to develop specific programs that build resilience and wellbeing, I believe that an understanding of the relevant factors and how they interact may allow teachers and adult leaders to utilize the frameworks to construct and augment their own programs in a way that is relevant to their target population, which they know the best!

My program for adolescent girls may or may not be relevant to your target population; however, there are a core set of activities, many of which have sound backing in psychological research, that I have found especially valuable within my group and may be relevant for use in most populations. I will describe ten essential activities below as well as note the wellbeing and resilience capacities they are intended to support.

1. Weekly 'get to know you' activities

EPOCH factors targeted: connection

Resilience factors targeted: connection

As noted in discussion of the frameworks, a sense of connection is both a wellbeing factor and resilience factor, and further is identified as a support for developing purpose and meaning in life. The simple act of meeting weekly as a group toward wellbeing undoubtedly builds connection; however, I make sure to specifically target it at every meeting in a warm-up activity.

In practice

Ice-breaker type activities for young teens abound and can be found easily on the internet. I will share two favorites of mine:

The first is using a giant beach ball and writing questions all over it with permanent marker – questions such as: 'what's the one thing you would have to have with you on a trip around the world?' and 'you wake up and it's ten years from now, what's your life like?' We toss the ball around the room to each other and wherever one's left thumb lands is the question read. This activity is one the girls always enjoy and can be used throughout the year. Collections of these types of questions also abound online.

Another activity that has greatly fostered connection is to ask the students to bring in baby pictures to share. I project them on a screen and we all guess whose image is shown, ask questions, and melt over the cuteness. In my group this is the warm-up activity to our work with the Dove Real Beauty Campaign materials which examines how women are portrayed in media and shows how their images are altered. Those materials are available at: www.dove.com/us/en/stories/campaigns.html

2. Exploring one's own character strengths and those of others

EPOCH factors targeted: all

Resilience factors targeted: all individual factors

Character education has been a valuable part of social-emotional training for centuries and remains a valuable foundation within many programs including my own. Character strengths are individuals' core characteristics that determine how they think, feel, and behave.[25] Many collections of core traits have been developed over centuries, but the model I have used with my students is the VIA (Values in Action) classification of strengths developed by Peterson and Seligman (2004) that categorizes 24 universal human strengths into the six virtues (groupings) of: wisdom, courage, humanity, transcendence, justice, and moderation (please refer to appendix for complete classification). Character strengths provide a foundation upon which all components of wellbeing and resilience can be bolstered, and further offer a language of positivity that students and teachers can use in reference to themselves and others. Indeed, the specific resilience components of connection,

---

25   Park, N. & Peterson, C. (2009): Character Strengths: Research and Practice. *Journal of College and Character*, 10(4).

optimism, self-regulation, and mental agility (open-mindedness) are also character strengths within the VIA, as are the wellbeing factors of perseverance, optimism, connectedness. The VIA character strengths assessment was created to measure the relative degree to which an individual exhibits each character strength and may be accessed for free with other valuable resources at: www.viacharacter.org/survey

In practice:

I have all my Girl Power members complete the online VIA survey early on in the program as the awareness of one's strengths, and the common language of strengths serves to inform all that follows. The survey is free online, is composed of 96 questions, takes about 25 minutes for the students to complete, and is available in other languages. At the end, the website provides the students with a report of their strengths, identifying their top five as their 'signature strengths'. The students are always excited to see their report and hold on to their top five like the 'golden ticket'. We then share as a group our top five and tally the group's results on a large poster. Furthermore, the girls always enjoy the opportunity to see with whom they share a signature strength, often surprised by the results. The activity serves to build a sense of connection early on and as noted provides important insight and language moving forward as we progress on to activities like goal-setting and choice-making.

3. Goal-setting

EPOCH factors targeted: engagement, persistence, and optimism

Resilience factors targeted: self-awareness, regulation, and efficacy; mental agility and optimism

As noted in the discussion of the frameworks, goal-setting that is done in a manner that is authentic, realistic, with clear planning, and assessment supports many pathways to overall wellbeing. Importantly, if one operationalizes hope as goals, pathways, and agency,[26] and considers such components as some of the precursors to a sense of meaning later in

---

26 Magyar-Moe, J. L. & Lopez, S. J. (2015): Strategies for accentuating hope. In S. Joseph (Ed.), *Positive psychology in practice: Promoting human flourishing in work, health, education, and everyday life* (2nd ed.) (pp. 483-502). Hoboken, NJ: Wiley.

life,[27] it seems essential that any program intended for wellbeing should include goal setting.

In practice

At our very first Girl Power meeting, I have the girls make vision boards – a poster-size collage of images and words pulled from magazines and printed from the internet – to start thinking about their futures. Where will they live? What work will they do? Who will their friends and families be? What passions and talents will they be engaging? The girls share their products with the group and take them home to remind them of their visions. Additionally, they can snap an image on their phone to keep it with them at all times. This meeting is followed by the session described above on exploring character strengths, after which we get into explicit goal-setting.

Goal-setting

The two formats I've found useful with my group are, firstly, the familiar acronym SMART Goals, which stands for specific, measurable, actionable, realistic, and timed. Secondly are the Character Lab's WOOP Goals, which stand for wish, outcome, obstacles, and plan. Both may be found online with good accompanying resources at the links below:

www.characterlab.org/woop

www.smartsheet.com/blog/essential-guide-writing-smart-goals

I include a version of the WOOP format in the appendices, modified with some clarifying questions that I have found useful. Furthermore, I introduce the reflection on personal goals with a script drawn from old Anthony Robbins goal-setting exercises as I've found it supports a deeper thought process (also found in the appendices). Both the WOOP and SMART platforms are useful in helping the user to hone in on concrete incremental goals and plan a way to track real progress. For example, the girls will often begin with a very broad goal such as 'getting in shape', which when placed within one of the suggested goal structures, may

---

27   Baumeister, R. F., & Vohs, K. D. (2002): The pursuit of meaningfulness in life. In C. R. Snyder & S. J. Lopez (Eds.), *Handbook of positive psychology* (pp. 608-618). New York, NY: Oxford University Press.

become as specific as walking two miles with my friend on the boardwalk on Tuesdays and Thursdays after school for the next two months.

Goals can also be tracked in personal journals (we decorate blank books for this purpose) with progress check-ins at later meetings. Toward this end, I have developed my own follow-up to WOOP called 'WOW!', which stands for: 'what's going well (or not)?', one thing I would change, and 'what's the next step?' Using goal-setting, my girls have improved grades, made more social connections, increased exercise time and changed eating habits; simultaneously this has increased self-efficacy, optimism, and supported development of purpose and meaning.

4. Making good choices

EPOCH factors targeted: persistence and optimism

Resilience factors targeted: self-awareness, regulation, and efficacy; mental agility and optimism

As noted above, the best programs are those that use the guiding frameworks in a manner most appropriate to the target audience, in this case adolescents. From personal experience, I note that adolescents are notoriously prone to living in the moment, reacting rather than acting, and failing to consider consequences. Accordingly, choice-making activities are essential and further may target self-regulation, an area typically developing in adolescence.[28] Having already considered our future visions, set goals, and identified supporting strengths, we can now practice making choices to support those goals.

In practice

This activity is based on a lesson my daughter Elizabeth used toward young women's empowerment while serving in the Peace Corps in the Pacific Island country of Vanuatu.

We place our girls in groups of four or more and give each group a large chart paper and markers. Each group then randomly selects a teacher-made 'hard choice' card – use what's right for your group. We go with

---

28   Oettengin, G. & Gollwitzer, M. (2015): Self-Regulation: Principles and Tool. *Self-Regulation in Adolescence*, pp. 3-29. New York, NY: Cambridge University Press.

some tough but realistic choices such as, 'your popular boyfriend whom you adore wants you to engage in intercourse with him or says he will end the relationship – do you do it?' It's important that each question be able to be answered as yes or no to support the chart activity. The groups set up their charts by writing the choice scenario at the top, then setting up four large quadrants, labelled across the top as yes or no, and along the sides as good or bad possible outcomes. An example is shown below:

Our choice situation:		
Possible outcomes:	If 'yes'	If 'no'
Positive:		
Negative:		

We encourage the girls to think in both short-term and long-term outcomes. The groups discuss and work together to fill in their poster, then each group shares to the whole group and all engage in full-group discussion. Simply seeing a visual of the outcomes balanced against one another and realizing that many will be quite long-term has had powerful effects on our group. In fact, girls have come back from the high school to tell us they've used the process to think about in-the-moment 'hard choices'.

5. Mindfulness practices

Mindfulness (non-judgemental focused attention to the present moment) has gained increasing popularity within school systems and other organizations due to its proven connection to increased self-awareness, self-regulation, strengthen attention, and reduce stress (Holzen et al, 2011). Depending on how it is used, mindfulness can also support various forms of engagement, build the relationships of connection, and contribute to positive emotions (happiness) when focused on gratitude. Mindfulness can be led by a group leader or can be practiced individually using simple scripts or employing one of the many available apps for that purpose.

In practice

In my case, I am fortunate to work with a colleague who teaches mindfulness meditation and conducts sessions with our girls – chances are you too may have a colleague who practices. We have used sessions as brief as five minutes, and as long as 20 with our group. We conduct sessions every few weeks and encourage the girls to practice on their own. My colleague also conducts meditations before school two mornings a week, which a few of the girls attend. Many scripts to lead a session are available online as are recorded meditation sessions. A script from UC Berkley's Great Good site is included in the appendix for getting started.

In addition to meditation, mindfulness can be used to focus on conversations to build relationships, academics (even standardized testing), or simply toward increasing joy by fully engaging in a pleasant experience such as taking a walk.

6. Active-constructive responding

EPOCH factors targeted: connectedness and happiness

Resilience factors targeted: self-awareness, self-regulation and connection

As defined within the relationship work of psychologist Shelly Gable, Active Constructive Responding (ACR) is one of four possible ways that people respond when someone shares good news with them. The ACR approach has been shown to lead to greater relationship satisfaction, trust, and fewer conflicts.[29] I have taught ACR as both a positive education trainer to adults, as well as to my adolescent girls, and in both cases have found it an easily graspable concept and one that is highly rated by the participants as making a difference in their lives.

In practice

The four quadrants of response types are shown below. I typically present the girls with this model and then ask two volunteers to model the styles – one person as the bearer of good news, the other the responder who tries out each style.

The news: 'Hey I just got hired as a waitress in that new restaurant for the summer!'

Table 1: The four quadrants of response types

	Constructive	Destructive
Active	Wow, that is great news! How did you get the job? What kind of food do they serve?	Oh no, you will have no free time at all this summer!
Passive	Oh, how nice. So, what's for homework tonight?	That's great. You know my sister got hired in the big fancy place where all the big tippers hang out!

The students usually have a laugh with this but are able to point out the features of each response type and generate their own examples. We also talk about how to engage in sincere ACR by using such strengths as curiosity. This topic too becomes a journal assignment: to pick two people to engage ACR with over the next week and notice if the relationship changes. Again, this is a very easy concept to grasp and one that seems to carry a lot of wellbeing bang for the buck! (Many additional great resources for ACR can be found on IPEN's website.)

---

29 Gable, S. L., Impett, E. A., Reis, H. T. & Asher, E. R. (2004): What do you do when things go right? The Intrapersonal and Interpersonal Benefits of Sharing Positive Events. *Journal of Personality and Social Psychology,* 87, pp. 228-245.

7. Explanatory style

EPOCH factors targeted: persistence, optimism, connectedness and happiness

Resilience factors targeted: self-awareness, self-regulation, mental agility, optimism and connection

As noted in the discussion of the wellbeing and resilience factors, optimism is defined, in part, as an optimistic explanatory style – the habitual way that a person explains the causes of the good and bad things that happen to them.[30] Optimism further has been associated with numerous health and wellbeing outcomes, and while some aspect is certainly biologically-determined, the explanatory style component can be targeted and improved. Furthermore, our explanatory patterns become habitual, often to the point that we don't assess situations accurately and feel badly about events when we don't need to. The point of targeting these patterns is to make us aware so that we can think and feel more accurately about a situation.

In practice

I like to think of the three dimensions of explanatory style as the 3 P's: personal (caused by me, or not me), pervasiveness (applies everywhere or just here), and permanence (always like this or just this time). This understanding works well for me personally, and may be useful with older children, but for my junior high girls I've found it helpful to break it down as follows:

Explaining why something happened:

Table 2: The 3 Ps

Personal:	Me	Not me
Pervasiveness:	Everywhere	Just here
Permanence:	Always	Just once

We begin by becoming aware of our own patterns by looking at scenarios relevant to adolescent girls, describing our initial reactionary responses as a group, and analyzing where they fall in each dimension.

---

30   Reivich, K. & Shatte, A. (2002): *The resilience factor: 7 Essential skills for overcoming life's inevitable obstacles.* New York, NY: Broadway Books.

Sample scenario

Two of your friends go to the movies and do not invite you. Why? How do you explain this?

Responses may vary from: 'they don't like me anymore and will no longer be my friends' (me, everywhere, always) to 'it was a movie about something they share, and they'll probably invite me another time' (not me, just here, just once).

We work with more relevant adolescent scenarios until the girls begin to realize that me, always, and everywhere are dangerous styles for explaining bad events. Conversely, if something good happens, a pattern of not me is also dangerous.

Then the girls work in groups with additional scenarios, share initial reactions with each other, and work to shift to the less pessimistic dimension, being careful to maintain a reality check (i.e. sometimes it is your fault and you acknowledge that, but also keep things in the realm of just here, and just this time) not a permanent condition. In the end, the girls tape a copy of the 3 P's dimensions in their journals to remain aware of patterns, toward building healthier styles. Oftentimes the simple awareness is very eye-opening for them and I often hear them correct themselves in their day to day interactions.

Although not described here, a valuable follow-up is to extend habitual thought patterns to consider one's 'thinking traps', related to unhealthy thought pattern such as over-generalizing, jumping to conclusions, and – everyone's favorite – mind-reading. Many resources by Reivich and Shatte, as well as other psychologists that are intended for use with students can be found online. IPEN also offers resources for these constructs. Again, awareness of one's unhelpful patterns can lead to change!

8. Team-building

EPOCH factors targeted: engagement, persistence, optimism, connectedness, happiness

Resilience factors targeted: self-awareness, self-regulation, self-efficacy, mental agility, optimism and connection

Wellbeing 'bang for the buck', team-building activities are an easy and rich source to target pretty much everything. Even the simplest team-building activity requires the participants to engage, persist, build optimism in successive improved attempts, connect with one another, and simply enjoy the experience. Similarly, all the self and interpersonal skills of resiliency are being addressed.

In practice

Most team-building activities require very little preparation or material input, just a challenging task and some space to do it in. Some of my favorite examples:

Task: Arrange yourselves in a straight line in alphabetical order by your mother's middle name without speaking.

Task: Three-person teams work together to find a missing object placed out in the distance in front of them. One person is the speaker who gives the directions, but must sit with their back to the object. One person can look at the object, but cannot speak and must gesture the directions to get to the object to the speaker. The third person is the actual searcher who walks to find the object, but is blindfolded and must rely on the words of the speaker who is going by the gestures of the one person who can see. Lots of fun in action!

Many similar team-building activities are available online. We play this last one on the beach near our school at the end of the year, and the girls always want to try it many times in each of the different roles.

We do team-building a few times a year, and the key each time is to debrief the process:

- How did the team work together?
- What strengths were used?
- How did the plan improve?
- How did each person contribute?
- Ties perfectly into Growth Mindset…

9. Growth Mindset

EPOCH factors targeted: persistence and optimism

Resilience factors targeted: self-awareness, self-regulation, mental agility and optimism

Many educators will be familiar with Dr. Carol Dweck's work on Growth Mindset, which is the belief that intelligence can be changed – that hard work contributes to academic performance (and most areas) more than biology. Dweck's work shows that having a Growth Mindset, as opposed to fixed, contributes, not surprisingly, to optimism and resilience.[31] Furthermore, awareness of one's mindset can contribute to change toward growth.

In practice

Many wonderful resources are available on Dweck's Stanford Growth Mindset website.[32] I like to start by watching a Will Smith video available on YouTube: www.youtube.com/watch?v=RIcQioPacXg

Here Smith talks about his work ethic and persistence, and the misconception that talent wins over hard work. We then discuss the attributes that let Smith succeed. We also talk about others who were not recognized early in their careers – people like Einstein and Henry Ford, for example – who were labeled as untalented and unintelligent, given up on. Next, we share examples of things we used to be unable to do, and now are able. For example, this could be anything from writing one's name to bike riding. We create a group poster of things we got better at. Then we turn to what we realistically want to work on and make a poster of what we're not good at yet. Dweck likes to call this 'the power of YET' This is a good time to revisit character strengths and goal-setting toward achieving the growth.

Again, IPEN's collection of resources provides additional activities for this.

---

31   Dweck, C. S. (2006): *Mindset: The new psychology of success.* New York: Random House.
32   Available at: www.mindsetkit.org/static/files/YCLA_LessonPlan_v10.pdf

10. Gratitude and other journaling opportunities

EPOCH factors targeted: connectedness and happiness

Resilience factors targeted: self-awareness, connection and optimism

Gratitude interventions were one of the earliest, evidence-based PIs, and remain consistently supportive of wellbeing.[33] Gratitude succeeds by boosting our own self-worth and then connecting beyond the self in thankfulness to the other. UC Berkeley's Great Good Science Center offers a brief and valuable introductory explanation.[34]

In practice

Gratitude practices are probably some of the easiest positive activities to include in one's program. We begin by asking the girls to bring in a personal artifact (i.e. 'show and tell') – an object of very personal worth to that individual. We place the girls in groups of four to six where they share their object and why it is special to them; we've seen instruments, books, photos, rocks, and more. We ask them to end their share with, 'this object makes me feel thankful for...'. They may be thankful for a person, experience, or their own personal character strengths.

The homework is to engage in the traditional (highly evidence-supported) daily practice of 'Three Good Things', which is also called 'Three Blessings' or 'What went well?' The girls record in their journals three things they are thankful for, and how they contributed to this benefit (targeting explanatory style as well). We share some of our examples with each other at the following meeting. Every year I am astounded by their ability to notice and appreciate the simplest things and come away with a new awareness myself.

Other journal activities

As noted above, one of our meetings is devoted to decorating the covers of blank books using paints and markers (I purchase hardcover books online at a cost of $1.99). This is a fun exercise in creativity, but further provides the platform for much of the planning, recording, and

---

33 Wood, A. M., Froh, J. J. & Geraghty, A. W. (2010): Gratitude and well-being: A review and theoretical integration. *Clinical psychology review*, 30(7), pp. 890-905.
34 Available at: www.greatergood.berkeley.edu/video/item/why_gratitude_works1

reflection associated with many of the activities. I provide the girls with copies of the relevant instructions and activity charts to remind them of the possibilities for using their journals. The girls paste these in their books to refer to during the year and beyond. This collection called 'what you can do in your journal' is included in the appendix.

A measurement plan

Although I now use the frameworks of wellbeing and resiliency as guideposts for my whole program, my first experience with formally using a wellbeing framework was as a measurement tool. Qualitatively, my colleagues and I observed early on that the girls in Girl Power progressed better academically, found engagement in high school and came back to tell us about it. I happily shared this information with anyone who would ask, including Dr. Martin Seligman, the founder of our MAPP program, to which he responded, 'Well that's all very nice Ginny … but are you measuring?'

I was not.

The following summer, I had the good fortune to attend the IPPA conference in Los Angeles and heard Dr. Peggy Kern speak about her newly-developed adolescent measure of wellbeing, the EPOCH questionnaire, closely aligned with the constructs of PERMA, with which I was already familiar. This instrument gave me what I needed to evaluate the program.

The measurement model

Given my noted frustration with the overemphasis on standardized testing in schools and the monocular focus on academic performance, I decided to not only assess gains in wellbeing for my girls, but further to track and correlate with academic performance, including standardized test scores, to bolster the case for an expanded focus on wellbeing. Dr. Peggy Kern graciously agreed to participate in this small study to provide analyses. While our design passed IRB muster, my school refused to sign off on releasing anonymous student test scores for a formal study. Ah, public schools. However, I conducted the measurement – following school survey protocols, of course – to satisfy our own curiosity, and frankly I believe there is value in such knowledge.

Design

The IT team at school put the 20-item EPOCH questionnaire[35] on the online survey website SurveyMonkey, along with other items that we chose to add, including self-reported academic performance in math and language arts, and questions about safety and basic needs being met – 24 items in total. I had all the 8th Graders, 89 boys and girls in total, complete the survey in the beginning of the school year. I had all the students take the survey again in June; 67 of which were able to be matched across time for both measures. The students included their student ID numbers for that purpose. This was a relatively simple way to collect the wellbeing data as SurveyMonkey provides the resulting data in an easily analyzable form.

To track standardized test scores, I used the 8th Grade students' state test scores from the previous year (during 7th Grade) in math and language arts as a baseline, to compare with their 8th Grade scores. This part was a bit tedious on my own as scores had to be entered with school ID numbers (not included in the state data) to be matched with their wellbeing scores. I imagine this process could be done much more easily with an on-board school system with a data analysis program in place.

Using these two sources of information, I had pre- and post-scores on both wellbeing and standardized math and reading tests for 67 students and could compare the results on both counts between my Girl Power participants (25 girls in total) and the rest of the 8th Grade (42 students). As noted, Dr. Kern of University of Melbourne, kindly utilized her statistical expertise to run the analyses, which again could certainly be accomplished within an existing school data system. I briefly describe the outcomes below.

Results

EPOCH wellbeing components, as well as overall wellbeing, increased substantially more in the Girl Power group from pre- to post-assessment. Furthermore, the greatest increase was in self-reported academic performance (graph 1).

---

35   Available for free at: www.peggykern.org/uploads/5/6/6/7/56678211/epoch_measure_of_adolescent_well-being_102014.pdf

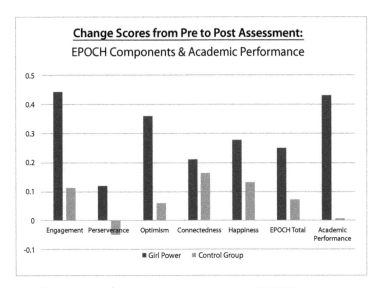

Graph 1: Change scores from pre- to post-assessment: EPOCH components & academic performance

Graph 2 shows the percentage increase in the number of students achieving proficiency in standardized testing for each group, with once again the Girl Power group gaining more students into the ranks of 'proficient' according to state testing.

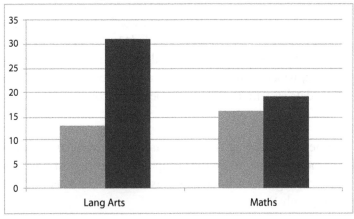

Graph 2: Percentage increase in the number of students achieving proficiency in standardized testing for each group

Finally, for me, the most interesting result was the correlational analyses shown in Table 3 below. From time 1 (pre-scores) to time 2 (post-scores) we found that across the whole sample (Girl Power and non-Girl Power), increases in standardized math scores were most correlated in connectedness. However, within the Girl Power group perseverance, connectedness, and overall wellbeing correlate with academic performance and standardized math test scores. Interestingly, the highest correlation for the math scores was again connectedness. According to Dr. Kern, although the sample size is small, the correlations are impressive.

'The table below correlates time 1 values with time 2 values. As we might expect, the wellbeing variables are correlated over time. Perseverance correlates with greater academic performance at time 2. In the full sample, connectedness correlates with greater math performance. In the Girl Power group, we actually see that perseverance, connectedness, and overall wellbeing correlate with better academic scores – despite a small sample size. In fact, the associations with achievement in the full sample are driven by the Girl Power group. This is an impressive result.' – Dr. Kern.

Table 3: Time 1 Variables with Time 2 Variables

Girl Power group		E_t2	P_t2	O_t2	C_t2	H_t2	EPOCH_t2	acad_t2	lacking_2	access_t2	safety_t2	need_t2	LA_t2	math_t2
engagement	r	.577**	0.357	0.268	0.212	0.207	0.345	0.285	0.139	0.144	-0.026	-0.004	0.104	0.134
	p	0.003	0.079	0.196	0.31	0.321	0.091	0.168	0.506	0.491	0.904	0.983	0.619	0.523
	N	25	25	25	25	25	25	25	25	25	25	25	25	25
perseverance	r	.635**	.907**	.733**	.702**	.469*	.773**	.900**	0.291	0.381	0.309	0.232	0.328	.434*
	p	0.001	0	0	0	0.018	0	0	0.158	0.061	0.132	0.265	0.109	0.03
	N	25	25	25	25	25	25	25	25	25	25	25	25	25
optimism	r	.494*	.597**	.669**	.491*	.487*	.612**	.569**	0.342	0.21	.518**	0.162	0.096	0.384
	p	0.012	0.002	0	0.013	0.014	0.001	0.003	0.094	0.315	0.008	0.44	0.647	0.058
	N	25	25	25	25	25	25	25	25	25	25	25	25	25
connectedness	r	0.333	.503*	.427*	.574**	.429*	.511**	.552**	0.344	0.181	.403*	0.081	0.393	.661**
	p	0.104	0.01	0.033	0.003	0.033	0.009	0.004	0.093	0.387	0.046	0.699	0.052	0
	N	25	25	25	25	25	25	25	25	25	25	25	25	25
happiness	r	0.287	.461*	.512**	.479*	.509**	.505**	0.391	0.282	0.147	.458**	0.128	0.066	0.314
	p	0.164	0.02	0.009	0.016	0.009	0.01	0.054	0.172	0.483	0.021	0.541	0.755	0.127
	N	25	25	25	25	25	25	25	25	25	25	25	25	25
EPOCH total	r	.598**	.768**	.716**	.682**	.575**	.746**	.736**	0.381	0.286	.471*	0.169	0.267	.539**

Frameworks as ongoing formative tools

In a bit of afterthought in my experiments in measuring outcomes, my colleagues and I decided to look at each activity the club had completed that year, and code them for the EPOCH wellbeing components addressed. Our purpose was to then quantify the percentage of meetings spent on each component to see where we were robust, and where we could stand to improve. That graph is shown below. We were strongest in engagement, and weakest in perseverance (I have since modified the curriculum).

What was even more interesting, is when I was assembling all the outcome data I happened to place the percentage of meetings spent on each topic (graph 3) next to the percentage increase in the group's wellbeing scores for each factor (graph 1). The distribution of the bars for the wellbeing components was nearly identical … indicating that we were targeting what we thought we were and it was coming out on the other end in the summative assessment!

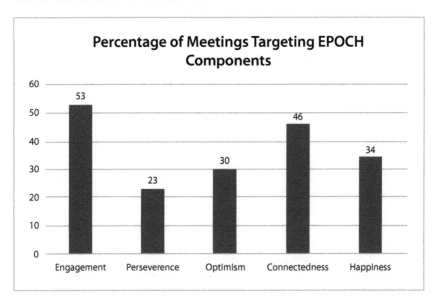

Graph 3: Percentage of meeting targeting EPOCH components

Conclusions

We can all work toward systemic change that is implemented proactively – not in response to some tragedy. In the meantime, just one caring individual in a school system can make a difference when informed by the right tools. Although my initial application of a wellbeing framework was as a means of measuring outcomes (and I got some good ones), the value of utilizing such a framework to plan and adjust the curriculum to respond to the needs of my students became apparent. I believe the frameworks I have described here, and the relationships between them offer valuable roadmaps of guidance in terms of identifying the needs of one's groups, as well as evaluating and creating the curriculum itself – yet we are flexible enough to allow appropriate structuring to best meet the needs of one's own best-known group. Many wonderful activities and exercises have been created by wise practitioners through the years. With the informed understanding of what constitutes resilience and wellbeing, we can select those that best support our immediate target population. With valuable and accurate guidance, even one who travels solo in challenging terrain can deliver resilience and wellbeing.

Further reading

Butler, J. & Kern, M. (2013): *The Perma Profiler.* Available at: www.peggykern. org/uploads/5/6/6/7/56678211/the_perma-profiler_092515.pdf

Centers for Disease Control and Prevention. (2008): Youth risk behavior surveillance. *Surveillance Summaries*, 59(SS-5).

Dweck, C. S. (2007): The perils and promises of praise. *ASCD*, 65(2), pp. 34-39.

Holzen, B. K., Lazar, S. W., Gard, T., Schuman-Oliver, Z., Vago, D. R. & Ott, U. (2011): How does mindfulness meditation work? Proposing mechanisms of action from a conceptual and neural perspective. *Perspectives on Psychological Science*, 6(6), pp. 537-559.

Maddux J. E. & Kleiman, E. M. (2016): Self-efficacy: A foundational concept for positive clinical psychology. In A. M. Wood & J. Johnson (Eds.), *The Wiley Handbook of Positive Clinical Psychology* (pp. 89-101). Hoboken, NJ: Wiley.

Masten, A. S. & Tellegen, A. (2012): Resilience in developmental psychopathology: Contributions of the project competence longitudinal study. *Development and psychopathology*, 24(2), pp. 345-361.

McLaughlin, M., Irby, M. & Langman, J. (1994): *Urban Sanctuaries: Neighborhood organizations in the lives and futures of inner-city youth.* San Francisco, CA: Jossey-Bass.

Peterson, C. & Seligman, M. E. P. (2004): *Character Strengths and Virtues: A handbook and classification.* 1(1). New York, NY: Oxford University Press.

Seligman, M. E. P. (2011): *Flourish: A visionary new understanding of happiness and well-being.* New York, NY: Free Press.

Werner, E. (2005): Resilience and recovery: Findings from the Kauai longitudinal study. *Research, Policy, and Practice in Children's Mental Health*, 19(1), pp. 11-14.

Appendices of Core Activity Resources

Appendix A: Values in Action Classification of Character Strengths

(Peterson & Seligman, 2004)

1. Wisdom and knowledge: cognitive strengths that entail the acquisition and use of knowledge.

- Creativity: thinking of novel and productive ways to do things.
- Curiosity: taking an interest in all of ongoing experience.
- Love of learning: mastering new skills, topics, and bodies of knowledge.
- Open-mindedness: thinking things through and examining them from all sides
- Perspective: being able to provide wise counsel to others.

2. Courage: emotional strengths that involve the exercise of will to accomplish goals in the face of opposition, external or internal.

- Authenticity: speaking the truth and presenting oneself in a genuine way.
- Bravery: not shrinking from threat, challenge, difficulty, or pain.
- Persistence: finishing what one starts.

- Zest: approaching life with excitement and energy.

3. Humanity: interpersonal strengths that involve 'tending and befriending' others.

- Kindness: doing favors and good deeds for others.
- Love: valuing close relations with others.
- Social intelligence: being aware of the motives and feelings of self and others.

4. Justice: civic strengths that underlie healthy community life.

- Fairness: treating all people the same according to notions of fairness and justice.
- Leadership: organizing group activities and seeing that they happen.
- Teamwork: working well as member of a group or team.

5. Temperance: strengths that protect against excess.

- Forgiveness: forgiving those who have done wrong.
- Modesty: letting one's accomplishments speak for themselves.
- Prudence: being careful about one's choices; not saying or doing things that might later be regretted.
- Self-regulation: Regulating what one feels and does.

6. Transcendence: strengths that forge connections to the larger universe and provide meaning.

- Appreciation of beauty and excellence: noticing and appreciating beauty, excellence, and/or skilled performance in all domains of life.
- Gratitude: being aware of and thankful for the good things that happen.
- Hope: expecting the best and working to achieve it.
- Humor: liking to laugh and tease; bringing smiles to other people.
- Spirituality: having coherent beliefs about the higher purpose and meaning of life.

Appendix B: Goal Discussion and Planning Page

Thinking about goals:

1. A goal I want to accomplish in the next six months is:
2. The things that are preventing me from reaching my goal are:
3. The negative outcomes from me not reaching my goal are:
4. If I accomplished the goal, the good outcomes would be:
5. The habit(s) that are holding me back from achieving my goal are:
6. A new habit(s) I could create to reach this goal is:
7. The things I could do to get rid of my bad habit are:
8. Do you commit to this goal? If so, when?

Based on Anthony Robbins work, as interpreted in MAPP 602, University of Pennsylvania, 2008.

Wish: What is an important wish that you want to accomplish in the next _____ (time period)?

Your wish should be challenging, but possible. Write your response in 3-6 words.

Outcome: What will be the best result from accomplishing your wish? How will you feel?

Obstacle: What is the main obstacle inside you that might prevent you from accomplishing your wish?

Plan: Select an effective action plan to tackle the obstacle:

If_____**, then**

I will _____.

If_____**, then, I**
will_____.

Think: who, what, where, and when.

Adapted from WOOP Goals, VIACharacterlab.org

Tracking goal progess:

WOW!

What's working, or not?

One thing I will change is:

What's my next step with this goal?

Millar (2018) based on WOOP Goals, via.characterlab.org

Appendix C: Sample Mindfulness Meditation Script

Mindfulness Body Scan Script from UC Berkeley Great Good Science Center: www.mindful.org/a-3-minute-body-scan-meditation-to-cultivate-mindfulness/

Begin by bringing your attention into your body.

You can close your eyes if that's comfortable for you.

You can notice your body seated wherever you're seated, feeling the weight of your body on the chair, on the floor.

Take a few deep breaths.

And, as you take a deep breath, bring in more oxygen enlivening the body. And, as you exhale, have a sense of relaxing more deeply.

You can notice your feet on the floor; notice the sensations of your feet touching the floor and the weight, pressure, vibration, and heat.

You can notice your legs against the chair: pressure, pulsing, heaviness, and lightness.

Notice your back against the chair.

Bring your attention into your stomach area. If your stomach is tense or tight, let it soften. Take a breath.

Notice your hands. Are your hands tense or tight? See if you can allow them to soften.

Notice your arms. Feel any sensation in your arms. Let your shoulders be soft.

Notice your neck and throat. Let them be soft. Relax.

Soften your jaw. Let your face and facial muscles become soft.

Then notice your whole body present. Take one more breath.

Be aware of your whole body as best you can. Take a breath and then, when you're ready, you can open your eyes.

Appendix D: What you can do in your journal...

(Paste this inside the cover of your journal)

1. Practice active constructive responding with someone, write about the experience:

- What helped you know what to say?
- How did it feel?
- How did the person respond?
- Do you think it changed your relationship?

Reminder of the response types:

	Constructive	Destructive
Active	Wow, that is great news! How did you get the job? What kind of food do they serve?	Oh no, you will have no free time at all this summer!
Passive	Oh, how nice. So what's for homework tonight?	That's great. You know my sister got hired in the really big fancy place where all the big tippers hang out!

2. Explaining why something happened: Keep track of the way you explain things that happen.

- Remember to watch out for reactions that are 'me, everywhere, always'.
- Try explaining in a realistic but different way that is 'not me, just here, just this time'.
- Write your new explanation:

Personal:	Pervasiveness:	Permanence:
Me	Everywhere	Always
Not me	Just here	Just once

3. Setting goals and tracking your progress:

WOOP Goals:

Wish: _____

Outcomes: _____

Obstacles: _____

Plan: _____

Who can help? What exactly will you do? Where will you do this? When will you do this? How will you know you've done it?

Tracking your goals – WOW!

What went well/or not? _____

One thing to change: _____

What's the next step(s)? _____

_____

4. Noticing what's good: three good things!

Write your responses each day.

Three good things:
What happened? Why?

1. _____

2. _____

3. _____

Chapter 4:

Intervention Leaders:
Defining positive attitudes

Rob Stokoe OBE & Mick Walsh

The wellbeing and happiness of students has always been a fundamental goal for great schools and passionate educators. The positive education movement does not seek to revolutionise education, rather it is simply drawing attention to the key fact that the emotional and physical wellbeing of all involved in school life is of prime importance. The greater focus upon wellbeing and happiness as a worthy goal is pertinent to successful schools, and rightly so, as the roots of adult happiness are said to form in childhood. Happy, confident and competent students are important to us all. The landscape around positive education is varied to say the least, as we talk of resilience, mindfulness, character strengths, and flow, and the research around this is both broad and complex. The purpose of this chapter is to propose an implementation process enabling schools to consider how wellbeing and positivity can impact upon classroom practice and the learning experience of those within.

Positive emotions broaden attention and engagement

According to Fredrickson (2001), positive emotion can broaden thoughts and actions in a way that supports effective and robust learning processes.[1] Two decades later, it is equally important – perhaps more so – that we foster and maintain a positive atmosphere in our schools and learning environments. The time our students spend in school is critical to them as adults and builds the foundations that will shape their futures. The increased awareness of and importance given to wellbeing and resilience has informed an increased appetite for integrating positive education programmes into our schools. Discrete teaching within health programmes is no doubt advantageous, if planned and delivered well, but a school-wide 'buy-in' and integrated approach is imperative for deep learning. That said, we need to tread carefully and thoughtfully – our curricula are overcrowded, and our teachers are feeling quite overwhelmed. They need to be provided with initiatives and processes, which can be readily accessed and translated into their individual learning and teaching contexts. Furthermore, our students are already exposed to stress all too early as, too often, they are subjected to internal benchmarking and testing, inspection, as well as the ongoing drive to sustain effort to ensure measurable progress. Coupled with increased perception of competition at all levels, this may lead to situations of self-doubt, adversity and unhappiness in their learning, and learning should never be a negative experience. When making decisions to engage in learning, every student should be able to begin with the notion of, 'I can do this, and I want to do this'. When our students adopt this growth-orientated mindset, they are more likely to achieve their learning goals and extend their potential.

Promoting positive self-image for every student

When we, as educators, focus upon strengths rather than weaknesses, upon what we can do rather than what we cannot do, then we will give both ourselves and our students a positive direction. By embracing optimism, encouraging perseverance, and cultivating stronger interpersonal attributes in our students, we will develop happier, more engaged learners, who will equip themselves with the skills to inform success; skills that will serve them well throughout their lives. The best schools, and the

---

[1] Fredrickson, B. (2001): The broaden-and-build theory of positive emotions. *American Psychologist*, 56(3), pp, 218-226.

best educators globally, go beyond the dissemination of knowledge and teaching of academic skills, to embrace the whole child, adapting their curriculum and teaching to support wellbeing, mindfulness and happiness, always promoting a positive self-image for every student. Our target must always be to develop academically, socially and emotionally capable young people, who can adapt their abilities and emotional competencies to help them to thrive in the 21st century. Young people who are emotional millionaires. To quote Howard Gardner, from his book Five Minds for the Future: 'The world doesn't need more of the brightest and the best, but more of those of good character.'[2] As we continually reflect it will be useful to redefine what 'best and brightest' means in the 21st century. Instead of prioritising academic high achievement, we need to place more store on the development of emotional intelligence and the acquisition of intelligent learning behaviours. By highlighting and celebrating characteristics such as curiosity (which inspires wonder and awe), creativity (of thought, design and action), purposefulness and perseverance, we expand the definition of 'best and brightest' from applying exclusively to academic high achievers to including all those who love to learn and are willing to learn bravely and flexibly. In our schools we also refer to the importance of becoming 'people for others' – thoughtful, selfless, caring, compassionate learners. These qualities also carry over into academic learning, with extremely positive outcomes.

A one-shoe-fits-all approach will not do

The challenge here is that no single framework can effectively meet these needs; a one-shoe fits-all approach simply will not do. The context we and our students face is unique. School-based programmes need to be diverse and flexible, adapting to meet the needs of the learners and educators within the organisation; in fact, they should be as rich and as eclectic as the school populations we serve. We need to develop programmes that offer experiences, support and guidance, which will develop in every student a portfolio of attributes and skills that will enable them to live better, happier lives.

---

2   Gardner, H. (2007): *Five Minds for the Future*. Boston, MA: Harvard Business Review Press.

These interventions must also be considered at a strategic or whole-school level. Geelong Grammar's project is a prime example, with all staff, teachers, administrators and cleaners all attending an initial training course with ongoing interventions beyond. The impact we need to see across our schools is the successful implementation of clearly defined and contextually appropriate responses and experiences, for and connected to our classrooms. We need to grow capable intervention leaders, who can disseminate good practice and integrate positive education successfully into our classrooms.

Implementation process

There is no silver bullet for building student and teacher wellbeing. Research indicates that it is the frequency of experiencing positive emotions, not their intensity, which has the greatest effect on enhancing the wellbeing of all of us. Encouraging students and teachers to look at life through their top character strengths, to self-assess on their efforts, and then to set new self-expectations, nudges them along the mindset continuum towards growth orientated mindsets. Thriving and flourishing school communities make a conscious choice to look for and celebrate the positive things they are doing; they do good to feel good. It also helps our young people to address their negatives/weaknesses by focusing on the positive actions or behaviours that would improve the situation.

To grow our brains' abilities, we need to strive to do more difficult things; bringing positive education alive in our schools is one of those things. There are rich personal growth rewards on offer while striving to achieve this difficult goal, and further benefits when it is achieved.

Step 1: As a member of staff reset your vision of what you want for your students.

Show the following four-minute clip about our reticular activating system. It is our neurological spam filter that only lets things through to our brain that we focus on and see as important. www.youtube.com/watch?v=QCnfAzAIhVw

In groups of three, ask what we want our students to act like, look like, sound like, know and be able to do because of our collective efforts and influence. (What usually comes up are things like: happy, resilient, respectful, lifelong learners, caring, and so on.)

Then for each descriptor, come up with three behaviours students would exhibit that would show it; they experience the world in behaviours, not descriptors. If we asked a 14-year-old boy to be resilient, he would be confused.

Then ask what actions we will take to cultivate those behaviours in our students.

As a side task, ask if these behaviours would apply to staff too.

Step 2: Identify things that you are already doing well to cultivate these behaviours in students and ourselves.

Audit our activities and monitor the degree of developmental challenge. Duplication may cause some difficulties but remember it's about what the individual students need.

It is important for you to hunt for the good stuff and appreciate what is going well at present in the wellbeing space.

You will usually find that they are not big things, but rather a collection of little gems students and staff are doing.

Step 3: Identify our champions, staff who are passionate about building student and staff wellbeing. They are our positive energy network for others to feed off.

Bring them together to celebrate the positive things we are doing to build both student and teacher wellbeing.

Identify areas that need our attention. A good strategy is to do a stock-take on what we are currently doing to build each of the evidence-based elements of wellbeing we are using. (There are many models of wellbeing to choose from; select one that is user-friendly for your school.)

Search the internet for resources and activities that will attend to those areas and cultivate the desired behaviours identified earlier.

Then, at the next staff meeting, introduce staff to these resources and activities and invite and encourage them to use one or more of them with their classes in their subject areas.

Step 4: Define accurate positive education language; this develops a robust wellbeing culture.

Show the glossary of positive education words, terms and meanings.

Explain that to develop a healthy positive education culture, which will benefit everyone, it is important to know how to talk about wellbeing accurately with students, parents and each other.

Ensure our champions deliberately and frequently use this language with students and colleagues. It needs to become a common language school-wide that is repeated frequently and accurately so it is internalised and becomes the language of our thoughts as well as well as our spoken words.

Step 5: Assign positive education tasks based on the strengths of individuals.

Having completed the VIA Character Strengths Survey, our champions meet to share their individual strengths.

Brainstorm tasks that need to be started (start small). Some would include: organising students and staff to complete the VIA Character Strengths Survey, putting up What Went Well (WWW) boards in staffrooms and some classrooms, letting students and staff know what this week's Wellbeing Fitness Challenge is.

Allocate tasks that suit each champion's strengths and get them started.

Step 6: Discover, share and celebrate successes, no matter how small (from little things, big things grow).

Share and celebrate the successes of individual students and staff in the staff bulletin, on What Went Well boards the staffrooms, on post-it notes in pigeon holes and on desks; just get these little successes out there, e.g. journaling acts of kindness we give and receive.

Set one goal for everyone to strive to achieve in the following week, e.g. complete the Resilience Builder.

Brainstorm with students the positive actions we can all do to show the weekly Character Strength at school in our every thought, word and action. This is a positive priming activity that benefits everyone.

Step 7: Cross silos in the school.

In social staffrooms install WWW whiteboards, inviting all staff to write on it or attach post-it notes on it to share what we are grateful for, how we went on the Wellbeing Fitness, challenge and their successes. WWW boards in classrooms work well.

One champion's weekly task is to summarise what is written on the boards and compile a term WWW booklet that is distributed to staff on the last day of term; staff love the positive feelings this act generates.

On the WWW boards, for each subgroup, e.g. Prep-Year 2, Year 3-4, Year 5-6, Year 7-8, Year 9-10, Year 11-12 and learning domains, use different coloured post-it notes or markers to increase relevance and interest for staff.

Step 8: Normalise the crossing of the silo borders.

Initiate and design a regular feedback loop, manage and feed upwards to energise leadership, communicate to all students, staff and parents the positive changes that are occurring in the school.

For example, a weekly WWW update on the school's website placed alongside a parent newsletter, e.g. a Year 10 class ran fun lunchtime activities with Year 7 students.

A different silo or subgroup is to share WWW each week at a staff forum for all to celebrate.

Step 9: The way we do things around here.

Fail well as a staff when things go wrong, as they certainly will at times. Then, try a new approach, to nudge everyone along the mindset continuum towards more growth orientated mindsets.

Share that neuroplasticity tells us that every experience rewires our brains; let's grow our brains together.

Ask and suggest, don't tell. Persevere, because nothing good in this life comes easily.

Concluding thoughts

Our purpose here is to share and to build upon current trends, identifying and sharing success globally. We need to look to future needs as we seek to define interventions and attitudes that will energise, engage and support the wellbeing and growth of our students, encouraging them to develop as robust capable and successful young people.

The promise of a wider and more effective implementation of positive psychology teaching in schools seems to be within reach. However, it will be up to the researchers of this generation to try to ensure that this becomes a reality. From what is now known, there is a clear link between psychological factors and is positive youth development also. Growing evidence suggests that school-based interventions can produce positive effects for student achievement and wellbeing. The diversity of interventions being studied and shared is impressive and we need to continue to communicate, share and grow together for the betterment of our young people.

Educating teachers on the importance of psychological factors in learning, highlighting the potential benefits of school-based programmes, and illustrating the concrete application of skills within the learning environment stands to greatly improve the number of teachers effectively integrating positive psychology into the classroom.

Hopefully the guidance here will give some structure to the 'champions' who will seek to bring a focus upon support and positive interventions. To all concerned, please remember that a focus upon humour, warmth and empathy will be adopted, as these are the leadership qualities, the leadership skills that foster and build positive learning environments, our pathway to a better future.

Glossary

- **Wellbeing** is a combination of equally important elements of wellbeing that works together as a team.

- **Signature Character Strengths** are natural ways we think, feel and behave, which enable us to become our best possible selves.

- **Gratitude** is about appreciating what is good in life and being thankful for those things.

- **Mindfulness** is connecting with our self, being in the present moment and accepting our thoughts.

- **Acts of Kindness** are behaviours that involve doing and receiving are doing kind things for others because they matter.

- **Growth Mindset** is understanding and believing that through lifting our efforts to learn new and try new difficult things, we can grow our brains' abilities in all areas of our life.

- **Fixed Mindset** is believing there is nothing we can do to change our abilities and intelligence; they are permanent.

- **Wellbeing Fitness Challenges** are fun activities to tackle each week to develop our self-awareness and self-regulation.

- **Flow** is an enjoyable state we experience when we are totally engaged in using our skillset to overcome a challenge that only stretches these skills.

- **Thriving and flourishing** is enjoying optimal wellbeing, feeling good by doing good things.

- **Resilience** is failing well and bouncing forward from setbacks, to welcome new challenges.

- **Active Constructive Responding (ACR)** is listening to someone tell their good news story so that they can relive their positive experience and responding in an encouraging and enthusiastic way.

- **Broaden and Build Theory** involves experiencing positive emotions to broaden our attention to think creatively, which builds increased engagement with our environment.

- **Savouring** is reliving or prolonging an enjoyable and fulfilling experience.
- **Resilience Builders** are activities to teach the seven learnable skills of resilience.

Many of Dubai's private schools already have well-developed programmes in place to support student wellbeing. These include:

A school that has developed a mindfulness and wellbeing room to help students mentally and emotionally by focusing on positivity. The room has smart tablets loaded with guided meditation routines, a gratitude tree for students to display what they are thankful for, a sensory room with a range of stimuli and a positive affirmation room.

A school where positive education is taught explicitly throughout, and which has appointed non-teaching Heads of Positive Education in Primary and Secondary, fully devoted to developing the curriculum and supporting the teachers. This has the potential to developing a collaborative, mindfulness collective which prioritises the growth and development of all teachers!

A Mindfulness Collective with the aim to collaborate and share existing programs in schools, to collect evidence to demonstrate best practice, and to provide support for schools who would like to implement mindfulness programs in the future.

Many schools have urban gardens that promote positive relationships and mindsets towards healthy food, especially, for example, vegetables.

Workshops by practitioners from the Institute of Positive Education in Australia for parents and schools to outline the benefits of positive education.

Chapter 5:
Positive Education in China

Yukun Zhao

Background

Positive education, in its very essence, is concordant with the tradition of Chinese education. Confucius said, 'The gentleman is not vessel.'[1] He advocated the 'whole-person' approach in education, rather than mere mastery of knowledge or techniques. The *Analects* started with a famous saying of his, 'To study and at due times practice what one has studied, is this not a pleasure?' Indeed, when Confucius talked about education, he emphasized the enjoyment and meaning far more than performance.

Furthermore, Chinese culture believes the power of preventive programs. As pointed out by the *Inner Canon of the Yellow Emperor*, the most ancient Chinese medical classic, 'The sages do not treat those who have already fallen ill, but rather those who are not yet ill'. Chinese understand the necessity of taking preventive measures before a person or a population becomes ill. The relationship between ill-being and wellbeing, to Chinese, is perfectly depicted by the relationship between 'yin and yang'. The best way to prevent ill-being is to nurture more wellbeing.

Therefore, the modern movement of positive education is widely welcome and quickly disseminating in China. But its popularity attributes to not

---

1   Confucius. (1979): *The Analects of Confucius*. London, UK: Penguin Books.

only the traditional Chinese philosophies, but also the fact that the Chinese education system has come to a time that requires a paradigm shift. On one hand, the Chinese education system is enormously successful. It produces the most engineers in the world, and the Chinese students consistently perform outstandingly in math and sciences compared to other countries. It's no overstatement that the Chinese education system is one of the main reasons behind the economic miracle of China in the past four decades.

On the other hand, however, the Chinese education system emphasized too much on academic performance and mainly relied on authoritarian discipline to achieve that. This resulted in the loss of interest of students in study, the ever-growing conflicts between students and parents as well as teachers, and, the worst of all, the rampant epidemics of psychological problems in the youth. A study in 2015 found that the six-month prevalence of any mental disorder among the students aged 6-16 years they surveyed was 15.24%.[2]

Positive education appears to be the right antidote for the dilemma. It focuses on both wellbeing and academic learning, which facilitates each other as predicted by research and proven by positive education practices in China.

Practices

In 2011, the Bureau of Education of Jiangyin, Jiangsu province, decided to explore a new education approach in elementary and secondary schools that can increase the happiness of the students. They chose the Jiangyin high school to design and test a standalone 'happiness course' for the 10th Graders that taught positive psychology concepts and techniques once a week. The results showed that students in the experiment group became happier, more optimistic, and gained better social and psychological capacities compared to the control group.

In 2012, the Bureau of Education of Beijing funded the 19th Middle School of Beijing to build a model of 'happy education'. They combined positive

---

2   Qu, Y., Jiang, H., Zhang, N., Wang, D. & Guo, L. (2015): Prevalence of mental disorders in 6-16 years old students in Sichuan province, China. *International journal of environmental research and public health*, 12(5), pp. 5090-5107.

psychology with traditional Chinese philosophy to design courses, train teachers, and remodel the school culture. Three years later, their rate of the first-class college entrances rose from 69.6% in 2012 to 75% in 2015. In 2014, the 19th High School of Beijing founded 'the League of Happy Schools of China' together with some other participating schools.

In 2014, the city of Zengcheng (now part of Guangzhou), Guangdong province, launched the biggest scale of positive education practices to date in China. Under the supervision of Ms. Ye Hong, then-vice mayor, more than 10,000 school principals and headteachers were trained in positive education theories and methods by the Positive Psychology Research Center of Tsinghua University (PPRC). Then they returned to their schools to disseminate and implement positive education. Dr. Martin Seligman was also invited to lecture to the educators of Zengcheng in 2015. Some headteachers continued to get online training and long-distance consulting from PPRC on how to design and teach positive education courses in the following years.

In 2015, Ms. Dou Guimei, the principal of the Tsinghua University Primary School (TUPS) decided to roll out a positive education program designed by PPRC in her school. This is a milestone in the positive education movement in China. Firstly, this marks the first attempt of a school practicing positive education in collaboration with an expert team with rigorous research background and theoretical guidelines. Secondly, the fact that TUPS, one of the most famous elementary schools in China, adopts positive education, sends a strong message to the Chinese education community that positive education has been accepted by the mainstream schools. Thirdly, unlike most other practicing schools who are funded and supported by government, TUPS decided to practice positive education and funded it by the school itself, largely due to Ms. Dou's prospective vision and commitment. Many other schools soon joined TUPS to adopt positive education by themselves.

In early 2017, the Qingyang district of Chengdu, Sichuan, started a whole-scale positive education project to engage all the schools in the area. Under the design of its leader, Ms. Liu Lipin, the Qingyang Bureau of Education organized all the psychology teachers from the district to be trained in positive psychology by PPRC. These teachers then went back to their schools to implement their own positive education programs and courses. Furthermore, the Shude Middle School and Paotongshu Elementary School, widely regarded as the best middle school and the best elementary school in the district, adopted the positive education framework of PPRC. After one year's experiment, both schools experienced increases in subjective wellbeing and positive characters among students. Because of these encouraging outcomes, five more schools from the Qingyang district will join them to implement the full-strength positive education framework, and the bureau of education is launching a large-scale training program to include more teachers who are not in the sector of mental health or moral development to learn positive psychology and how to use them in their daily teaching. It's estimated that in 2018, positive education will cover more than 80,000 students, 4000 teachers, and 100,0000 parents in Qingyang.

To further disseminate positive education, PPRC also launched a non-profit program called 'Happy Gardener' (gardener is the common metaphor of teacher in China) that trains schools principals for free, thanks to the Beijing Happiness Foundation. The program has trained six classes in positive education, benefitting more than 600 principals, who came to Tsinghua University for a five-day training in positive education.

The positive education framework

The positive education framework promoted by PPRC consists of four main components:

1. Assessments

PPRC measures psychological indicators of students and teachers, including wellbeing, anxiety/depression, learning motivation, resilience, growth mindset, grit, parenting styles etc. They are measured three to four times per year, at the beginning and the end of each semester. PPRC uses these measurements to evaluate the effectiveness of the positive education program and generate a report for the school to help them better understand the strengths and weaknesses of their students and teachers, often down to each class.

2. Training

PPRC offers comprehensive trainings in positive psychology and positive education to the schools. All the teachers teaching the positive education courses are required to attend. In most cases, all the teachers in the whole school will at least participate part of the training. This prepares the teachers for the next two components.

3. Positive education courses

These are the standalone courses developed by PPRC and taught to the students one session per week. It's based on the PERMA theory of Martin Seligman that stresses positive emotion, engagement, relationships, meaning, and accomplishments as the five pillars of wellbeing, with character strengths and virtues as the foundation.[3] Since individuality and self-awareness is less emphasized in Chinese culture, a new pillar of positive self was added to the model. And since the importance of physical education is often ignored in Chinese schools, a new foundation of positive health was added to the foundation. The new model is called the '6+2' model, with two core elements and six areas. Furthermore, it teaches practical techniques in the following six categories: social and emotional capacities, optimism and self-efficacy, resilience, grit and self-regulation, growth mindset, and engagement.

4. Positive school culture

PPRC works with each school to build a more positive culture on things varying from physical environments like decorations, building and room designs, signs and pictures, to events like charity activities, sport games, home-school interactions, non-academic assignments, etc. Teachers are also encouraged to adopt a positive education language (e.g. growth mindset) in their classrooms.

Schools from all over China are adopting the positive education framework. In Beijing, the Tsinghua University Primary School and its Central Business District branch, the Tsinghua University Middle School, the University of International Business and Economics Primary School.

---

3   Seligman, M. E. P. (2011): *Flourish*. Boston, Massachusetts: Nicholas Brealey Publishing.

In Jiangsu, Jiangyin Technical Secondary School, Jiangyin Yunting Middle School, Xuzhou Development District High School, Suzhou Zhenchuan Middle School. In Tianjin, Beichen Experimental Elementary School and Beichen Experimental Middle School. In Chengdu, Shude Middle School and Paotongshu Elementary School. And Taohuajiang Elementary School in Hunan, Puyang Youtian 5th Elementary School in Henan, Yuncheng Professional Technology University in Shanxi.

Empirical evidence

Positive education has become a main theme in the field of positive psychology research in China. Each of the first three biannual China International Positive Psychology Conference has a forum in positive education. The fourth one, held in August 2017, was co-hosted with the International Positive Education Networks and mainly dedicated to positive education. Some research papers were also produced during the positive education practices (e.g. Zeng et. al., 2016).[4] The empirical evidences of positive education are encouraging.

First, positive education programs have been proven effective to the students' mental health. For example, after one year's 'happiness course' in the three experiment classes in Jiangyin High School, the students showed higher increase of happiness and more decrease of depression. Happiness was measured by the Subjective Well-being Scale (Diener, 1984).[5] Depression was measured by the Children's Depression Inventory (Kovacs, 1992).[6] As illustrated in Fig. 1, the students who received positive education course exhibited significant higher happiness level after the one-year intervention ($M = 11.07$, $SD = 2.24$) compared to before the intervention ($M = 9.73$, $SD = 2.53$, $F (1,451) = 16.359$, $p = 0.000$). The students in the 'business-as-usual' classes also gained more happiness within the same period (from $M = 10.08$, $SD = 2.37$ to $M = 10.70$, $SD = 2.37$, $F (1, 451) = 4.730$, $p = 0.000$), but the relative gain was less than half of that of the experiment group.

---

4   Zeng, G., Hou, H. & Peng, K. (2016): Effect of Growth Mindset on School Engagement and Psychological Well-Being of Chinese Primary and Middle School Students: The Mediating Role of Resilience. *Frontiers in psychology*, 7.

5   Diener, E. (1984): Subjective well-being. *Psychological bulletin*, 95, p. 542.

6   Kovacs, M. (1992): *Children's Depression Inventory* (CDI). Toronto, ON: Multi-Health Systems Inc.

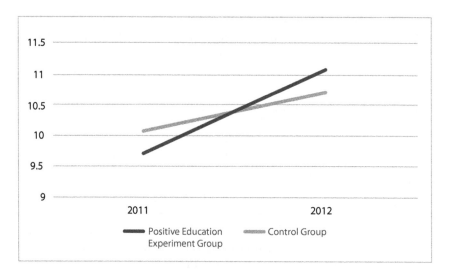

Figure 1: Change of subjective wellbeing of the positive education experiment group compared to the control group

Secondly, positive education can also help to build the positive psychological resources of students. In Yuncheng Vocational College, positive education courses were taught to the freshmen once a week, for eight weeks. In China, a vocational college is often considered 'inferior' to the normal colleges, attended by those academic 'losers' who can't get admitted by other schools. Therefore, their students are typically low in self-efficacy and hope. PPRC measured their resilience using the Brief Resilience Scale,[7] growth mindset using the Growth Mindset Scale,[8] and hope using the Adult Hope Scale.[9] As shown in the Table 1, the students who received the eight-week course showed significant increase in growth mindset and hope, while the control group had no significant changes. On the other hand, the resilience level of students in the control group dropped significantly, probably due to the tough challenges in

---

7   Smith, B. W., Dalen, J., Wiggins, K., Tooley, E., Christopher, P. & Bernard, J. (2008): The brief resilience scale: assessing the ability to bounce back. *International journal of behavioral medicine*, 15(3), pp. 194-200.

8   Dweck, C. S. (2006): *Mindset: The new psychology of success.* London, UK: Random House.

9   Snyder, C. R., Harris, C., Anderson, J. R., Holleran, S. A., Irving, L. M., Sigmon, S. T., et al. (1991): The will and the ways: Development and validation of an individual-differences measure of hope. *Journal of Personality and Social Psychology*, 60, pp. 570-585.

the first year, while the students in the experiment group showed no significant changes in resilience, which means the positive education program can protect students' resilience.

Trait	Group	M (SD)$_{before}$	M (SD)$_{after}$	t	df	p
Resilience	Experiment	3.31 (±.64)	3.29 (±.62)	-.38	123	.70
	Control	3.35 (±.69)	3.20 (±.56)	-2.42	104	.017**
Growth Mindset	Experiment	3.16 (±.47)	3.24 (±.47)	1.91	123	.058*
	Control	3.14 (±.55)	3.14 (±.49)	-.069	104	.95
Hope	Experiment	2.74 (±.51)	2.84 (±.45)	2.11	123	.037**
	Control	2.78 (±.48)	2.75 (±.63)	-.539	104	.59

Table 1: The change of positive psychological resources of students in positive education experiment group compared to the control group

* $p < 0.1$, **$p < 0.05$.

Thirdly, positive education program can make the students' learning motivation more autonomous. In TUPS, two classes from the 2nd, 3rd and 5th Grade participated took the weekly positive education classes for nine weeks. PPRC measured the students' learning motivation using the Academic Self-Regulation Questionnaire.[10] The questionnaire is based on the Self Determination Theory[11] that distinguishes the intrinsic learning motivation from extrinsic learning motivation. It further divides the extrinsic motivation into three different regulatory styles: external, where students are motivated by rewards and punishments; introjected, where students learn to meet other people's expectations; integrated, where students find the meaning and value of learning. The Relative Autonomy Index (RAI) was calculated based on the theory as 2 x intrinsic + integrated – introjected – 2 x external. It is an indicator of how autonomously a student's learning motivation is. It turned out that after nine sessions of positive education courses, the students in the

---

10 Ryan, R. M. & Connell, J. P. (1989): Perceived locus of causality and internalization: Examining reasons for acting in two domains. *Journal of Personality and Social Psychology*, 57, pp. 749-761.

11 Ryan, R. M. & Deci, E. L. (2000): Self-determination theory and the facilitation of intrinsic motivation, social development, and well-being. *American psychologist*, 55(1), p. 68.

experiment group became significantly more autonomous in learning motivation (from M = 1.43, SD = 0.20, to M = 1.91, SD = 0.19, F (1,491) = 6. 59, p = .01), while the students in the control group had no significant change (from M = 1.63, SD = 0.20, to M = 1.87, SD = 0.20, F (1,491) = 1. 70, p = 0.19).

Summary

Positive education is rapidly taking off in China. A practical model of positive education that's tailored for Chinese schools has emerged and widely applied. Empirical evidences showed that the positive education programs can enhance not only students' wellbeing and mental health, but also their positive psychological resources and learning motivation. That's why positive education is well received in China. It could be the right addition for the existing effective yet psychologically expensive educational system.

To further the movement of positive education in China, however, more work need to be done. Firstly, the word needs to be spread out; positive education is very new. Teachers, students, and parents like it instantly when they practice it, but for those who never tried it or even heard of it, they can't get the benefit. And they are still most of the Chinese education community. Secondly, we need more support from the government to push positive education, as the government has the most resources in China. Yet we must not rely only on the government. We need to convince the individual principals, teachers, and parents to adopt positive education. They are the real driving force of education. Thirdly, we need to integrate the latest technology with positive education more closely. That could be in assessment, using large scale online platform or to build a big data of student positive psychology inventory. And it could be in the classroom, using wearable devices with biological feedback technologies to evaluate the students' engagement and enjoyment in real time. Or it could be in educational tools, using VR and AI to develop interactive applications to help the students build more positive psychological resources. We need to get the ride of the new technology to make positive education benefitting more students in a more rapid and more effective way.

Further reading

Diener, E. (1984): Subjective well-being. *Psychological bulletin*, 95, p. 542.

Dweck, C. S. (2006): *Mindset: The new psychology of success*. London, UK: Random House.

Ryan, R. M. & Deci, E. L. (2000): Self-determination theory and the facilitation of intrinsic motivation, social development, and well-being. *American psychologist*, 55(1), p. 68.

Ryan, R. M. & Connell, J. P. (1989): Perceived locus of causality and internalization: Examining reasons for acting in two domains. *Journal of Personality and Social Psychology*, 57, pp. 749-761.

Qu, Y., Jiang, H., Zhang, N., Wang, D. & Guo, L. (2015): Prevalence of mental disorders in 6 to 16-year-old students in Sichuan province, China. *International journal of environmental research and public health*, 12(5), pp. 5090-5107.

Seligman, M. E. P. (2011): *Flourish*. Boston, Massachusetts: Nicholas Brealey Publishing.

Smith, B. W., Dalen, J., Wiggins, K., Tooley, E., Christopher, P. & Bernard, J. (2008): The brief resilience scale: assessing the ability to bounce back. *International journal of behavioral medicine*, 15(3), pp. 194-200.

Snyder, C. R., Harris, C., Anderson, J. R., Holleran, S. A., Irving, L. M., Sigmon, S. T., et al. (1991): The will and the ways: Development and validation of an individual-differences measure of hope. *Journal of Personality and Social Psychology*, 60, pp. 570-585.

Zeng, G., Hou, H. & Peng, K. (2016): Effect of Growth Mindset on School Engagement and Psychological Well-Being of Chinese Primary and Middle School Students: The Mediating Role of Resilience. *Frontiers in psychology*, 7.

Chapter 6:
Positive Transitioning

Amba Brown

'The only way to make sense out of change is to plunge into it, move with it, and join the dance.' – Alan Watts

Positive transitioning: flourishing with change

Positive transitioning is not about ignoring the struggle that comes with change. The struggle, of course, is part of it. It's about dealing with the expected transitions of life in a solution-focused way, to prepare, support and inspire individuals through the time of change.

Within this chapter, we will explore this critical, and often overlooked, aspect of positive education known as 'positive transitioning'. We will start with a working definition, followed by a discussion addressing its relevance today. We will then explore both the general principles for supporting positive change in youth and the specific tools that can be implemented for three of these momentous transitions: starting school, transitioning to high school and preparing students for a life after school.

A working definition

The definition: 'positive transitioning' can best be explained using a combination of the two words it's made up of.

Firstly, the word 'positive' can be derived from a definition of the overarching scientific meaning of 'positive psychology'. While there are currently various definitions, the most fitting is defined by Gable et al. (2005) as 'the study of the conditions and processes that contribute to the flourishing or optimal functioning of people, groups, and institutions'.[1]

Secondly, the word 'transitioning' is well defined in the Oxford Dictionary as 'the process or a period of changing from one state or condition to another'.

Combined, my working definition of positive transitioning is 'the study of the conditions and processes that contribute to the flourishing or optimal functioning of people, groups, and institutions when undertaking the process or period of change from one state or condition to another'.

It's also useful to explain the term 'expected life transitions', being the times in which we are implementing these positive transitioning tactics. Life transitions are periods of time we move from one life experience to another, often experiencing various changes, e.g. finishing school. While independently the stages of school and life after school are common experiences, the accompanying change faced through the transition can bring about feelings of uncertainty and instability as one navigates these new times.

Coping with expected change

Today, 'mental health' is defined by the World Health Organisation (2004) as 'a state of wellbeing in which every individual realises his or her own potential, **can cope with the normal stress of life,** can work productively and fruitfully, and is able to contribute to his or her community'.

No longer do we merely see mental health as being the absence of disease but, instead, a state of optimal wellbeing that we can all strive for. The growing emphasis on positive education is certainly somewhat intertwined with this shift in how we view mental health.

---

1   Gable, S. L. & Haidt, J. (2005): What (and Why) Is Positive Psychology? *Review of General Psychology,* 9(2), pp. 103-110.

The attention is, therefore, no longer only directed towards times of trouble, or towards students displaying alarming signs. It's on all students and the importance of them receiving a holistic educational experience, where skills for wellbeing are taught in addition to traditional academic content.

While there are many factors to consider, as outlined above, the specific intention herein is to investigate how we can best prepare and support youth through the expected life transitions. As opposed to only focusing on unexpected life transitions, such as death, separation, moving schools, etc.

Pittman (2000) accurately sums up the need for this approach with his statement 'problem-free is not fully prepared',[2] suggesting that change is inevitable, vital and a universal human experience.

Around the world, students differ in their ability to cope with these planned life transitions. For example, one student may view the start of high school as an exciting opportunity to achieve independence, whereas another may struggle with a loss of identity or support. At times, the experience of major change, regardless of being expected, can be too much to cope with, resulting in significant issues in adjusting and overwhelming stress responses, which can affect both physical and mental wellbeing.

Below are examples of signs and symptoms youth may display when not coping well with change.

- Exhaustion or trouble sleeping.
- Overwhelmed and difficulty coping.
- Feeling isolated or the desire to isolate oneself.
- Confused and lacking self-confidence.
- Stressed and the constant weight of the world on one's shoulders.
- Frequently upset, anxious, irritable, down or moody.

---

2   Pittman, K. J. & Wright, M. (1991): *Bridging the Gap: A Rationale for Enhancing the Role of Community Organizations in Promoting Youth Development.* Washington, DC: Center for Youth Development and Policy Research.

It's critical we shift the focus to a preventive approach to reduce the prevalence of stress and anxiety in youth.

In contrast to the idea that individuals are resistant and adverse to change, the science of positive psychology has taught us the concept of human growth and our inherent ability to adapt to change. We are, in fact, able to control our behaviour and attitude, which act as survival mechanisms to help us grow and adapt over time.

Studies illustrate the impact of a positive emotional state on supporting our ability and willingness to adapt when uncertainty is increased. Research undertaken by Fredrickson and Branigan (2005) has also shown that a positive emotional state is linked to increased social behaviour, exploration and curiosity.[3]

On the other hand, negative emotional states were found to narrow our thought-action repertoires with the activation of the 'fight or flight' response.[4] Hence the significance of promoting positive emotions and mental wellbeing during transitions.

Other factors found to improve youth wellbeing through challenging times include resiliency, gratitude, meaning, flow, positive relationships and character strengths (discussed further below).

How we can best support transitioning youth

While typically, expected life transitions are more likely to be challenging for students from families who are financially disadvantaged, with disabilities, and culturally isolated, all students can benefit from increasing their preparedness and skills for adjusting to change. 'Readiness' for these transitions is found to increase wellbeing, and long-term academic and occupational achievement.

To achieve optimal wellbeing during change, it's key to go beyond nurturing the academic needs of youth, and tap into their emotional, social and personal developmental needs.

---

3   Fredrickson, B. L. & Branigan, C. (2005): Positive emotions broaden the scope of attention and thought-action repertoires. *Cognition & Emotion*, 19(3), pp. 313–332.

4   Fredrickson, B. L. (1998): What Good Are Positive Emotions? *Review of General Psychology: Journal of Division 1, of the American Psychological Association*, 2(3), pp. 300–319.

Below I've identified three key pillars for positive transitioning:

1. 'The Practical Pillar' includes informing youth about the differences they can expect and normalising these experiences.
2. 'The Social Pillar' which addresses the role of social networks for supporting the individual through the transitions.
3. 'The Psychological Pillar' which includes a positive transitioning emotional toolkit to build youth resiliency and facilitate a growth mindset.

These are described in depth below.

The three pillars of positive change

1. The Practical Pillar: information is key

The practical pillar includes all the essential information for adjusting to change. That is, the facts we can pass on to prepare youth. This is about managing expectations, to help normalise the new experiences that can make us feel out of our comfort zone. There are various sources that can be utilised to reduce the stress and uncertainty of the future, including attending open days, speaking with students and/or teachers from the new educational stage, visiting school's websites, support books and local information sessions.

After the differences are explained and the feelings normalised, recognise the various positive outcomes related to the change. For example, it might be stressful finishing school and being uncertain about a decision but it's positive they have the freedom of choice and can explore something they're interested in.

Then identify any areas of stress through discussion with the child, so steps can be put into place to overcome. For example, if a student is feeling worried about making friends at their new school they can join a sports team to help facilitate.

It's also helpful to engage youth in relevant decision-making. Depending on the transition, youth will have varying levels of control over their lives. For example, when starting school, they will likely have little input in deciding where they will go, whereas when finishing school, this transition is largely their decision. So how do we prepare them to confidently decide? The more we involve youth in change, the more confident and empowered they will be when making decisions as they mature.

Imagine a child that really enjoys dancing – helping them to identify this is something that makes them happy and encouraging them to select a senior school that has this as an option, is a great way of building on past experiences and building confidence in themselves.

As students learn more about the next stage of life, they should be encouraged to look forward with both an optimistic and realistic lens, to consider how they could overcome adversity.[5] This balanced outlook, including the reality of future difficulties has been found to better prepare students when these times arise.[6]

2. The Social Pillar: we all play a part

Growing up, youth are largely influenced by the expectations placed on them by society and culture. This has a natural influence on their interpretation and decision-making. The characteristics of our social settings also help to protect youth from various problems. Examples include a supportive family, parental engagement, role models and high expectations.[7]

A blend of effective strategies implemented by educators, parents and students is believed to be most effective. The following table shows strategies by various stakeholders.

5   Baumeister, R., Vohs, K. & Oettingen, G. (2016): Pragmatic prospection: How and why people think about the future. *Review of General Psychology*, 20(1), pp. 3-16.

6   Gollwitzer, P. & Kinney, R. (1989): Effects of deliberative and implemental mind-sets on illusion of control. *Journal of Personality and Social Psychology*, 56(4), pp. 531-542.

7   Benson, P. L. (1997): *All kids are our kids: What communities must do to raise caring and responsible children and adolescents*. San Francisco, CA: Jossey-Bass.

STRATEGY	PARENTS	SCHOOLS	STUDENTS
Consider non-academic needs	Encourage them to develop positive supportive friendships and engage in activities they enjoy.	Talk about positive attitudes, self-control strategies, and ways to deal with emotions, provide counselling.	Socialise with others, build friendships, recognise the things you enjoy and identify own emotions.
Discover interests	Encourage hobbies, ask engaging questions like what do you enjoy learning? What do you like and dislike about school?	Provide various extra-curricular options and encourage participation in different topics.	Take part in activities they enjoy and try new things.
Build relationships	Encourage relationships with others (talking with a teacher, a counsellor, family, friends) to build and diversify their support network.	Create group or paired activities, arrange peer support system and open communication channels.	Speak with others to share worries, concerns, dreams, goals or to simply ask questions.
Making decisions	Provide information and share relevant experiences. Encourage exploration, decision making, and planning.	Discuss moral dilemmas and provide information about the options and next steps.	Develop self-awareness by considering answers surrounding who they are, what they enjoy, etc.
Set individual expectations	Expect the child's best effort at all times. Explain an important aspect of growing through change is floundering and making unplanned choices.	Involve the parent and child in setting realistic and achievable expectations.	Establish personal definition of success and consider ways to achieve this.

Table 1: Strategies by various stakeholders

3. The Psychological Pillar: building an emotional toolkit

Emotional readiness is a key component for promoting a positive transition, as change can be difficult for young children, bringing about various emotional reactions. To do this, we must prepare them with an emotional toolkit, which includes (but isn't limited to) confidence, mindfulness, happiness, and resiliency.

Confidence: Build self-confidence by encouraging their involvement in extra-curricular activities that help to build inner confidence of their abilities.

Mindfulness: Taking a moment to be aware of our feelings, thoughts and actions is instrumental in managing the various emotions that come with change. Research has proven this increases social skills and promotes mental and general wellbeing in youth.[8]

Positive emotions: Encourage involvement in things that induce positive emotion (excluding survival acts, e.g. eating or sleeping). Activities such as exercising and spending time with friends help us feel good. The sooner youth identify and apply such positive practices, the faster they will incorporate them as healthy coping strategies more regularly, reducing the desire to opt for unhealthy coping techniques, such as drugs and alcohol.

Resiliency:

Resiliency is the capacity in which we adapt to stressful events in a healthy and flexible manner. The application of the ABC model is well researched in building resiliency in youth. Students are taught how beliefs (B) about adversity (A), not the adversity itself cause the consequential (C) feelings.[9] The fact that emotions don't follow external events, but instead follow the thoughts of those events. This helps to emphasise the power of thoughts and strength in managing them.[10]

---

8   Zhou, K., Liu, Q., Niu, G., Sun, X. & Fan, C. (2017): Bullying victimization and depression in Chinese children: A moderated mediation model of resilience and mindfulness. *Personality and Individual Defferences*, 104, pp. 137-142.

9   Seligman, M. E. P. (2011): *Flourish*. Boston, MA: Nicholas Brealey Publishing.

10 Haggerty, K. P. & Shapiro, V. B. (2013): Science-Based Prevention Through Communities That Care: A Model of Social Work Practice for Public Health. *Social Work in Public Health*, 28, pp. 349–365.

Navigating specific transitions

Mostly, youth navigate transitions without excessive stress, however a significant number do struggle, and this is often found to continue well into young adulthood. While there are several universal factors we can apply to all ages to promote positive transitioning, we must also consider individual age variants. I'll now apply the fundamentals of the three pillars to three key transitions: starting school, starting high school and finishing school.

Starting school

For most children, school begins around the age of five, with many already having taken part in some type of educational program beforehand. We hear a lot about 'school readiness', but a more accurate expression is 'child coping readiness'. After all, it's more about preparing the child for life and the many changes ahead than simply preparing them for school.

The checklist hosts all the obvious items like organising a uniform, a backpack and collecting all the other bits and bobs that go in it, but we must ensure that we include the development of the social and emotional skills required to deal with the upcoming changes. The physical schooling environment and all the rules and procedures that come with it, along with the new social context and academic expectations.

It makes sense how it can be overwhelming when we clump it all together, but the process for digesting and adapting can be broken down over time. All we need is the awareness and time to prepare.

Why should we bother? Internationally, research has found students who have trouble settling into their first year at school are at higher risk of learning difficulties throughout their schooling years and more likely not to graduate. From a positive point of view, students who have a positive beginning are found to be more relaxed, develop stronger relationships, improved learning and hold a stronger sense of belonging.[11]

---

11   Milburn, C. (2018): *Preparing kindergarten children for school*. Essential Kids. Available at: www.essentialkids.com.au/education/school/starting-school/preparing-kindergarten-children-for-school-20090215-88ki

Here are two tips to prepare students in the lead up to the big first day:

1. Introduce and prepare the child for how things will be

Months prior, provide information and explain what their new school schedule will look like. What time will they begin school, take breaks and finish? Logistics aside, point out the positives of going to school. Such as, meeting new friends, learning, and teach them why going to school is a privilege. This perspective promotes gratitude and gives context around the wider meaning of the fact children go to school to enhance their own lives.

After explaining how it works, arrange for a practice day where the student can experience it hands-on. This exposure helps reduce various unknowns, such as: the rules and procedures, the size of the school, its distance from home, and where the bathrooms and canteen are, etc. These details may feel minute to us adults but they are important factors in building the child's confidence and familiarity with their new environment.

During the years leading up to the child's first year of school, it's also helpful for the parent/caregiver to gradually build the child's confidence and prepare them by developing their academic skills (encouraging learning at home), independence skills (encouraging them to take more responsibility in daily activities such as getting ready), and social skills (by arranging play dates and teaching social skills such as sharing, being respectful and taking turns), which will all contribute to an increased confidence in their abilities and sense of self-competence.

2. Develop emotional skills and provide support

During the weeks leading up to the start of school, encourage regular check-ins with the child to see how they're feeling about their pending transition. What are they looking forward to? Help to shift any negativity bias by focusing on the positives that lay ahead. Psychologist William James notably said, 'the greatest weapon against stress is our ability to choose one thought over another.' Additionally, research has found that positive future expectations are linked with enhanced social and emotional adjustment to school.[12]

---

12   Wyman, P., Cowen, E., Work, W. & Kerley, J. (1993): The role of children's future expectations in self-system functioning and adjustment to life stress: A prospective study of urban at-risk children. *Development and Psychopathology*, 5(4), p. 649.

Like anyone, the child may not always want to talk, as the discussion itself can evoke anxiety. However, ensure that a conversation is had at some point prior to starting school and the child feels the caregiver is approachable.

Closer to the first day, extra support may be required if the child begins showing signs of worry and vulnerability. Encourage the child to identify and express their emotions as they come up and label their intensity. This can be initiated by offering different emotions they could be feeling or giving examples of times when you felt similar emotion to build their emotional vocabulary. Effective emotional communication will become more and more useful as their social network begins to widen and their interpersonal skills develop.

Starting high school

Depending on the country you reside in, the next major expected transition will either be starting middle school or high school. These transitions arguably face the largest amount of change at any one time as external changes overlap internal changes. Students face biological changes through puberty, social changes with relationships, and psychological changes, as they gain an increased independence and learn to navigate their teenage years.

The management of this transition is specifically important, as such rapid change can increase the possibility of positive and negative outcomes. A positive transition for this age group has been correlated with positive future outcomes, including career and academic achievement.[13]

Youth's preparedness for their first year of high school plays an important role in establishing their future teen preparedness. In this section we will explore two specific tips:

1. Teach them what differences to expect

In the same respect as the transition above, explain the differences they can expect from their new educational environment, and provide the opportunity for them to visit the new environment before their first day.

---

13   Kern, M. L. & Friedman, H. S. (2008): Early educational milestones as predictors of lifelong academic achievement, midlife adjustment, and longevity. *Journal of Applied Developmental Psychology*, 30(4), pp. 419–430.

Remind them it's normal to wonder about the future and have anxiety around unknowns. Common worries include difficulty coping with homework, getting lost and making new friends. Ask what worries they have and explain these can be eased by either developing a new skill, a way of coping or applying stress management techniques such as mindfulness, meditation and yoga. Establish an open dialogue where the teenager can ask any questions and provide honest and informative responses. The more informed youth are the better placed they are to make healthy decisions.

2. Building independence

With high school comes a teens desire to seek out increased independence. The continuation of establishing and modifying new boundaries will be required during this period. A structured routine and clear communication of the expectations of youth is effective in encouraging them to build their independence and self-care academically, socially and psychologically. Working together with the teen to discuss and create a routine teaches awareness of their needs and social expectations and develops self-discipline. Factors to include are school and home expectations, self-care and things they can do using Seligman's (2011) PERMA model (positive emotions, engagement, positive relationships, meaning and achievement) to increase their wellbeing, which is explained further below.

While the focus is on the teen's new independence, parental and teacher engagement is still undoubtedly critical in supporting this transition. Their involvement demonstrates care and attention, providing a supportive foundation for the teen, which can help foster security and self-worth.

www.beyondblue.org.au
www.lifeline.org.au

Finishing school

Today there is much discussion around the difficulties in navigating a life post-school due to the very real first world problem of choice overload.

The transition is becoming increasingly complicated, with the options being less structured and new career paths popping up all the time.

At the end of the day, the decision around next steps rests with the school-leaver, it's important for parents and educators to positively support the decision-making process.

Follow these practical approaches to prepare students for the transition after school:

1. Change the way we look at the question: 'what do you want to do after school?'

Today it's simply not possible for students to understand all their options, with a reported 65% of students expected to work in jobs that don't yet exist.[14] So, this reported overwhelming experience of not being able to make a well-informed decision is understandable. Times are also changing with the norm today being to have more than one career and multiple jobs before retirement. So, this question, 'what you want to do after school?', is redundant.

As a society, we can shift this expectation by rephrasing the question for a more realistic and insightful response. Questions like 'what do you enjoy?', 'what are your strengths?' and 'how are you feeling towards your first step out of school?'

In the event a youth is asked the age-old question ('what you want to do after school?'), we should encourage a response like: 'I'm interested in … and I'll see where it leads me.'

At the end of the day, life is a journey and if the choice does not end up being forever, that's ok. There is still time to learn, grow and move onto something else.

2. Making the decision: using Martin Seligman's PERMA Model for a positive after school transition

Using Seligman's PERMA Model as a framework, we can explore the five elements of wellbeing to support youth in navigating this final transition.

---

14   Stillman, D. & Stillman, J. (2017): *Gen Z @ work*. London, UK: HarperCollins.

P – Positive emotion

Encourage students to recognise and note down all they enjoy. These responses are a great insight into areas of interest that should be explored further in terms of the various available pathways; working, studying, travelling or creating their own project.

E – Engagement

Consider what activities they find themselves most engaged or trigger a state of flow. The experience of flow is a key contributor to our wellbeing, examples include art and sport. Becoming aware of these activities are useful for the consideration of next steps after school, but also to have as healthy ways to spend their down time.

R – Relationships

The role of positive relationships is known to increase wellbeing. During decision-making it's helpful for discussing the various options and emotions, sharing ideas and viewpoints and normalising experiences.

M – Meaning

A key ingredient for wellbeing is living a life with meaning. Encourage youth to understand what they find meaningful. That is, something they care about that's bigger than them. Questions like, 'what would you like to do to improve the world?' can unlock passion and career paths.

A – Accomplishment

With the above responses considered, students can begin to create realistic and achievable goals. Ticking off goals works as a self-fulfilling prophesy, as you recognise your abilities and become motivated to reach more goals, ultimately contributing to your overall wellbeing.

Supporting students from start to end

An all-inclusive education is made up of more than the hours in the curriculum; it encompasses the transitions between the institutions. In the words of Lana Lang: 'Life is about change. Sometimes it's painful. Sometimes it's beautiful. But most of the time, it's both.'

Despite research for positive transitioning being in its infancy, there is no question we need to learn and share more to educate and support youth through these well-known times.

Above all, know it's normal for transitions to bring with them a mixed bag of emotions. Not only for the children but also their careers. For some these heightened emotions may take longer to subside than others, as the adjustment phase is different for everyone. Like any new beginning, there may be a level of sadness around leaving the past behind, anxiety around the many unknowns and the excitement of the future. Combined together it can lead to a roller coaster of emotions, but it is just one more step on the long road of growth ahead.

Further reading

Baumeister, R., Vohs, K. & Oettingen, G. (2016): Pragmatic prospection: How and why people think about the future. *Review of General Psychology*, 20(1), pp. 3-16.

Benson, P. L. (1997): *All kids are our kids: What communities must do to raise caring and responsible children and adolescents.* San Francisco, CA: Jossey-Bass.

Fredrickson, B. L. (1998): What Good Are Positive Emotions? *Review of General Psychology: Journal of Division 1, of the American Psychological Association*, 2(3), pp. 300–319.

Fredrickson, B. L. & Branigan, C. (2005): Positive emotions broaden the scope of attention and thought-action repertoires. *Cognition & Emotion*, 19(3), pp. 313–332.

Gable, S. L. & Haidt, J. (2005): What (and Why) Is Positive Psychology? *Review of General Psychology*, 9(2), pp. 103-110.

Gollwitzer, P. & Kinney, R. (1989): Effects of deliberative and implemental mind-sets on illusion of control. *Journal of Personality and Social Psychology*, 56(4), pp. 531-542.

Haggerty, K. P. & Shapiro, V. B. (2013): Science-Based Prevention Through Communities That Care: A Model of Social Work Practice for Public Health. *Social Work in Public Health*, 28, pp. 349–365.

Kern, M. L. & Friedman, H. S. (2008): Early educational milestones as predictors of lifelong academic achievement, midlife adjustment, and longevity. *Journal of Applied Developmental Psychology*, 30(4), pp. 419–430.

Milburn, C. (2018): *Preparing kindergarten children for school*. Essential Kids. Available at: www.essentialkids.com.au/education/school/starting-school/preparing-kindergarten-children-for-school-20090215-88ki

Pittman, K. J. & Wright, M. (1991): *Bridging the Gap: A Rationale for Enhancing the Role of Community Organizations in Promoting Youth Development*. Washington, DC: Center for Youth Development and Policy Research.

Seligman, M. E. P. (2011): *Flourish*. Boston, MA: Nicholas Brealey Publishing.

Stillman, D. & Stillman, J. (2017): *Gen Z @ work*. London, UK: HarperCollins.

World Health Organization. (2004): *Promoting mental health: concepts, emerging evidence, practice*. Summary Report. Geneva: World Health Organization. Available at: www.who.int/mental_health/evidence/en/promoting_mhh.pdf

Wyman, P., Cowen, E., Work, W. & Kerley, J. (1993): The role of children's future expectations in self-system functioning and adjustment to life stress: A prospective study of urban at-risk children. *Development and Psychopathology*, 5(4), p. 649.

Zhou, K., Liu, Q., Niu, G., Sun, X. & Fan, C. (2017): Bullying victimization and depression in Chinese children: A moderated mediation model of resilience and mindfulness. *Personality and Individual Defferences*, 104, pp. 137-142.

Chapter 7:
The Value of Self-Acceptance, of Being Enough

Rob Stokoe

Your wellbeing and a positive outlook are key ingredients of a great life. Wellbeing is complicated, probably its best thought of as person centric quality, continually shifting and evolving in the dynamics of our social and personal contexts. What is clear is that we need to pay attention to the quality of our inner selves. It's about learning how to accept, value and make conscious choices about how we become more fully aware of ourselves as we strive for happiness, love, success and purpose in our lives. At the heart of this are our personal values; values that are energised by the competence of valuing ourselves, which in turn allows us to value and be generous to others as we strive to achieve our goals that are unique to each of us. We all need to strive to live with joy, purpose and perseverance as we strive for our goals, valuing both ourselves and those around us.

Know your own values and passions
The Oxford Dictionary defines 'values' as 'principles or standards of behaviour; one's judgement of what is important in life'. To embrace the challenges life offers we must take the time to listen to our hearts

and begin to consider what is meaningful and important to us, insights that allow us to understand our unique values and passions. Our core values are unique and important to each of us, they highlight what we stand for, guiding our behaviour and decision making. As individuals we develop our belief systems in the light of our experiences that inform our values and attitudes. Being mindful of our values is the driver that give our lives purpose and a sense of self-determination, allowing us to live with integrity as we follow our inner compass. This focus will encourage a high level of alignment between our values and actions, which leads to high levels of integrity. The extent to which our lives align with our values, they define what is of importance to us as we strive to find our place in the world, to live a happy, aligned and contented life.

Our values influence our sense of what is worthwhile and this will shift and change as we embrace our individual journey. As we live our lives we will transition into new phases and our definition of our wellbeing and success changes and adapts to the circumstances we face. We will face challenges through events that conflict with our values and this may lead to frustration. If we can face these circumstances positively we may begin to better understand the source of frustration, this will help us to move forward. To cultivate a purpose driven mindset, we need to live our values, accept where you have been and positively confront challenges, taking responsibility; understanding that our wellbeing is interwoven into our values and acceptance of your whole self. Choosing to build strength into your emotional capability will encourage the potential to accept challenge, additionally, you will pay attention to being emotionally and physically well; to create a contented, purposeful future that is full of possibility.

Wellbeing is a multi-faceted quality

There are many facets of life which have the potential to influence our wellbeing. Carol Ryff identified six areas of influence: self-acceptance, positive relationships, autonomy, environmental mastery, purpose in life and a sense of personal growth. In truth we all face ups and downs throughout our lives. Yet as we consider ourselves, striving to find or place in the world we all too often tend to dwell upon the negatives in our lives and the apparent strengths we perceive in others. Terry Prince put it well when he wrote: 'Your life is your garden and your thoughts are your seeds, so if your life isn't awesome you've been watering the weeds.' We need to learn to elevate ourselves, to feel positive about who we are, accepting the unique potential that we all carry. Accepting that wellbeing is a variable we all need to understand that we must continually feel positive about ourselves and how others view us. We will often encounter difficulties and problem, however, that does not mean that we are the problem, but we are responsible for finding positive solutions. As individuals rarely do we control the events that influence our lives, but what we can control is our response and how we feel about them. Our wellbeing, our emotional mastery will be informed by accepting responsibility for self as well as living with the positive character attributes of integrity and humility.

We all desire to realise our potential and to have a good life. Self-acceptance, or self-compassion, is key to this and refers to actions which contribute to the maintenance of our wellbeing and promotion of growth.[1] Instead of focusing upon what is wrong, self-acceptance promotes focus upon what is right. That each of us understands and has the capacity to utilise and develop our strengths. That said, this must always be considered in the context of not only our strengths but also our limitations as we develop and pursue our values.

The value of self-acceptance, of being enough

When faced with constant opportunity and challenge as we walk the path of life, we seek constant success, ongoing achievement and affirmation. As we look inwards considering ourselves, we need more often to consider and acknowledge the positive attributes and growing talents within. If we have difficulties or poor judgement in our lives, we need to reflect, understanding that we must bring a strong and positive response.

To counter such situations, we must face them with self-awareness, acceptance and kindness. An approach to self-awareness and self-

---

1   Neff, C. (2010): Self-Compassion: An Alternative Conceptualization of a Healthy Attitude Toward Oneself. *Self and Identity*, 2, pp. 85-101.

acceptance is supported by the broaden-and-build theory proposed by Fredrikson (2001).[2]

This theory builds upon the fact that over time experience of positive emotions can shift people's daily experiences toward more positive emotions. Consequently, if we take some time (no more than ten minutes) to consider your positive experiences every day, most importantly, write them down. Over time this approach will encourage individuals to become self-accepting, developing positive habits and patterns thinking that will become automatic. It usually takes about six months to achieve this, but the outcomes are long-term and self-empowering, allowing you to focus upon the positives in life.

Everyone has ups and downs, that is part of being human, being aware that everyone struggles from time to time. So, cut yourself some slack, give yourself permission to be imperfect. The solution begins with being responsible for you and being kind to yourself, after all you are the most important person in your life.

Focus upon what is right, rather than what is wrong

Today we live in what Seligman describes as a, 'worry culture', where we tend to focus upon what is wrong rather than what is right. When we fall short of our own expectations we tend to be self-critical, even harsh in our self-judgement. In the context of schools even the best teachers may not recognise or accept their individual talent. Their skills and professional attributes may be invisible to them. Coaches and psychologists refer to this as, 'expert induced amnesia', teachers can become blind to their competencies. Teachers tend to have a self-critical disposition, aware of shortfalls or areas for growth rather than the brilliance they bring to their classrooms. To counter this and to raise levels of positive affirmation we need leaders who focus upon what is right rather than what is wrong. Leaders who will intentionally activate, recognise and advise their colleagues, actively support and find reasons to celebrate great teaching. This approach will inform greater acceptance

---

2   Fredrickson, B. L. (2001): The role of positive emotions in positive psychology: The broaden-and-build theory of positive emotions. *American psychologist*, 56(3), pp. 218-226.

of self, giving teachers the positivity and confidence, which will inform growth and self- determination. After all, if you were coaching Lionel Messi you would not focus upon his tackling, you would focus upon what he does when he is on the ball, as well as the fact he is the best in the world. This approach of internal collaboration, focusing upon what is right rather than what is wrong is critical to the development of effective schools as it supports teacher improvement and development. It creates environments of possibility for self and for others, informing an authentic environment where risk taking is fine, where we learn from mistakes and celebrate success, continually challenging ourselves to thrive. Let's face it, the best teachers want to be part of schools that help them to improve and provide contentment, enhancing the capacity for growth. Schools that help, acknowledge, support, and assist because they understand that it is their job to get better, a career-long task.

Relate to ourselves wisely with kindness and positivity

Being positive and self-aware encourages us to treat ourselves with understanding and kindness, focusing upon how much we can do, acknowledging effort and how close we are to achieving our goals. When we choose the path of considerate self-awareness we are accepting a balanced view of the problems we face, forgiving ourselves for what we have or have not done. We are learning to move on, accepting the best of any given situation. After all its not just the problems you face in life, it's how you deal with them. Offering kindness and forgiveness to yourself allows you to be forgiving and kind to others, that said, you must be friends with yourself first. 'Rather than harshly judging oneself for personal shortcomings, the self is offered warmth and unconditional acceptance.'[3] Over the last decade or so, research has consistently shown a positive correlation between self-compassion and wellbeing. People who have self-compassion also have greater social connectedness, emotional balance and overall life satisfaction.

Self-compassion accepts the key principal that we are always a work in progress, not so much imperfect, rather striving continually for new

---

3   Neff, C. (2010): Self-Compassion: An Alternative Conceptualization of a Healthy Attitude Toward Oneself. *Self and Identity*, 2, pp. 85-101.

horizons. Relating to ourselves honestly in a way that respects our values, with kindness and positivity is essential for our emotional consistency and wellbeing. This goes much further than mindfulness as it deepens understanding beyond awareness of the difficulties we, and others face. It brings an element of emotional wisdom as we culture tenderness towards ourselves and trust in our individual potential. Ultimately this engenders the strength to trust in our insight, allowing us to progress not in isolation, rather developing a deeper connection with self and others. Self-compassion sustains the notion of caring for others, informing a happier more content and engaged self, more capable of making a positive difference.

Connecting to yourself engages your ability to connect with others and this impacts positively upon our wellbeing. To engage in benevolent activities, giving to others offers us in return a 'high heart'. This is of critical importance to the complexity of wellbeing as: 'Giving to others is beneficial to your individual wellbeing.'[4] Acts of kindness inform a well lived life, after all, when we give we feel good and it is an emotion that persists.

Make gratitude a habit, have an 'attitude of gratitude'

Why? Because as we pursue happiness and life satisfaction, gratitude offers a positive and long-lasting effect. Put simply, the more gratitude we offer and receive the happier our lives will be. As we consider and learn to recognise the positive contribution of others to our wellbeing then we strengthen our sense of abundance. We do this by taking time to notice and reflect upon the things we're thankful for. Consequently, we experience more positive emotions, feel more alive, sleep better, express more compassion and kindness, a positive outcome.

According to Peterson & Seligman (2004), gratitude is one of the key character strengths we have as individuals, and one which can be developed. It can be described as mindful awareness of the benefits of your life, it is an emotion that promotes wellbeing and is linked to the value of benevolence; it encourages trust, informing strong relationships.

---

4   Weinstein, N. & Ryan, R. M. (2010): When helping helps: Autonomous motivation for prosocial behavior and its influence on well-being for the helper and recipient. *Journal of Personality and Social Psychology*, 98(2), pp. 222-244.

Like any other human virtue, it must be modelled and practiced as it helps us to recognise the good things offered, helping us offset and deal with difficulties we face, sustaining a positive impact upon our wellbeing. We all react positively to the goodness of others and reciprocate in a timely way as opportunities arise. Deliberately cultivating an attitude of gratitude increases our wellbeing as it is grounded in humility and negates the impact of lost opportunities. Through demonstrating our gratitude for the moment, we can free ourselves from regrets and other negative emotions such as envy. Research indicates that gratitude reduces envy, facilitates positive emotions, and even makes us more resilient.[5]

Positive gratitude interventions

When we pay attention to what is good in our lives, counting our blessings rather than our burdens, noticing what we already have then we are more likely to feel positively about ourselves and our place in the world. Paying attention to what is good through simple acts as saying 'thank you', writing a letter of appreciation or dedicating a few minutes a day to journal what we are grateful for enhances our happiness, both long and short term by over 10%.[6] This can be as simple as writing three good things, events or moments that happened during the day. These positive gratitude interventions have many positive influences as gratitude offers you happiness that lasts, not least to our physical wellbeing as it has been shown to increase sleep effectiveness as well as optimising exercise.[7] Writing or simply reflecting upon what we are grateful for just before we sleep help us sleep better, fall asleep faster and sleep for longer.

Gratitude has a positive impact upon our wellbeing, helping us to feel better about our circumstances, which in turn, leads to feeling better about yourself. It also encourages us to think more positively and to develop a greater capacity for happiness. Gratitude is something that

---

5   Amin, A. (2014): *The 31 benefits of gratitude you didn't know about: How gratitude can change your life. Happier Human.* Available at: www.happierhuman.com/benefits-of-gratitude

6   Seligman, M. E. P., Steen, T. T., Park, N. & Peterson, C. (2005): Positive psychology progress: Empirical validation of interventions. *American Psychologist*, 60, pp. 410-421.

7   Emmons, R. A. & McCullough, M. E. (2003): Counting blessings versus burdens: an experimental investigation of gratitude and subjective well-being in daily life. *Journal of personality and social psychology*, 84(2), p. 377.

leads to much more sustainable forms of happiness because it is not based in that immediate gratification; it is a way of being. If you commit to an 'attitude of gratitude' you will better balance your emotions, feel better and be happier – a happiness that lasts.

Summary

The flow of life will offer the unknown, the good and sometimes disappointments, nevertheless it is important for us to increase our value and experience of positive emotions. In life others will let you down, but if events are dealt with in a robust and positive way these situations will enhance and even transform your understanding of yourself. Accept that you are worth respect and be kind to yourself, especially when things are not as you hoped. Being kind and positive about yourself will help you to meet the challenges of the today and the future with optimism and self-belief. As we more often offer ourselves candour, trust and even forgiveness, we will develop a greater sense of where we are and where we are going, of intellectual and emotional self-assurance. Accept that the hardest person to lead is yourself but be appreciative of what you bring and how others see you. Have the courage to write you own story.

We are all unique and continually evolving, tested and adapting to the trials that every single new day brings. Gaining emotional awareness and learning to accept value ourselves through positive choices is integral to becoming what we can be. Life will continually offer us challenges that will always test us, but if we accept responsibility for ourselves we can meet those challenges with optimism, believing and intentionally feeling positive about who we are and how others see us. Simply putting aside ten minutes a day to note what went well and why will support us in developing and maintaining a positive mindset. Your self-awareness, self-compassion and acceptance will support us on our journey, after all the greatest competence is being kind to yourself. This is a journey that is about building our personal capacity, where change is meaningful, and we continually grow our own brilliance, success beyond success.

Further reading

Amin, A. (2014): *The 31 benefits of gratitude you didn't know about: How gratitude can change your life. Happier Human.* Available at: www.happierhuman.com/benefits-of-gratitude

Barnard, L. & Curry, J.F. (2010): Self-Compassion: Conceptualizations, Correlates and Interventions. *Review of General Psychology*, 15(4), p. 289.

Emmons, R. A. & McCullough, M. E. (2003): Counting blessings versus burdens: an experimental investigation of gratitude and subjective well-being in daily life. *Journal of personality and social psychology*, 84(2), p. 377.

Fredrickson, B. L. (2001): The role of positive emotions in positive psychology: The broaden-and-build theory of positive emotions. *American psychologist*, 56(3), pp. 218-226.

Neff, C. (2010): Self-Compassion: An Alternative Conceptualization of a Healthy Attitude Toward Oneself. *Self and Identity*, 2, pp. 85-101.

Seligman, M. E. P. (2011): *Flourish.* London, UK: Nicholas Brealey Publishing

Seligman, M. E. P., Steen, T. T., Park, N. & Peterson, C. (2005): Positive psychology progress: Empirical validation of interventions. *American Psychologist*, 60, pp. 410-421.

Weinstein, N. & Ryan, R. M. (2010): When helping helps: Autonomous motivation for prosocial behavior and its influence on well-being for the helper and recipient. *Journal of Personality and Social Psychology*, 98(2), pp. 222-244.

Chapter 8:
Positive Places for Learning

Matthew Easterman

We have probably all experienced it at some point. We've been trying to concentrate in class and someone puts their hand up to complain that it's too hot, that the sun is in their eyes, or that it's too dark, too cold, or there's a funny smell, or their chair legs are wobbly. Perhaps the teacher sent a memo, letter or email to the janitor to have a noisy fan fixed, or perhaps the school took the time to refurbish a room that was on the edge of collapse. Sometimes, just sometimes, we got a whole new building with new features. But, even then, we sometimes found it was too bright, too noisy, too **something** or not enough. Although humans are adaptable, we are also susceptible to our surroundings. We often need a Goldilocks space – not too hot and not too cold – for our brains and bodies to perform at their best. When it comes to learning, the physical environment is the stage on which we perform, the cave in which we hide, the world inside the world where amazing changes happen. Surely, we should know that the environment is conducive to the best types of learning and teaching we can muster.

All roads lead to the present

It is a slight fallacy that all classrooms, especially in the developed world, are based on an 'industrial' model of education that was rolled out at some point in the 19th century to train factory workers.

There have been many competing types of schools and school designs depending on the socio-cultural and political environments in which they grew. Indeed, it could be argued that it has only been the recent push towards standardisation of curriculum, teaching approaches, assessment and accountability through 'reforms' in many jurisdictions that real industrial-scale standardisation has occurred.[1] Many teachers lament the fact that they can't 'have fun anymore' in their practice because of – often well-founded – changes to laws and policies that support a safer and more protective environment for students.[2]

The physical environment we build for ourselves is a direct reflection of the dominant culture of the time in which it was designed and built.[3] For many students today, they are learning in places designed and built in the immediate post-war era, where baby booms paired with centralised planning led to standardisation of designs to meet a need that had never existed.

'Cells and bells' were the order of the day in the 1940s-1960s in much of the developed world, where the priority was educating as many students in as efficient as possible manner for a reasonable economic cost.[4] Although there have been some attempts to stimulate new movements of design and innovation in recent decades, they often lapsed into a more standardised approach that can be easily tracked, mapped and held accountable. This happened in England during the Building Schools for the Future (BSF) programme, which went from innovative world-leading and locally-driven design projects to a series of increasingly small and underfunded projects that was finally cancelled under a new conservative government in the 2010s. In Australia, the success of the Building the Education Revolution (BER) programme was wide and varied, with many (often government run) schools being given a list of

---

1   Sahlberg, P. (2006): Education Reform for Raising Economic Competitiveness. *Journal of Educational Change*, 7(4), pp. 259-287.

2   Bahr, N. & Mellor, S. (2016): Building Quality in Teaching and Teacher Education. *Australian Education Review*, 61.

3   Joye, Y. (2007): Architectural Lessons from Environmental Psychology: the case of biophilic architecture. *Review of General Psychology*, 11(4), pp. 305-328.

4   Shaw, A. (2016): *Factory Model vs 21st Century Model of Education*. Available at: www.linkedin.com/pulse/factory-model-vs-21st-century-education-anne-shaw

options to choose from, even when those options were inappropriate for the context. There was little attempt to make positive places of learning but rather roll out a centralised, standardised set of buildings to house more students. A few brave souls bucked the trend and pushed back, and the results have been much more useful and pleasing environments for their students.

Some streams of education have taken different routes, 'alternative' places of learning such as Montessori or Steiner schools. In many of these places, the architecture reflects their approach to learning and teaching, as well as the wider philosophical, moral and social perspectives offered by the school. The natural world often features quite heavily as a priority in these designs, as well as accommodating flexible furniture for students and teachers.

Regardless of the educational traditions that seem to ebb and flow as they are discovered, rediscovered, reworked and adapted by different groups in different contexts, there are always opportunities to undertake design processes from within the school (if it is already established) or within the local community (if a new build). Both are valuable cores of a design process to get the most relevant, useful and vibrant learning spaces possible for the people that will use them.

Recently, the Australian states of New South Wales and Victoria have intentionally focused on designing new schools and significantly refurbishing existing sites with a more aspirational mindset than 'cells and bells'. Their respective school building authorities strive to create places that are better for learning, better for diverse approaches to learning and, in short, better for humans.

Where are we now?

Humans are fantastically adaptable. Over tens of thousands of years, we have learned how to build shelters, cities and civilisations for ourselves to move from 'survive' to 'thrive'. The social networks, the institutions and, yes, the physical spaces and places around us all contribute to our opportunities for growth. Part of this is the construction of schools and the school experience for increasing numbers of people in all societies. The places we design for learning are a direct reflection of our (economic) needs, our dreams and our willingness to invest in younger generations. Where we are affects how we learn and, whilst we adapt to our surroundings, there are some things we can do every day to grow and maintain positive places for learning.

Where we learn affects how we learn. There are many factors and issues relating to our environment, our surroundings, that can affect us physically, emotionally and psychologically and thus affect our ability to learn. Issues such as light, fresh air, noise, access to the outdoors, navigation, flexibility and amenities can all help or hinder the individual student and teacher experience of learning in complex and changing ways.[5] Studies such as Clever Classrooms (2016) from Salford University identified significant learning gain differences between students in 'better' environments to those in 'poorer' environments. This difference can be over a year's worth of time in the classroom. To put it another way, students completing the same courses in less conducive environments are over a year behind students in better classrooms even before the lesson begins. The three factors found to be 'significantly influential' in this study were: light, temperature and air quality. Each one should be able to be managed by those who run the facilities in which their students learn.

Indeed, a well-designed, well-maintained and appropriately used place for learning can have positive emotional benefits on students. As Graetz (2016) that: 'environments that elicit positive emotional responses may lead not only to enhanced learning but also to a powerful, emotional attachment to that space. It may become a place where students love to learn, a place they seek out when they wish to learn, and a place they remember fondly when they reflect on their learning experiences.'[6]

Isn't that what we want for our students? To love their learning throughout their life? How often do we consider the impact of where they learn as a hindrance to this noble goal?

---

5   Tanner, K. (2009): Effects of School Design on Student Outcomes. *Journal of Education Administration*, 47(3), pp. 381-399.

6   Graetz, K. (2016): *Psychology of Learning Environments*, in Oblinger (ed.) Learning Spaces, published online via Educause. Available at: www.educause.edu/research-and-publications/books/learning-spaces/chapter-6-psychology-learning-environments

Goldilocks spaces

Some spaces are 'too' something: too hot, too cold, too moist, too exposed, too draughty, too stuffy, too light, too dark.[7] Temperature extremes are an obvious and useful factor to identify, gather data, analyse and report on the impact.[8] We need to find our 'Goldilocks conditions', within the context, so that the space is not an inhibitor to learning but a physical environment that makes us more disposed to learning.

As a socio-cultural experience, schools need to be places where students not only feel physically safe, but also feel excited, stimulated, challenged and pushed beyond their comfort zone. The physical environment does not exist in a vacuum from other factors. We ourselves, the 'users' of a physical environment are both part of and separate to its function, form and aesthetic appeal. A classroom is not fully a classroom without students and teachers. A school, similar. Just walk around a school site after everyone has gone home and one can feel that something has been 'switched off', or is absent. We have known this for centuries and it has been seriously studied for several decades. The key aspect of the physical environment is whether it has been designed for the purposes and functions required by the users, or not. Schools, by and large, have been accused of looking more like prisons than playgrounds. And, even when schools are designed to look great, if we don't regularly engage with the people inside them they may not be fit for purpose. Indeed, one student remarked to me that her experience of school was as a 'beautiful prison'.

It is, therefore, essential to include the users of the new spaces in the design process from the earliest moments. The best architects of schools, for example, will run workshops and feedback sessions as one of the very first steps in their approach to ensure that the voice of the user is valued and absorbed into the thinking of the design team. Though never a guarantee of total success of every element and feature of the design, it will mitigate many of the issues of 'post-occupancy' by having established a partnership with the teachers, students and other users

---

7   Al-Sallal, K. A. (2010): Daylighting and visual performance evaluation of classroom design in the UAE. *International Journal of Low-Carbon Technologies*, 5, pp. 201-209.

8   Ahman, M., Lundin, A., Musabasic, V. & Soderman, E. (2000): Improved Health After Intervention in a School with Moisture Problems. *Indoor Air*, 10, pp. 57-62.

who have a deep and clear understanding of the potential of the pitfalls and the purpose of the spaces into which they move. The design process itself can be a positive experience, leading to more positive use and indeed wider positive impact over other projects and experiences at the school.[9] An example of this is the quite pervasive use of design thinking methodologies in areas well outside the traditional areas of 'design', into leadership strategy, curriculum design and assessment development.

A slightly worrying trend (in Australia at least) is the intention to 'learn the lessons' of health and medicine in terms of how research is applied in practice, as well as developing policy based on the evidence provided by the research alone. In terms of the built environment, this should be some cause for concern if adopted wholesale and without critical analysis, leadership and judgement by educators, students and other users of the space as to what is appropriate. At the very core of the purpose of the design of hospitals is to make the experience as painless, seamless, and rapid as possible; to get in and get out of the process with the least pain and the most support. The main goal of a hospital is to never need one, and when we do need one, for that need to be dealt with as efficiently as possible.

On the other hand, schools are places where we want students to want to be. We want students to feel an urge to run to school (not just run home) and we want them to feel not only safe and 'cared for' but also stimulated, challenged, engaged and enticed to come back the next day with a new sense of purpose. We are trying to infuse students with a love of learning and a love of the place of learning at the same time. In education, we want them to keep coming back. This is fundamentally different to the world of health or indeed many other organisations and physical environments.

Designing for wellbeing

Whilst schools are not hospitals, we do want them to be places that provide for our basic needs, the lowest rungs of Maslow's hierarchy, so that we can achieve the higher levels of Maslow and start exploring the more complex, deeper, networked web of thinking that forms higher order thinking.

---

9   Woolner, P. (2018): *Collaborative Re-Design*, a seminar presented at the Centre for Research on Learning and Innovation at the University of Sydney.

'In teaching, you can't do the Bloom's stuff before you take care of the Maslow's stuff.' – Alan E. Beck

We know that students' physical health can be affected by the environments in which they learn. Many studies have investigated this, from the basic features of light, noise, temperature and so on through to the air quality that may affect students with asthma,[10] risk taking behaviour,[11] teacher attendance, and, of course, student achievement.[12]

The places at schools which support wellbeing do not need to be expensive, elaborate and highly specialised 'wellness centres'. These places can be formed with simple changes to how existing spaces are used. For example, by allocating a classroom for quiet reflection during lunchtimes. Other attempts to make school spaces more 'homely' have had great success, such as creating a relaxation corner in a classroom with used or donated furniture to improve the allocated space; or moving a class to a library space or performance area to display with work or engage in different types of learning experiences. Changing space, even in minor ways, can have significant impacts on how we think about the space, how we use the space and how we feel about the use of that space. In turn, the space becomes part of our design of learning experiences as much as a textbook, a website, or any other resource or tool at our pedagogical disposal.

Bridging the physical and the digital worlds

Access to digital learning spaces has become essential to learning and teaching in the modern global, hyper-connected context. The digital services available to teacher and students are now quite prolific. Learning management systems (LMS), online discussion platforms, social media and email are just a few of the means by which we can communicate to and with students in a variety of settings. Most schools will subscribe

10   Henebery, B. (2016): *How learning environments affect student health.* The Educator: Australia. Available at: www.theeducatoronline.com/au/news/how-learning-environments-affect-student-health/226815

11   Jamal, F., Fletcher, A., Harden, A., Wells, H., Thomas, J. & Bonell, C. (2013): The school environment and student health: a systematic review and meta-ethnography of qualitative research. *BMC Public Health*, 13.

12   Brooks, D. C. (2011): Space matters: The impact of formal learning environments on student learning. *British Journal of Educational Technology*, 42(5), pp. 719-726.

to set of technologies (LMS + storage + communications) to provide a baseload of access and security to their staff and students. Some schools provide students with devices to use and some allow students to 'Bring Your Own Device' (BYOD).

For a long time, many looked at digital services as an 'other' thing. It was something optional, something external, something distinct and separate to the school experience. The 'real' world was the classroom, the books and the face-to-face relationships that were essential to engaging in even the most basic of learning and living. Now we have the means to connect with people from around the world and in all kinds of forms and forums. We have fused the physical and the digital worlds so that one affects the other and sometimes in immediate and confronting ways.

We need to remember that the digital worlds we create for ourselves are as real as the physical world. What we do in our public, private or secret online worlds is tethered to what we do and say in our physical world.[13] This will only become more prevalent as we begin to make more and more global connections as part of schooling, work and life. The need for digital citizenship programs and genuine engagement with people in meaningful relationships has never been more necessary. This is where having safe spaces – both physical and digital – can play a key role.

Our reputation and social footprint is altered by our actions and words even more so in the digital space. There, we are archived and stored for those with access to mine our recorded thoughts and experiences online. There, nothing is easily forgotten. We need to be proactive in helping student navigate this other layer of their reality.

Ideas for school leaders

Build a shared purpose: begin conversations early about what kind of teaching and learning experiences you intend to support and what kinds of spaces and resources might be required. Decide on a strategy, prototype it, reflect on it, tweak it and try again.

---

13   Martin, F., Wang, C., Petty, T., Wang, W. & Wilkins, P. (2018): Middle School Students' Use of Social Media. *Journal of Educational Technology & Society*, 21(1), pp. 213-224.

Be a leader of learning: make sure you understand what it is like to teach in all areas of the school, whether indoor or outdoor, practical or theory lessons. Walk around the school and visit classrooms to truly understand your current position and readiness for change.

Be inclusive: create and chair an active committee of colleagues and students who can help inform the future planning for teaching, learning and spaces in the school.

Bring learners into decision-making: let students explore different options for furniture, arrangement, size and type of rooms, fixtures and features. As they will be spending most of their time in these spaces it is important for them to help build protocols and understandings around each space.

Ideas for teachers

Be curious and brave: try something new each week and reflect on how it works (or doesn't work). If you are allocated to a new space, think about different ways of teaching and learning that you and your students might be able to engage with. There are many resources online to help teachers explore different pedagogical approaches that can help expand a teacher's repertoire beyond a 'chalk and talk' mentality.

Work together: invite other teachers to team-teach or observe your lessons. Give each other specific feedback and focus on building skills in a manageable amount of areas (don't try to do everything at once). Share your experiences on social media or in your staff meetings so that you can develop a culture of dialogue between colleagues.

Be vocal and visible in your thinking: explain to your students why and how you will attempt to use space in a different way. Ask for their feedback and train them to develop a deeper understanding of the uses and possibilities of new and existing spaces for learning.

Ideas for students and parents at home

Rate your spaces: think about which spaces in your home are ideal for learning and those that are not ideal. There could be an opportunity to develop a mini-timetable at home where students can use key places in the home for assignment work or private study, whereas at other times it is open to the whole family. Make this clear and consistent so that the whole household knows the protocols.

Consider lights, noise and heat: how conducive is the home to learning? Is it possible to keep a room or space cool, with enough light to study but also with enough noise reduction so that the learner is not distracted or uncomfortable?

A few final thoughts

If teachers attempt to experiment – even just a little – with the light levels, location, seating arrangements (including on the floor or standing), changing groupings or using music or other background sounds, the mood of the class can shift and have a significant impact on the learning experience. Just remember to capture the experience, gather feedback from students and colleague, debrief and discuss then plan the next experience.

There are no silver bullets when it comes to classroom design for wellbeing as the experience is a conversation between people and place, constantly changing along with our moods, preferences, past experiences and goals.

If we truly value our wellbeing, we will prioritise it and make every space a reflection of how we dream our futures of learning can be created.

Further reading

Ahman, M., Lundin, A., Musabasic, V. & Soderman, E. (2000): Improved Health After Intervention in a School with Moisture Problems. *Indoor Air*, 10, pp. 57-62.

Al-Sallal, K. A. (2010): Daylighting and visual performance evaluation of classroom design in the UAE. *International Journal of Low-Carbon Technologies*, 5, pp. 201-209.

Bahr, N. & Mellor, S. (2016): Building Quality in Teaching and Teacher Education. *Australian Education Review*, 61.

Blackmore, J., Bateman, D., Loughlin, J., O'Mara, J. & Aranda, G. (2011): *Research into the connection between built learning spaces and student outcomes: Literature review.* Melbourne, Australia: Department of Education and Early Childhood Development.

Brooks, D. C. (2011): Space matters: The impact of formal learning environments on student learning. *British Journal of Educational Technology*, 42(5), pp. 719-726.

Graetz, K. (2016): *Psychology of Learning Environments*, in Oblinger (ed.) Learning Spaces, published online via Educause. Available at: www.educause.edu/research-and-publications/books/learning-spaces/chapter-6-psychology-learning-environments

Henebery, B. (2016): *How learning environments affect student health.* The Educator: Australia. Available at: www.theeducatoronline.com/au/news/how-learning-environments-affect-student-health/226815

Jamal, F., Fletcher, A., Harden, A., Wells, H., Thomas, J. & Bonell, C. (2013): The school environment and student health: a systematic review and meta-ethnography of qualitative research. *BMC Public Health*, 13.

Joye, Y. (2007): Architectural Lessons from Environmental Psychology: the case of biophilic architecture. *Review of General Psychology*, 11(4), pp. 305-328.

Martin, F., Wang, C., Petty, T., Wang, W. & Wilkins, P. (2018): Middle School Students' Use of Social Media. *Journal of Educational Technology & Society*, 21(1), pp. 213-224.

Sahlberg, P. (2006): Education Reform for Raising Economic Competitiveness. *Journal of Educational Change*, 7(4), pp. 259-287.

Shaw, A. (2016): *Factory Model vs 21st Century Model of Education.* Available at: www.linkedin.com/pulse/factory-model-vs-21st-century-education-anne-shaw

Tanner, K. (2009): Effects of School Design on Student Outcomes. *Journal of Education Administration*, 47(3), pp. 381-399.

Woolner, P. (2018): *Collaborative Re-Design*, a seminar presented at the Centre for Research on Learning and Innovation at the University of Sydney.

Chapter 9:

Creating Educational Context that Supports Wellbeing and a Love of Learning

Dr. Helen Street

It could be said that, when it comes to education, we are living in 'emotional times'.

Over the past 30 years, schools worldwide have embraced a myriad of topic focused and whole-school wellbeing programs, including positive education. This growing wellbeing trend has resulted in many schools spending increasing time, effort, and money teaching students how to 'be happy and healthy', as well as how to achieve great academic results. However, despite having great intentions, many of the wellbeing initiatives and positive education programs schools are heavily investing in, are simply not working as well as expected, wanted, or needed.[1] Moreover, many are not working at all.[2] [3] [4]

1   Street, H. (2017): Measures of success: Exploring the importance of context in the delivery of wellbeing and social and emotional learning programs in Australian primary and secondary schools in Frydenberg, E. Martin, A.J. and Collie R.J. (Eds) *Social and Emotional Learning in Australia and the Asia Pacific*. Singapore: Springer Science and Business.
2   Weare, K. & Nind, M. (2011): Mental health promotion and problem prevention in schools: What does the evidence say? *Health Promotion International*, 26(1).
3   West, S. L. & O'Neal, K. K. (2004): Project D.A.R.E. outcome effectiveness revisited. *American Journal of Public Health*. 94(6), pp. 1027–1029.
4   Wysong, E. & Wright, D. W. (1995): A decade of DARE: efficacy, politics and drug education. *Sociological Focus*, 28(3).

In addition, mental health issues remain alarmingly high in Australia and the rest of the developed world with nearly 25% of our adolescents, and one in six of our younger children, seriously clinically distressed.[5][6] It seems that we have never done so much to support wellbeing in schools, yet poor mental health in schools has never been so prevalent.

In 2011, a comprehensive investigation of 52 reviews and analyses of school-based wellbeing programs, found that although there was little negative impact of the programs, any positive impact was highly variable.[7] In fact, in many instances, evidence-based wellbeing programs and initiatives had not had a significant positive impact at all.

Along far more vehement lines, educational psychologist Professor Kathryn Ecclestone wrote an article for the UK Conversation in which she suggested that school wellbeing programs are largely a waste of time and resources.[8] Professor Ecclestone states that she 'has found that some of these interventions actually have negative effects. In general, the research field is fragmented, one-sided, inconclusive and methodologically flawed'.

This is not to say that there is not great value in the development of whole school wellbeing and positive education. There is also an increasing body of research supporting the value of these programs.[9] In particular, research has found that the most effective school programs as those that are universal and aimed at the entire school population.[10][11]

5   Australian Bureau of Statistics. (2015): National Health Survey, 2014-15. Available at: www.abs.gov.au/ausstats/abs@.nsf/Lookup/by%20Subject/4364.0.55.001~2014-15~Main%20Features~Psychological%20distress~16

6   Mission Australia. (2018): *The 2017 Mission Australia Youth Survey.* Available at: www.missionaustralia.com.au/publications/annual-reports/annual-report-2017

7   Weare, K. & Nind, M. (2011): Mental health promotion and problem prevention in schools: What does the evidence say? *Health Promotion International,* 26(1).

8   Ecclestone, K. (2015): *Well-being programmes in schools might be doing children more harm than good.* The Conversation. Available at: www.theconversation.com/well-being-programmes-in-schools-might-be-doing-children-more-harm-than-good-36573

9   Greenberg, M. T., Domitrovich, C. & Bumbarger, B. (2001): *Preventing Mental Disorders in School Aged Children. A Review of The Effectiveness of Prevention Programmes.* Pennsylvania State University, PA: Prevention Research Center for the Promotion of Human Development, College of Health and Human Development.

10 Wells, J., Barlow, J. & Stewart-Brown, S. (2003): A systematic review of universal approaches to mental health promotion in schools. *Health Education,* 103, pp. 197–220.

11 Weare, K. & Nind, M. (2011): Mental health promotion and problem prevention in schools: What does the evidence say? *Health Promotion International,* 26(1).

Yet, the positive impact of these programs is still far less than it is intended to be or believed it could be.[12] [13]

I firmly believe that the reason for such mediocrity stems from a failure to create school contexts that reflect the values, attitudes and behaviours inherent in the pursuit of wellbeing. Certainly, it is of little surprise that the most effective programs appear to be those that have the biggest impact on overall school culture and climate. Both research and experience are telling us that however great a wellbeing program's ideals may be, they will not translate into positive outcomes if they are not better supported within the context in which they are delivered

For example, positive education emphasises the importance of positive emotion, engagement, relationships, meaning and achievement in the maintenance of wellbeing (PERMA); with an emphasis on developing character strengths rather than 'removing weakness'.[14] However, the day to day reality of school life tells students a very different story. School contexts around the world emphasise the importance of 'winning' and doing better than others to be successful in life. They frequently embrace inequitable practices such as homework and 'gifted and talented' programs that favour academic high achievers over others. Many support forced competition through compulsory participation in competitive sport and in-class activities. Many undermine self-determination and embrace a constant need for approval with prizes, rewards, and awards. Many even offer awards for demonstrating good values that turns the pursuit of wellbeing into a competition to be judged by others. Many schools also give weakness priority over strengths; with more time and attention given to poor academic performance, than to success, when students are struggling.

12   Street, H. (2017): Measures of success: Exploring the importance of context in the delivery of wellbeing and social and emotional learning programs in Australian primary and secondary schools in Frydenberg, E. Martin, A.J. and Collie R.J. (Eds) *Social and Emotional Learning in Australia and the Asia Pacific*. Singapore: Springer Science and Business.
13   Street, H. (2017): Motivation outside in, inside out. In Slemp, G; Murray, S & White, M., (Eds) *Future Directions in Well-being: Education, Organizations, and Policy*. New York, NY: Springer.
14   Norrish, J. (ed) (2015): *Positive Education: The Geelong Grammar School Journey*. New York, NY: Oxford University Press.

In addition, stressed and overloaded staff are often expected to 'teach' social and emotional skills and role model positive behaviours.

My all-time favourite theory of living well, is Ryan and Deci's self-determination theory (SDT). SDT looks to understand self-determination and motivation within a social context. The theory proposes that a sense of autonomy, relatedness to others and the things we do, and a sense of competency are all required for the development of wellbeing and connection with life. As such, this well-researched theory goes a long way to explaining the inadequacy of current educational context in supporting either lasting happiness or a love of learning. Autonomy is severely compromised in contexts that encourages compliance and obedience. Relatedness is compromised with contexts that supports competition and outcomes over process. Competency is compromised, for all but a few, within contexts that revers high grades and awards.

I do not believe that we can place individuals into unhealthy social systems and then expect them to be healthy and well. It seems a total anomaly for a school to embrace competition, behavioural control, and high outcomes; and then expect students to learn about collaboration, autonomy, and doing your 'personal best'. Moreover, I believe we are creating a troubling dichotomy if we put young people into school systems that create despondency and disengagement and then try to teach them about the importance of positive emotion and flow. This is a bit like feeding a child chocolate and ice cream daily and then trying to improve their diet with the addition of salad.

If we can develop school context in a positive and sustainable way, we can create an environment that helps everyone to flourish. I call this positive development of a healthy context 'Contextual Wellbeing'.[15] In schools, 'Contextual Wellbeing' is simply defined as a state of health, happiness, and positive engagement (in learning) that arises from membership of an equitable, inclusive and cohesive (school) environment. Contextual wellbeing supports the explicit teaching of wellbeing in schools in addition to providing a means of creating a flourishing community from the ground up.

---

15 Street, H. (2018): *Contextual Wellbeing: Creating Healthy School Contexts to Nurture Flourishing Students and Staff.* The Positive Times. Available at: www.positivetimes.com.au

The Contextual Wellbeing model provides a framework for understanding how each of four key domains of a social context can better support a flourishing community. The People (e.g. staff and students); physical space (e.g. classroom set-up, outdoor spaces); policies and practice (e.g. homework policy, behavioural management practices) and social norms (e.g. whether to trust others, how to treat others). The healthy development of each of these key contextual domains is described as follows:

People

Attention paid to supporting the wellbeing and social emotional learning of teachers and school leaders, can help all help members of the school community thrive. For example, socially competent staff with manageable levels of stress, and high levels of wellbeing will model positive behaviour to the entire class.[16] [17]

I firmly believe that the support of staff wellbeing needs to be made an absolute priority in every school. A shiny, well-resourced school will not thrive without good educators. In contrast, good educators can surpass most of the problems of a run-down school, and still help students to flourish.

When school staff experience wellbeing, manageable stress levels and social and emotional competency, they can far more effectively support positive relationships and social emotional learning in their students.[18]

Physical space

The physical space comprises the buildings and grounds of the school as well as the wider geographical space impacting on the school culture and climate. This includes the classrooms, library and reception, staff room and other rooms within the school complex, as well as recreational

---

16   Collie, R. J. (2017): Teachers' Social and Emotional Competence: Links with Social and Emotional Learning and Positive Workplace Outcomes in Australian primary and secondary schools. In Frydenberg, E. Martin, A. J. & Collie R. J. (Eds) *Social and Emotional Learning in Australia and the Asia Pacific*. Singapore: Springer Science and Business.

17   Roffey, S. (2012): Pupil wellbeing – teacher wellbeing: Two sides of the same coin? *Educational & Child Psychology*, 29(4), pp. 8-17.

18   Spilt, J. L., Koomen, H. M. & Thijs, J. T. (2011): Teacher Wellbeing: The Importance of Teacher–Student Relationships. *Educational Psychology Review*, 23, pp. 457–477.

areas such as the canteen and outside areas such as the school oval or playgrounds.

A healthy school physical context is one that promotes cohesion, community, and a sense of belonging, rather than competition, hierarchies, and a focus on gaining the approval of others. For example, an outside work of art created by all members of a class presents healthy messages about the importance of community and collaboration. In stark contrast, a trophy cabinet or 'school leader' board clearly states that some members of the school community are more highly revered than others.[19] Similarly, posters depicting school values can act as a powerful reinforcement of desired social norms; whereas a public display of rewards presented for example, 'acts of kindness,' creates competition and emphasises the importance of others approval.

Policy and practice

The policy and practice of a school includes written policies describing set rules, in addition to overt practices carried out by staff. For example, most schools will have both a behavioural management policy and a homework policy. If these policies are to support wellbeing as well as academic learning, they need to be in line with current research, rather than embedded in history and a sense of 'having always done things that way'. For example, many primary (elementary) schools still have a homework policy recommending that children do regular academic work at home. This occurs despite a plethora of research stating that there is no benefit to learning outcomes for primary school homework.[20] [21] The research also finds that homework amplifies inequity (e.g. some children have parental support while others do not), and diminishes opportunity for vital family time, sport, and creative play.[22]

19   Kohn, A. (1999): *Punished by Rewards*. New York, NY: Houghton Mifflin Harcourt.

20   Victorian Department of Education. (2014): *Inquiry into the approaches to homework in Victorian schools*. Available at: www.parliament.vic.gov.au/file_uploads/ETC_Homework_Inquiry_final_report_PWkrPPVH.pdf

21   Victorian Department of Education. (2014): *Inquiry into the approaches to homework in Victorian schools*. Available at: www.parliament.vic.gov.au/file_uploads/ETC_Homework_Inquiry_final_report_PWkrPPVH.pdf

22   Whitebread, D. (2012): *The Importance of Play: a report on the value of children's play with a series of policy recommendations*. Cambridge, UK: University of Cambridge.

There are many other common policies and practices that promote inequity, competition, and a relentless focus on 'working hard'. These include the use of extrinsic rewards in and out of class, award ceremonies, in-class grades, compulsory participation in competitive sport and the minimising of time for play and creativity. It is vital that schools create a flourishing community with policy and practices that build cohesion, equity, and engagement in the process of learning.

Social norms

Social norms are the unwritten rules that guide behaviour. They shape attitudes among members of the school community and reflect the strongest values of the school. Researchers have repeatedly found that social norms accurately predict class behaviour.[23]

Frequently identified unhealthy social norms include treating others with mistrust, talking in class, disrespecting teachers, and seeing learning as a socially undesirable activity. In contrast, healthy social norms include trusting and being respectful to others and seeing engagement in academic learning as a positive behaviour.

Healthy social norms need to be actively and openly nurtured within every aspect of the school community. It is imperative that schools take time to establish healthy norms and then regularly build cohesion to ensure that all students internalise these norms. Time is especially needed to ensure that vulnerable students feel a sense of belonging within their class groups and within the wider school community.

I believe that context matters in the pursuit of school-based wellbeing, far more than we might care to admit. I can't help but wonder how much more successful positive education programs would be if they were actively reflected in and supported by the context in which they are embedded. Rather than focusing on the acquisition or delivery of the newest program, schools could usefully focus on building a healthy equitable context to support wellbeing in their students.

---

23   Mercer, S., McMillen, J. & DeRosier, M. (2009): Predicting change in children's aggression and victimization using classroom-level descriptive norms of aggression and pro-social behaviour. *Journal of School Psychology*, 47, pp. 267–289.

The Contextual Wellbeing model offers a framework that schools can use to build their own equitable, cohesive context. A context where everyone can flourish. It has often been said that it takes a whole village to raise a child, I certainly believe it takes a healthy, whole school context to help a child to flourish. With passion, careful planning and perseverance, great things develop.

Contextual wellbeing matters because every child matters.

To find out more about Contextual Wellbeing please visit www. contextualwellbeing.com.au or get in touch via helen.street@uwa.edu.au

Further reading

Australian Bureau of Statistics. (2015): National Health Survey, 2014-15. Available at: www.abs.gov.au/ausstats/abs@.nsf/Lookup/by%20Subject/4364.0.55.001~2014-15~Main%20Features~Psychological%20distress~16

Canadian Council on Learning. (2009): *A systematic review of literature examining the impact of homework on academic achievement.* Available at: www.edu.au.dk/fileadmin/edu/Udgivelser/SystematicReview_HomeworkApril27-2009.pdf

Collie, R. J. (2017): Teachers' Social and Emotional Competence: Links with Social and Emotional Learning and Positive Workplace Outcomes in Australian primary and secondary schools. In Frydenberg, E. Martin, A. J. & Collie R. J. (Eds) *Social and Emotional Learning in Australia and the Asia Pacific.* Singapore: Springer Science and Business.

Deci, E. L. & Ryan, R. M. (1985): *Intrinsic Motivation and Self-determination in Human Behaviour.* New York, NY: Plenum Publishing.

Deci, E. L. & Ryan, R. M. (1987): The support of autonomy and the control of behavior. *Journal of Personality and Social Psychology,* 53(6), pp. 1024–1037.

Ecclestone, K. (2015): *Well-being programmes in schools might be doing children more harm than good.* The Conversation. Available at: www.theconversation.com/well-being-programmes-in-schools-might-be-doing-children-more-harm-than-good-36573

Greenberg, M. T., Domitrovich, C. & Bumbarger, B. (2001): *Preventing Mental Disorders in School Aged Children. A Review of The Effectiveness of Prevention Programmes.* Pennsylvania State University, PA: Prevention Research Center for the Promotion of Human Development, College of Health and Human Development.

Kohn, A. (1999): *Punished by Rewards.* New York, NY: Houghton Mifflin Harcourt.

Mercer, S., McMillen, J. & DeRosier, M. (2009): Predicting change in children's aggression and victimization using classroom-level descriptive norms of aggression and pro-social behaviour. *Journal of School Psychology,* 47, pp. 267–289.

Mission Australia. (2018): *The 2017 Mission Australia Youth Survey.* Available at: www.missionaustralia.com.au/publications/annual-reports/annual-report-2017

Norrish, J. (Ed) (2015): *Positive Education: The Geelong Grammar School Journey.* New York, NY: Oxford University Press.

Roffey, S. (2012): Pupil wellbeing – teacher wellbeing: Two sides of the same coin? *Educational & Child Psychology,* 29(4), pp. 8-17.

Spilt, J. L., Koomen, H. M. & Thijs, J. T. (2011): Teacher Wellbeing: The Importance of Teacher–Student Relationships. *Educational Psychology Review,* 23, pp. 457–477.

Street, H. (2017): Measures of success: Exploring the importance of context in the delivery of wellbeing and social and emotional learning programs in Australian primary and secondary schools in Frydenberg, E. Martin, A.J. and Collie R.J. (Eds) *Social and Emotional Learning in Australia and the Asia Pacific.* Singapore: Springer Science and Business.

Street, H. (2017): Motivation outside in, inside out. In Slemp, G; Murray, S & White, M., (Eds) *Future Directions in Well-being: Education, Organizations, and Policy.* New York, NY: Springer. (2)

Street, H. (2018): *Contextual Wellbeing: Creating Healthy School Contexts to Nurture Flourishing Students and Staff.* The Positive Times. Available at: www.positivetimes.com.au

Victorian Department of Education. (2014): *Inquiry into the approaches to homework in Victorian schools.* Available at: www.parliament.vic.gov.au/file_uploads/ETC_Homework_Inquiry_final_report_PWkrPPVH.pdf

Weare, K. & Nind, M. (2011): Mental health promotion and problem prevention in schools: What does the evidence say? *Health Promotion International,* 26(1).

Wells, J., Barlow, J. & Stewart-Brown, S. (2003): A systematic review of universal approaches to mental health promotion in schools. *Health Education,* 103, pp. 197–220.

West, S. L. & O'Neal, K. K. (2004): Project D.A.R.E. outcome effectiveness revisited. *American Journal of Public Health,* 94(6), pp. 1027–1029.

Whitebread, D. (2012): *The Importance of Play: a report on the value of children's play with a series of policy recommendations.* Cambridge, UK: University of Cambridge.

Wysong, E. & Wright, D. W. (1995): A decade of DARE: efficacy, politics and drug education. *Sociological Focus,* 28(3).

Chapter 10:
Gross Domestic Product, Happiness and Soft Skills

Roy Blatchford

When Francis Fukuyama published his now infamous tome *The End of History and the Last Man* in 1992, the western liberal democracies thought they had things sorted at last. Working in an American university at the time, I recall vividly the stir the book caused among faculty staff. Fukuyama wrote soothingly and persuasively:

'What we may be witnessing is not just the end of the Cold War, or the passing of a period of post-war history, but the end of history as such: that is, the end-point of mankind's ideological evolution and the universalisation of Western liberal democracy as the final form of human government.'

For the baby boomers of the West who had enjoyed free education, free love and freedom from world war, who had watched the Berlin Wall fall and the break-up of the USSR, Fukuyama's verdict rang true. So far as old conundrums such as ideology and identity were concerned, nobody really cared any more. What mattered was ramping up material prosperity. President Bill Clinton declared in his first presidential campaign: 'It's the economy, stupid.'

25 years on from President Clinton's election mantra the world's developed economies are wealthier than ever – estimated to be more than 70% larger in real terms than they were in 1992. Yet Fukuyama's prediction of end-game stability has been racked by social strife, political division and ideological conflict across the globe, within and between countries, undoubtedly fuelled by 24/7 social media. Moreover, glimpsed from the East, fractured western democracies appear less enviably prosperous than perhaps once they were. Karl Marx, of course, predicted that communism would replace capitalism.

Turmoil, churn and unpredictable voting patterns in the West have led many social commentators and political scientists to challenge familiar definitions of what it is to be a well-balanced and thriving society. In particular, the familiar use by governments of Gross Domestic Product (GDP) to measure national economic wellbeing has come in for serious questioning.

David Pilling, for example, in his fascinating book *The Growth Delusion* explains some of the limitations of applying GDP in today's global society. According to Pilling, economic growth, as normally defined, is just a measure of the expansion of goods and services produced during a given period. When poor countries are transforming themselves into wealthier ones, growth as measured by GDP can be a decent proxy for wellbeing. But, Pilling argues compellingly, 'once countries reach a certain level of prosperity, the relationship between economic growth and wellbeing tends to break down. To put it colloquially, more stuff doesn't automatically equate to more happiness.'

Alternative models to GDP have emerged, seeking to weigh thoughtfully the competing claims of qualitative and quantitative data. The Human Development Index is now widely used in international development, while Richard Layard of the London School of Economics has advanced an index with measures of happiness. The Legatum Prosperity Index has gained considerable traction with world leaders, measuring as it does a basket of eight aspects of a good society:

- Economy
- Social capital
- Entrepreneurship and opportunity
- Health
- Education
- Personal freedom
- Safety and security
- Governance

It is against a backcloth of debate about how we measure the 'success' of contemporary societies that much of the debate around soft skills, in the workplace and in educational institutions, is taking hold. Which brings me to my experiences within the UK education system: as teacher, principal, Her Majesty's Inspector, and academy sponsor.

Confidence, resilience, independence – these companion attributes have become a rallying cry for the many commentators on social mobility in UK schools. The argument runs: get all young people to feel more confident about themselves, to develop their resilience and to hone their independent skills – then so-called 'achievement gaps' will be closed.

Is this the elusive recipe for enhancing social mobility? Is it that easy? And what realistic part can schools play?

The subject of desirable character traits and soft skills is firmly on the political agenda. While in office, Prime Minister David Cameron got Whitehall thinking carefully about measuring happiness in society. The Department for Education produced a well-argued report in August 2017 titled 'Developing character skills in schools'; the Education Policy Institute studied employability and soft skills in its excellent research paper 'Educating for our Economic Future'.

And two insightful books on the same subject are well worth dipping into: *Taught Not Caught* by former Secretary of State for Education Nicky Morgan, and *The Character Conundrum* by Matt Lloyd-Rose.

What are we talking about here in practice?

Take the following extract from a thoughtfully worded advertisement for new employees to join a five-star international hotel:

The type of person we are looking for can demonstrate:

- **A desire to improve themselves in terms of skills, knowledge and experience.**
- **Good organisational skills and high service standards.**
- **Patience, a sense of humour and an ability to accept and act on constructive feedback.**
- **An ability to work on their own initiative and to be a good team player.**
- **Excellent and pro-active communication skills.**
- **An eye for detail and a willingness to improve all aspects of the service we offer.**
- **A positive attitude to all aspects of the job including enthusiasm, a professional and common-sense approach and a dedication to the interests of the business.**

If most 18 year olds were to feel confident enough to apply for such a position, we would probably hail that their parents and their teachers had done a pretty fine job, caught and/or taught.

Take another scenario. Imagine meeting one of your pupils, now aged 11, when they are 25. You meet by chance in a cafe and open a conversation. What do you wish to hear? You may well hope to hear that they continued to enjoy a good education beyond your classroom. More important, you probably want to find out that they are healthy in body and mind, confident, happy and fulfilled – a realisation of many of the soft skills that matter in life.

I have posed this scenario to hundreds of audiences around the world. Irrespective of culture and context, teachers comment on the 'character stuff' and rarely on, say, the young adult's higher education qualifications. I recall the principal of an international school affirming that by age 25 he expected all his former students to be active and honest citizens, entrepreneurial in their chosen fields, and global in outlook.

It is rare to enter a school or college which does not – intellectually at least – value 'soft skills'. Whether the institution actually teaches the following, implicitly or explicitly, varies markedly: people skills, etiquette, attitudes, social and emotional intelligence, problem-solving, conflict resolution, time management, and so on.

Some school leaders contest that these skills and attributes are largely innate, that they are 'caught' from parents, peers, teachers and social media models, and cannot be 'taught'. Others argue that while the nature and nurture elements are strong, it is eminently possible to design courses through which soft skills can be taught – indeed, must be taught in order that many pupils can enhance their self-esteem and employability.

From years of teaching and observing a range of personal and social education classes, I conclude that, whilst often fun, engaging and containing valuable learning points, such courses do not contribute significantly to the broader soft skills agenda.

Rather, the best schools develop pupils' innate character through carefully designed and implemented whole-school values, through their daily ethos, through the dignity of positive relationships between adults and students, through the consistency of high expectations.

And not forgetting to deliver what the 2009 Ofsted Framework described incisively: 'The school's curriculum provides memorable experiences and rich opportunities for high quality learning and wider personal development and wellbeing.'

Two concluding reflections on this subject.

First, I came across the following agenda in an outdoor adventure centre. It made me reflect that perhaps soft skills are most effectively addressed away from formal classrooms. The centre judges its own success on the extent to which visiting students leave having absorbed and demonstrated these during their stay.

10 Things That Require Zero Talent[1]

Being on time

Work ethic

Effort

Body language

Energy

Attitude

Passion

Being coachable

Doing extra

Being prepared

Second, may there always be space for the originals and mavericks of this world! They might have been inspired by loving or dysfunctional parents, by poor or accomplished teachers, but in the end, they shape hard and soft skills to their own inimitable ends. Steve Jobs captured these people best, in relaunching Apple in 1997. Watch him on YouTube for the full impact of his words!

Think Different

'Here's to the crazy ones.

The misfits.

The rebels. The troublemakers.

The round pegs in the square holes.

The ones who see things differently.

They're not fond of rules.

And they have no respect for the status quo.

---

1   Acknowledgements to Mark Evans MBE, Executive Director of Outward Bound Oman.

You can quote them, disagree with them,

glorify or vilify them.

About the only thing you can't do is ignore them.

Because they change things.

They push the human race forward.

While some may see them as the crazy ones,

we see genius.

Because the people who are crazy enough to think,

they can change the world, are the ones who do.'

Further reading

Fukuyama, F. (1992): *The End of History and the Last Man.* London, UK: Penguin Books.

Layard, R. (2011): *Happiness: Lessons from a New Science.* London, UK: Penguin Books.

Lloyd-Rose, M. (2017): *The Character Conundrum.* Abingdon, UK: Routledge.

Morgan, N. (2017): *Taught Not Caught.* Woodbridge, UK: John Catt Educational Ltd.

Piling, D. (2018): *The Growth Delusion.* London, UK: Bloomsbury Publishing.

Chapter 11:
Growth Goal-Setting in Positive Education

Emma Burns, Andrew Martin &
Rebecca Collie

Positive education seeks to apply the principles of positive psychology to teaching in order to support and promote improved wellbeing among students (Seligman, Ernst, Gillham, Reivich, & Linkins, 2009; Waters, 2011). By embedding positive psychology within pedagogy, positive education strives to develop a synergistic relationship between student wellbeing and achievement (Seligman et al., 2009). In this way, positive education seeks to improve student wellbeing while also supporting academic outcomes. Alongside resilience, hope, and gratitude, positive psychology also places an emphasis on recognising personal growth (Seligman & Csikszentmihalyi, 2000). By recognising growth, individuals can acknowledge positive occurrences and make personal growth-related choices that are essential for personal thriving (Fredrickson, 2001; Seligman & Csikszentmihalyi, 2000).

Additionally, there has been an increased focus on growth approaches to education and how they can support student wellbeing and academic performance (Anderman, Anderman, Yough, & Gimbert, 2010; Anderman, Gimbert, O'Connell, & Riegel, 2015; Dweck, 2012; Elliot, Murayama, &

Pekrun, 2011; Martin, 2015; Travers, Morisano, & Locke, 2015). Growth goal-setting is one such approach that enables students to make personal growth-related choices (by way of the goals they set and strive for) that help them reach their personal level of academic excellence (Martin, 2006). This chapter looks at growth within positive education, specifically growth goal-setting among students.

What is growth goal-setting?

Growth goal-setting entails utilising goals that are intended to improve one's personal growth in life (Travers et al., 2015). By and large, growth goal-setting among students has been investigated by way of personal best (PB) goal-setting (for summary, see Burns, Martin, & Collie, 2018a; see also Elliot et al., 2011 for self-based goals and Phan, Ngu, & Williams, 2016 for optimal best goals). PB goal-setting refers to the use of specific, challenging, and competitively self-referenced goals towards which students strive to surpass their past best performances or efforts (Burns et al., 2018a; Martin, 2006; Martin & Liem, 2010; Travers et al., 2015). PB goal-setting emphasises the importance of self-referenced challenge and continued self-improvement.

In today's educational climate there is an increasing focus on high-stakes standardised testing and normative grading (Anderman et al., 2010; Martin, 2006). Such assessment schemes are associated with increased student anxiety and inter-student competition (McNeil, 2000). Similarly, the use of normative grading schemes means that success is experienced by a relative minority of students, despite the individual progress students' experience (Covington, 1992). As such, it is important to have effective educational strategies, such as PB goal-setting, that encourage students to value and focus more on their personal growth, and less on external measures of academic success. Because PB goal-setting encourages students to strive to outperform their past best efforts and focus on personal excellence (Martin & Elliot, 2016a), PB goal-setting creates personal benchmarks, rather than external benchmarks (Martin, 2006). Thus, by promoting a focus on the self (both personally and academically), PB goal-setting is one way to promote student wellbeing while not compromising academic achievement.

Types of PB goal-setting

Broadly speaking, there are two types of PB goal-setting: process PB goal-setting and outcome PB goal-setting (Martin, 2010). Process PB goal-setting refers to exceeding one's best efforts in an activity, task, or domain. These focus on behaviours that are conducive to personal improvement, and examples include: spending more time on one's homework than previously; reading an extra resource for an assignment than one normally would; asking or answering a question in class when one is typically silent; staying in one's seat more often in class this week than last week; and, arriving to class on-time more often this week than the previous week. In these cases, PB goal-setting involves the way students go about their schoolwork and conduct themselves in their academic life. Outcome PB goal-setting refers to the results of one's actions and efforts that demonstrate self-improvement. Examples of outcome PB goal-setting include: getting a higher mark in one's yearly exams than one's half-yearly exams; getting more sums correct in one's mathematics work than in previous attempts; and spelling more words correctly in one's weekly spelling quiz than in previous quizzes. In these cases, the PB goal-setting refers to outcomes and results.

Mechanisms involved in PB goal-setting

There are four reasons why PB goal-setting is thought to motivate students, support wellbeing, and promote achievement. First, the specific self-referenced nature of PB goal-setting enables students to focus on themselves and their performance, rather than the performance of others (Martin & Elliot, 2016a). There are several benefits of this. Goals that are self-referenced remove the ambiguity of the desired outcome and allow the goal to be more specific to the individual. Ambiguous goals (e.g. 'do your best goals') have subjective targets and provide little to no guidance of what is required (Locke & Latham, 2002), and such goals have been found to have a demotivating effect on individuals (Locke & Latham, 2013). Specific self-referenced goals, on the other hand, clearly define both the target (i.e. level of past performance) and the amount of effort required to meet that target (i.e. more than previous effort; Locke & Latham, 2002; 2013). In this way, these goals are more likely to sustain commitment, as they clearly outline what is required (Klein, Cooper, Monahan, 2013). Thus, the specific self-referenced nature of PB goal-setting allows students to pursue clear goals that emphasise personal improvement.

Second, PB goal-setting entails goals that are optimally difficult for the individual (Martin, 2006). Because PB goal-setting relies on competing against past personal performances, the goals are tailored to the individual, rather than tied to external benchmarks. Optimally difficult goals have been found to engender determination, persistence, and effort (Locke & Latham, 2013). Goals that are too easy or too hard undermine motivation and often lead to lack of commitment (Locke & Latham, 2013; Polivy & Herman, 2002). Additionally, students who achieve goals that are optimally difficult (as well as personally relevant) are more likely to experience increased self-satisfaction and self-esteem (Locke & Latham, 2002; Martin, 2011). In this way, the optimally difficult nature of PB goal-setting may help students remain motivated while also developing important life skills (e.g., determination).

Third, the personal benefits of meeting self-referenced and optimally challenging goals (e.g., self-satisfaction) are self-reinforcing (Bandura, 2002). This means that students are more likely to re-engage with PB goal-setting, leading to more positive outcomes (Martin, 2011). In this way, PB goal-setting be an iterative process (Burns et al., 2018a): students identify their personal best, set PB goals (which clearly outline their required effort), students pursue their PB goals, and students meet their PB goals, ultimately creating a new personal best. The cycle then begins again (Burns et al., 2018a; see Bandura, 1991 for in-depth conceptualising). The process of PB goal-setting is active and promotes continual personal progress and academic improvement. As such, PB goal-setting is a process that helps students recognise and value their personal growth and thriving.

Lastly, PB goals create a dissonance between where a student is now and where he or she wants to be. Individuals are motivated to reduce dissonance as dissonance is uncomfortable (Oettingen, Pak, & Schnetter, 2001). Thus, setting a PB goal creates a gap that the individual is motivated to close (Bandura, 1991). This motivation comprises both the energy and the direction for goal pursuit, leading to enhanced likelihood of goal attainment (Locke & Latham, 2002; Martin, 2006).

Benefits of PB goal-setting

A central aim of positive education is to foster and improve student wellbeing without sacrificing academic outcomes (Norish, Williams, O'Connor, & Robinson, 2013; Seligman et al., 2009). As such, it is important to utilise holistic approaches that support both aims equally. Given that PB goal-setting has been associated with numerous positive academic and wellbeing outcomes for students, it can be considered one such holistic approach. The following section summarises a body of research (survey and experimental) that has documented the impact of PB goal-setting on student functioning.

Achievement and achievement-related outcomes

PB goal-setting has been shown to be significantly linked with students' academic outcomes, namely achievement, class participation, and disengagement. More precisely, past work has shown that students who use PB goal-setting demonstrate higher levels of achievement (Burns et al., 2017; 2018a; Martin, Collie, Mok, & McInerney, 2016; Martin & Elliot, 2016b; Martin & Liem, 2010). Indeed, a series of intervention studies in mathematics found that students who used PB goal-setting (compared to those who were not asked to set goals) had significantly higher rates of mathematics achievement, even after accounting for prior achievement and relevant socio-demographic factors (e.g., gender, age; Ginns, Martin, Durksen, Burns, & Pope, 2018; Martin & Elliot, 2016b). This suggests that PB goal-setting may be an effective strategy for promoting improved personal achievement.

In addition to academic achievement, PB goal-setting has also been linked with important classroom behaviours related to achievement. Classroom participation is considered to be a critical element of academic engagement and subsequent achievement (Fredricks, Blumenfeld, & Paris, 2004; Skinner, Kindermann, & Furrer, 2009). Students who participate in the classroom are more likely to pay attention and remain on task (Finn & Zimmer, 2012). This contrasts with academic disengagement, which reflects a withdrawal of effort and interest in the classroom and academic life (De Castella, Bryne, & Covington, 2013; Finn, Pannozzo, & Voelkl, 1995; Martin, Marsh, & Debus, 2003). Students who experience academic disengagement tend to attain lower achievement and are less likely to complete school (Finn et al., 1995; Schwinger, Wirthwein, Lemmer, & Steinmayr, 2014). PB goal-setting has also been shown to positively predict classroom participation (Burns et al., 2018a; Collie, Martin, Ginns, & Papworth, 2016; Martin & Liem, 2010) and negatively predict academic disengagement (Liem, Ginns, Martin, Stone, & Herrett, 2012, Martin & Elliot, 2016a). Thus, PB goal-setting is an effective strategy for promoting academic achievement both directly and indirectly through achievement-related behaviours, such as improving classroom participation and decreasing academic disengagement.

Wellbeing related outcomes

Beyond academic outcomes, PB goal-setting has been consistently linked with a variety of adaptive behaviours that are essential for student wellbeing and growth. The behaviours of focus in this chapter are those explicitly related to the three realms of happiness as denoted by positive education (Seligman, 2002; Seligman et al., 2009): the pleasant life (i.e. enjoyment), the engaged life (i.e. flow, buoyancy, persistence), and the meaningful life (i.e. future aspirations, interpersonal relationships). Seligman and colleagues (2009), argue that these three realms reflect distinct and skill-based approaches to understanding and promoting happiness.

The 'pleasant life' refers to cultivating positive emotions (Seligman, 2002). Building positive emotions has the potential to expand and strengthen individuals' cognitive, emotional, and behavioural resources (Fredrickson, 2001). Thus, when individuals are faced with challenging circumstances, they have a wider and more positive range of cognitive, behavioural, and emotional responses (Fredrickson, 2001; Pekrun, Goetz, Titz, & Perry, 2002). In terms of education, fostering positive attitudes towards school, such as school enjoyment, is one such way to promote the pleasant life in students. Indeed, school enjoyment is considered an important element of student wellbeing (Waters, 2011). Martin and Liem (2010; see also Burns et al., 2018a) found that PB goal-setting significantly predicted school enjoyment over time. It may be that the self-referenced nature of PB goal-setting helps make academic tasks more personally relevant to students, which may increase their overall enjoyment.

The 'engaged life' refers to the ability to become absorbed in tasks (Seligman, 2002), such that one enters a state of 'flow' (Csikszentmihalyi, 1990). Flow is considered an important element of academic learning, as it reflects a state of deep engagement, and relies on students' ability to persevere in the face of academic difficulty (i.e. persistence) and daily challenges and set-backs (i.e. buoyancy; Csikszentmihalyi, 1990; Liem et al., 2012). Academic persistence refers to the extent to which students remain engaged and keep trying at difficult or challenging tasks (Martin, 2007). Academic buoyancy refers to a student's capacity to deal with typical everyday stresses, such as poor grades or difficulty meeting due dates (Martin & Marsh, 2008). Thus flow, as well as persistence and buoyancy, can be considered essential elements of the engaged life. Indeed, PB goal-setting has been found to positively predict all three over time (Burns et al., 2018b; Liem et al., 2012; Martin & Liem, 2010; Yu & Martin, 2014). Because PB goal-setting focuses on creating goals that are optimally difficult for the individual, it may be that the pursuit of such goals engenders persistence and buoyancy – and helps individuals enter a state of flow (Liem et al., 2012).

The 'meaningful life' refers to developing meaningful connections with others, as well as having meaningful intentions for the future (Seligman et al., 2009). Thus, the meaningful life refers to the ways in which individuals 'transcend the self' (Seligman et al., 2009, p. 296). For students, this may include developing meaningful relationships with others, such as their teachers, peers, and parents, as well as thinking about their academic intentions for the future. Interpersonal relationships (i.e. those with teachers, peers, and parents) provide students with both academic and emotional support (Collie et al., 2016; Martin & Dowson,

2009). Academic intentions for the future (e.g. attending university) help students conceptualise possible future selves, which can motivate students towards that envisaged positive future (Hoyle & Sherrill, 2006). PB goal-setting has been significantly linked with both interpersonal relationships and academic intentions. Not only has PB goal-setting been associated with positive teacher, peer, and parent relationships (Collie et al., 2016; Burns et al., 2017, 2018a), it has also been found to predict positive teacher-student relationships over time (Liem et al., 2012). PB goal-setting encourages students to focus on their personal improvement and to see others as collaborators rather than competitors (Martin, 2006). Thus, it may be that PB goal-setting helps foster more positive interpersonal relationships. Additionally, PB goal-setting is consistently linked with academic intentions (Collie et al., 2016; Burns et al., 2017, 2018a). Because PB goal-setting is an iterative process that encourages students to look forward to achieving their next personal best, it may be that PB goal-setting helps students more clearly conceptualise possible academic futures for themselves.

Summary

Taken together, PB goal-setting is positively implicated in adaptive student functioning. Not only does PB goal-setting promote important achievement related outcomes (i.e. academic achievement, classroom participation, decreased academic disengagement), it also fosters outcomes essential to student wellbeing (i.e. school enjoyment, flow, persistence, buoyancy, interpersonal relationships, academic intentions). In this way, PB goal-setting presents an effective strategy under the positive education umbrella for fostering student thriving.

How to promote growth goal-setting

PB goal-setting can be one means for promoting student wellbeing and academic achievement. As such, it is important for educators to understand how to promote PB goal-setting in the classroom. The research summarised above suggests that effective promotion of PB goal-setting, either as a component of teacher/classroom practice or through targeted individual intervention, may yield positive outcomes for students. The following section discusses important factors and strategies for promoting PB goal-setting in the classroom.

Martin (2006) has identified four considerations for implementing PB goal-setting. First, it is important that students accurately identify their personal best. This is critical for creating self-referenced goals that are optimally challenging for the individual (Martin, 2006). It is not uncommon for students to over- or under-estimate their optimal level of difficulty, which can lead to goals that are too easy or too hard (Polivy & Herman, 2002). As discussed above, such goals have been shown to be demotivating (Locke & Latham, 2002; Polivy & Herman, 2002). Thus, when encouraging students to utilise PB goal-setting, it is critical that students receive help in identifying their personal best. Teachers can help students with this by providing constructive and specific self-referenced feedback to students about their current performance or effort as relative to their past performances or efforts (rather than feedback that is comparative/relative to others). Such feedback has been found to positively impact personal goal-setting, in that such feedback helps students upwardly revise their goals (Ashford & De Stobbelier, 2013; Iles & Judge, 2005; Johnson, Turban, Pieper, & Ng, 1996; Shih & Alexander, 2000).

Second, accurately assessing students' progress toward their PB goals is an essential component of PB goal-setting. Accurate assessment is key not only for ensuring that students remain on track, but also for maintaining student motivation (Locke, 1996). Students are more likely to maintain their goal commitment if they can see the progress they are making (Klein, et al., 2013; Locke, 1996). Although assessing personal progress can be difficult, especially if the tasks are not the same or highly similar (Martin, 2006), recent work in growth goal-setting has found that reflective diary/record keeping is one strategy that helps students effectively track their progress across different tasks (Travers et al., 2015). As such, teachers may encourage students to record their progress in personal diaries. Similarly, in line with the first consideration, teachers may discuss this documented progress with students when providing feedback.

Third, effective goal management strategies are crucial for goal attainment (Locke & Latham, 2002), especially if students set long-term outcome PB goals. Indeed, some outcome PB goals may take quite a long time to attain (e.g. approximately 4-6 months if one is wanting to improve on one's half-yearly exam results). In contrast, process PB goals can be attained somewhat quickly – often from one day or week to the next. As such, it is important for students to understand that outcome PB goals (e.g. getting a higher grade on the next exam) are best met by setting and achieving process PB goals (e.g. studying for longer than yesterday; Martin, 2015). Additionally, for struggling students, reasonably immediate successes can be important and motivating (Martin, 2013). As such, and in line with the second consideration, teachers may encourage students to set process PB goals, especially in the beginning, and track progress on both these and their outcome PB goals.

Fourth, it is important to consider the social elements of PB goal-setting. As discussed above, PB goal-setting is closely associated with interpersonal relationships. Similarly, Travers and colleagues (2015) found that support from and accountability to others plays a salient role in growth goal attainment. This suggests social support and even collaboration on PB goal pursuit is beneficial for students. As such, and as found by Martin and Elliot (2016b), teachers may consider using daily reminders that encourage students to achieve their PB goals and to be supportive of their peers' pursuit. Taken together, these considerations indicate the importance of providing feedback about students' PB goals, tracking PB goal progress, PB goal management, and encouraging social support for PB goal-setting.

Conclusion

In this chapter, an effective growth-oriented strategy under the positive education umbrella was discussed: PB goal-setting. We summarised what PB goal-setting is, identified various types and examples of PB goal-setting, its benefits for students, and how it can be promoted in the classroom. Additionally, we reviewed the ways in which PB goal-setting promotes both academic functioning and personal wellbeing. In summary, PB goal-setting is an important growth-oriented construct that encourages students to value their personal growth and place less attention on external measures of academic success. Moreover, it is one strategy for promoting both achievement and wellbeing among students. Thus, the focus of PB goal-setting aligns well with the core tenets of the positive education field.

References

Anderman, E. M., Anderman, L. H., Yough, M. S. & Gimbert, B. G. (2010): Value-added models of assessment: Implications for motivation and accountability. *Educational Psychologist*, 45, pp. 123-137.

Anderman, E. M., Gimbert, B., O'Connell, A. A. & Riegel, L. (2015): Approaches to academic growth assessment. *The British Journal of Educational Psychology*, 85, pp. 138-153.

Ashford, S. J. & De Stobbeleir, K. E. M. (2013): Feedback, goal setting, and task performance revisited. In E. A. Locke & G. P. Latham (Eds.), *New developments in goal setting and task performance* (pp. 51-64). New York, NY: Routledge.

Bandura, A. (1991): Social cognitive theory of self-regulation. *Organizational Behavior and Human Decision Processes*, 50, pp. 248-287.

Bandura, A. (2002): Social cognitive theory in cultural context. *Applied Psychology: An International Review*, 51, pp. 269-290.

Burns, E. C., Martin, A. J. & Collie, R. J. (2017): Understanding the role of adaptability and personal best (PB) goals in students' academic outcomes: A social cognitive perspective. *BJEP Monograph Series II*, 12, pp. 111-143.

Burns, E. C., Martin, A. J. & Collie, R. J. (2018a): Adaptability, personal best (PB) goals, and gains in students' academic outcomes: A longitudinal examination from a social cognitive perspective. *Contemporary Educational Psychology*, 53, pp. 57-72.

Burns, E. C., Martin, A. J. & Collie, R. J. (2018b): Understanding the role of personal best (PB) goal setting in students' declining engagement: A latent growth model. *Submitted for publication*.

Collie, R. J., Martin, A. J., Papworth, B. & Ginns, P. (2016): Students' interpersonal relationships, personal best (PB) goals, and academic engagement. *Learning and Individual Differences*, 45, pp. 65-76.

Covington, M. V. (1992): *Making the grade: A self-worth perspective on motivation and school reform.* Cambridge, UK: Cambridge University Press.

Csikszentmihalyi, M. (1990): *Flow: the psychology of optimal experience.* New York, NY: Harper & Row.

De Castella, K., Byrne, D. & Covington, M. (2013): Unmotivated or motivated to fail? A cross-cultural study of achievement motivation, fear of failure, and student disengagement. *Journal of Educational Psychology,* 105, pp. 861-880.

Dweck, C. S. (2012): Mindsets and human nature. *American Psychologist,* 67, pp. 614-622.

Elliot, A. J., Murayama, K. & Pekrun, R. (2011): A 3 × 2 achievement goal model. *Journal of Educational Psychology,* 103, pp. 632-648.

Finn, J. D., Pannozzo, G. M. & Voekl, K. E. (1995): Disruptive and inattentive-withdrawn behavior and achievement among fourth graders. *The Elementary School Journal,* 95, pp. 421-434.

Finn, J. D. & Zimmer, K. S. (2012): Student engagement: What is it? Why does it matter? In S. Christenson, A. Reschly, & C. Wylie (Eds.), *Handbook of research on student engagement* (pp. 97-131). Boston, MA: Springer.

Fredricks, J. A., Blumenfeld, P. C. & Paris, A. H. (2004): School engagement: Potential of the concept, state of evidence. *Review of Educational Research,* 74, pp. 59-109.

Fredrickson, B. L. (2001): The role of positive emotions in positive psychology. *American Psychologist,* 56, pp. 218-226.

Ginns, P., Martin, A. J., Durksen, T. L., Burns, E. C. & Pope, A. (2018): Personal Best (PB) goal-setting enhances arithmetical problem-solving. *The Australian Educational Researcher.* Advance online publication.

Hoyle, R. H. & Sherrill, M. R. (2006): Future orientation in the self-system: Possible selves, self-regulation, and behavior. *Journal of Personality,* 74, pp. 1673-1696.

Ilies, R. & Judge, T. A. (2005): Goal regulation across time: The effects of feedback and affect. *Journal of Applied Psychology,* 90, pp. 453-467.

Johnson, D. S., Turban, D. B., Pieper, K. F. & Ng, Y. M. (1996): Exploring the role of normative- and performance-based feedback in motivational processes. *Journal of Applied Social Psychology*, 26, pp. 973-992.

Klein, H. J., Cooper, J. T. & Monahan, C. A. (2013): Goal commitment. In E. A. Locke & G. P. Latham (Eds.), *New developments in goal setting and task performance* (pp. 65-89). New York, NY: Routledge.

Liem, G. A. D., Ginns, P., Martin, A. J., Stone, B. & Herrett, M. (2012): Personal best goals and academic and social functioning: A longitudinal perspective. *Learning and Instruction*, 22, pp. 222-230.

Locke, E. A. (1996): Motivation through conscious goal setting. *Applied and Preventive Psychology*, 5, pp. 117-124.

Locke, E. A. & Latham, G. P. (2002): Building a practically useful theory of goal setting and task motivation: A 35-year odyssey. *American Psychologist*, 57, 705-717.

Locke, E. A. & Latham, G. P. (2013): Goal setting theory: The current state. In E. A. Locke & G. P. Latham (Eds.), *New developments in goal setting and task performance* (pp. 623-630). New York, NY: Routledge.

Martin, A. J. (2006): Personal bests (PBs): A proposed multidimensional model and empirical analysis. *British Journal of Educational Psychology*, 76, pp. 803-825.

Martin, A. J. (2007): Examining a multidimensional model of student motivation and engagement using a construct validation approach. *British Journal of Educational Psychology*, 77, pp. 413-440.

Martin, A. J. (2010): *Building classroom success: Eliminating academic fear and failure*. New York, NY: Bloomsbury.

Martin, A. J. (2011): Personal best (PB) approaches to academic development: Implications for motivation and assessment. *Educational Practice and Theory*, 33, pp. 93-99.

Martin, A. J. (2013): Improving the achievement, motivation, and engagement of students with ADHD: The role of personal best goals and other growth-based approaches. *Australian Journal of Guidance and Counselling*, 23, pp. 143-155.

Martin, A. J. (2015): Growth approaches to academic development: Research into academic trajectories and growth assessment, goals, and mindsets. *British Journal of Educational Psychology*, 85, pp. 133-137.

Martin, A. J., Collie, R. J., Mok, M. M. C. & McInerney, D. M. (2016): Personal best (PB) goal structure, individual PB goals, engagement, and achievement: A study of Chinese- and English-speaking background students in Australian schools. *British Journal of Educational Psychology*, 86, pp. 75-91.

Martin, A. J. & Dowson, M. (2009): Interpersonal relationships, motivation, engagement, and achievement: Yields for theory, current issues, and educational practice. *Review of Educational Research*, 79, pp. 327-365.

Martin, A. J. & Elliot, A. J. (2016a): The role of personal best (PB) and dichotomous achievement goals in students' academic motivation and engagement: A longitudinal investigation. *Educational Psychology*, 36, pp. 1285-1302.

Martin, A. J. & Elliot, A. J. (2016b): The role of personal best (PB) goal setting in students' academic achievement gains. *Learning and Individual Differences*, 45, pp. 222-227.

Martin, A. J. & Liem, G. A. D. (2010): Academic personal bests (PBs), engagement, and achievement: A cross-lagged panel analysis. *Learning and Individual Differences*, 20, pp. 265-270.

Martin, A. J. & Marsh, H. W. (2008): Academic buoyancy: Towards an understanding of students' everyday academic resilience. *Journal of School Psychology*, 46, pp. 53-83. doi.org/10.1016/j.jsp.2007.01.002

Martin, A. J., Marsh, H. W. & Debus, R. L. (2003): Self-handicapping and defensive pessimism: A model of self-protection from a longitudinal perspective. *Contemporary Educational Psychology*, 28, pp. 1-36.

McNeil, L. (2000): *Contradictions of school reform: Educational costs of standardized testing.* New York, NY: Routledge.

Norrish, J. M., Williams, P., O'Connor, M. & Robinson, J. (2013): An applied framework for positive education. *International Journal of Wellbeing*, 3, pp. 147-161.

Oettingen, G., Pak, H. J. & Schnetter, K. (2001): Self-regulation of goal-setting: Turning free fantasies about the future into binding goals. *Journal of Personality and Social Psychology*, 80, pp. 736-753.

Pekrun, R., Goetz, T., Titz, W. & Perry, R. P. (2002): Academic emotions in students in self-regulated learning and achievement: A program of qualitative and quantitative research. *Educational Psychologist*, 37, pp. 91-105.

Phan, H. P., Ngu, B. H. & Williams, A. (2016): Introducing the concept of optimal best: Theoretical and methodological contributions. *Education*, 136, pp. 312-323.

Polivy, J. & Herman, C. P. (2002): If at first you don't succeed: False hopes of self-change. *American Psychologist*, 57, pp. 677-689.

Schwinger, M., Wirthwein, L., Lemmer, G. & Steinmayr, R. (2014): Academic self-handicapping and achievement: A meta-analysis. *Journal of Educational Psychology*, 106, pp. 744-761.

Seligman, M. E. P. (2002): *Authentic happiness: Using the new positive psychology to realize your potential for lasting fulfillment.* New York, NY: Free Press.

Seligman, M. E. P. & Csikszentmihalyi, M. (2000): Positive psychology: An introduction. *American Psychologist*, 55, pp. 5-14.

Seligman, M. E. P., Ernst, R. M., Gillham, J., Reivich, K. & Linkins, M. (2009): Positive education: Positive psychology and classroom interventions. *Oxford Review of Education*, 35, pp. 293-311.

Shih, S. & Alexander, J. M. (2000): Interacting effects of goal setting and self- or other-referenced feedback on children's development of self-efficacy and cognitive skill within the Taiwanese classroom. *Journal of Educational Psychology*, 92, pp. 536-543.

Skinner, E. A., Kindermann, T. A. & Furrer, C. J. (2009): A Motivational perspective on engagement and disaffection. *Educational and Psychological Measurement*, 69, pp. 493-525.

Travers, C. J., Morisano, D. & Locke, E. A. (2015): Self-reflection, growth goals, and academic outcomes: A qualitative study. *British Journal of Educational Psychology*, 85, pp. 224-241.

Waters, L. (2011): A review of school-based positive psychology interventions. *The Australian Educational and Developmental Psychologist*, 28, pp. 75-90.

Yu, K. & Martin, A. J. (2014): Personal best (PB) and "classic" achievement goals in the Chinese context: Their role in predicting academic motivation, engagement and buoyancy. *Educational Psychology*, 34, pp. 635-658.

Chapter 12:

Wellbeing:
A predictor of success

Rob Stokoe

This chapter was originally published in my first book, *Leaders of Learning*. Undoubtedly this is one of the chapters which I enjoyed writing. Happy to share it with you all.

'Each morning when I open my eyes I say to myself: I, not events, have the power to make me happy or unhappy today. I can choose which it shall be. Yesterday is dead, tomorrow hasn't arrived yet. I have just one day, today, and I'm going to be happy in it.' – Groucho Marx

As we face the challenges of rapid change and developing strategies for learning in the 21ˢᵗ century we must never lose sight of the fact that people matter. They can inform the future success of any school; their wellbeing and engagement are essential if a school is to develop or improve its performance. The future requires that the wellbeing of the whole staff is nurtured as an energizer for change. As leaders we must focus upon change that will bring about positive outcomes, we have power to influence those around us, and in return, be influenced ourselves, we live with a purpose and in that context wellbeing matters. The concept of wellbeing comprises feeling good and functioning well. Feelings of happiness, contentment, enjoyment, curiosity and engagement are characteristic of individuals who have a positive outlook on life. Equally important for wellbeing is our sense of purpose and place, our function in the world. Experiencing positive relationships, having some control over one's life and having a sense of purpose are all important attributes of wellbeing. However, wellbeing is not an outcome; it is something that broadens our perspective, a predictor of future success.

We all want to be happy

The state of wellbeing and satisfaction largely depends upon the thinking of an individual, yet the quest for wellbeing, for happiness, is universal as everyone wants to be happy. I think we would all agree that wellbeing and happiness put us on the road to fulfillment accepting that happiness is a journey, not a destination. We must acknowledge how complex it is as it is always influenced by traits such as optimism, gratitude, zest, curiosity, and love regardless of age or financial context. All these traits can be nurtured and encouraged; there are many routes to happiness. The word happy is an emotionally positive word, it offers a positive message, opening dialogue and always a driver that helps us drive to make a better world. Yet we need to understand this, is happiness a trait, 'I am a happy person', or a state, 'I am happy today'. Happiness is complex, is it an emotion, a reflection of people lives. We all need to understand what makes us happy and our accounts of wellbeing. Considering happiness gives us a momentum for change where knowledge and engagement become empowering tools, even discussing happiness is a win, win.

Every school is unique and special and as leaders we must always be open and honest, paying attention to and being mindful of the wellbeing of our community. Mindful leaders are self-aware, ethical, clear-sighted and relationally transparent. They are both trusted and are effective and they create the environment for great learning. Professional development to support teacher wellbeing has become an emergent theme, one that supports better and more secure learning. Positive, optimistic, happy people are mentally, physically, and emotionally healthier more able to access new learning. They are more resilient, have better relationships, are more successful at work, they are satisfied with their lives and careers. Research suggests they even live longer! Being mindful will always have a positive impact upon wellbeing (Huppert & Johnson, 2010). Wellbeing makes us feel good and if we feel good we can display happiness, contentment interest and affection. The positivity of wellbeing encourages in each of us the ability to make choices and offers resilience in the face of challenges, enhances curiosity and creativity.

The positive impact of wellbeing

In recent years there has been a growing acceptance that the wellbeing of a school community has a positive impact upon the formal outcomes of school activity, it directly informs student capacity for learning and achievement. As leaders we must understand how we are perceived on a day to day basis and the impact we have on our educators. The very designation of headteacher is an impediment, accepting that we must always demonstrate awareness and be proactive in considering and bring a steady focus upon staff wellbeing. As leaders we need to have a progressive and empowering mindset in order that we foster positivity and understand the expectations of our talented staff. The best thing for any school is an engaged, happy and motivated staff, who knows they are valued by their leaders. As leaders we must aspire to create a context which allows, indeed encourages our staff to flourish. Flourishing creates a positive effect. According to Fredrickson and Losada (2005), to flourish means to live with an optimal range of human functioning, one that connotes goodness, growth and resilience. Keyes (2002) argues that people can move from languishing to flourishing and function well if they develop positive emotional wellbeing, positive social wellbeing and positive psychological wellbeing. We may be lucky enough to have teachers who display high levels of social and emotional competence; it is likely that we model and nurture these attributes, but do we need to create the opportunity to provide explicit training in the development of skills such as compassion, gratitude and empathy. I would not under estimate either the value or the challenge of such development as developing social and emotional skills in adults is a complex process. For our teachers, these skills are imperative not only for their personal wellbeing but to improve student learning.

Teacher wellbeing is relevant

The best thing for students is a happy, motivated staff. Teacher wellbeing is relevant for whole school wellbeing, informing a stable, secure social and learning environment for students. Murray-Harvey (2010) found that both academic outcomes and social and emotional wellbeing in school were 'unambiguously influenced' by the quality of relationships between teachers and students. By putting the motivation and engagement of staff alongside the students, you are doing the best you can do for the students. Yes, we put the needs of the students, but they are far from our sole responsibility if we do not pay attention to our educators and support staff we are doing our learners a disservice. When teachers are at ease with their responsibilities, when they have a sense of professional autonomy they project that same sense of wellbeing into their learning environments making learning an enjoyable act, a goal to which all of us are dedicated. We must access the creativity and potential within our teaching teams supporting and encouraging our talented teachers to both inform and thrive in positive, collaborative environments. The outcomes include positive effects for children's knowledge and attainment and teachers' professional commitment, knowledge and satisfaction (Goddard, Hoy & Woolfolk, 2004).

The report goes on to outline seven pathways to wellbeing in a school:

- Building a respectful and supportive school community.
- Developing pro-social values.
- Providing a safe learning environment.
- Enhancing social-emotional learning.
- Using strengths-based approaches.
- Fostering a sense of meaning and purpose.
- Encouraging a healthy lifestyle.

Listening

We all know people who are good listeners. No matter what the context they always know what to say, how to say it and when to say it. They offer a high level of care and consideration; they are active listeners able to put aside their own viewpoint trying to see things from another perspective. Not only do they listen with their ears, they listen with their eyes and their heart as they consider not only what is being said, but what the other person feels. Active listening brings the focus of attention to the speaker and what they have to say, a way of listening and responding to another person that promotes mutual understanding. Leaders who have a high degree of emotional intelligence are effective listeners; they can offer positive solutions without causing offence or upset. They are caring, considerate and others usually leave feeling valued, motivated, and optimistic. This mindful listening is deeply powerful, it involves listening with integrity and honesty and responding with compassion and understanding. Mindful listening offers kindness and insight to both colleagues and students in times of need and is critical to mutually supportive relationships.

A smile is a charity

A smile is a universal means of communicating, it's also one of the most basic expressions of all, smiles are cross-cultural and have the same meaning in different societies. More than 30% of us smile more than 20 times a day and, for some, less than 14% of us smile less than five times a day. In fact, one of the reasons schools are such great places to work is that children smile as many as 400 times daily, great for us as educators as our natural reflex is to return a smile, it's contagious and happiness is activated when we smile. The brain, in seeing a smile, has already considered the reward attained. More often we need to access the power of authentic smiles, according to Gutman (2011) it can connect us with others, you will be happier and healthier. 'Too often, we underestimate the power of a touch, a smile, a kind word, a listening ear, an honest compliment, or the smallest act of caring, all of which have the potential to turn a life around.' – Leo F. Buscaglia

Recognition, acknowledgement and unexpected kindness

Recognition is hugely important, just two hours a week in acts of unexpected kindness will inform an emotionally literate school. A school where leaders find teachers doing great things, have the time to listen, to prompt, to encourage and to demonstrate care for their teachers and give positive feedback for their efforts will inform great learning for students. Therefore, you must seek out colleagues, catch them doing great things and tell them why and how well they are doing. We all like praise. I know I need to tell people more often how much I appreciate them, but I keep trying, I can never do enough.

Something special is happening here

We all feel good when someone thanks us. Our purpose should always focus upon the special things that happen in our schools. Recognising that 'something special is happening here', is highly rewarding and motivating for all concerned. We need to build the happy gene! Key to effective leadership is to maintain and develop positivity and high morale; we need to be systematic and fair in recognising, celebrating and sharing the accomplishments of our students and teachers. Recognition supports motivation across any school, fuelling high performance and reinforcing desired behaviours, building a culture of high performance and high levels of motivation. As leaders we need to utilise and value recognition, acknowledging that whether recognition works for us is not the point, it works for others. Simply recognising the effort staff commit to their work will raise levels of motivation and morale. My point here is that recognition is a leadership tool; the work of Robert Cialdani identifies recognition as an effective device that can be used to lead and motivate people other than you. You never know, someone may just come along and acknowledge you someday. Ultimately, you must admit that it is good for you, if it's is good for your school, and it is the right thing to do. Our parents were right all along, it's just polite to say, 'thank you' and is a great way to build relationship capital, or to create a reciprocity pool.

In saying recognition is the right thing to do it must be deserved and our response to excellence must be authentic, not automatic; you must mean it. When we apply recognition, we have a positive impact upon areas such as engagement, attendance, collaboration, retention and most importantly learning and teaching. We need to make time to get into our classrooms, catch people doing exemplary work, sharing great experiences. We then need to thank them and tell them how they are doing such a great job. Our professional colleagues merit constructive feedback and positive affirmation or simply saying, 'thank you' for a job well done. Recognising the great things happening around you in your school will make it a happier place to be, for everyone, put simply; it feels great to work in an organisation where morale is high!

Being mindful is an inherent human capacity. But it doesn't always come naturally, it requires discipline and practice to focus on the 'here and now' and not get side-tracked by past mistakes or future results. (Bell, 2012) Mindful leaders can achieve this; they are less concerned about individual success and self-esteem issues and are better able to form deeper meaningful connections and relationships with those they lead. We are all mindful to one degree or another, moment by moment. Effective leaders are attentive, aware of and value the opinions of colleagues and their experiences, engaging in conversations that cross the boundaries of function and hierarchy, this way they gain new perspectives from as well as trust and deeper engagement from staff. Promoting positive wellbeing amongst colleagues makes a huge difference. When staff feel appreciated and empowered, they are willing to share their practice and demonstrate greater empathy for the learners in their care. This enhances the capacity of any school to nurture and developing students' potential. Children with higher levels of emotional, behavioural, social, and school wellbeing, on average, have higher levels of academic achievement.

Student wellbeing

As leaders we must acknowledge the difference we can make by embracing the notion of student wellbeing within and beyond the academic context. We need to foster wellbeing because there is a link between wellbeing, academic and personal success. Implicit modelling of wellbeing may already be the source of positive engagement with our students, but we must consider whether we can be deliberate, explicit in our approach and target the wellbeing domains following the example of Geelong Grammar School who have actively implemented a positive education program in recent years. In a school wide context, they target six wellbeing domains, including positive emotions, positive engagement, positive accomplishment, positive purpose, positive relationships, and positive health, underpinned by a focus on character strengths (Norish et al, 2013). Positive Education is essentially traditional education focused on academic skill development complemented by approaches that nurture wellbeing and promote good mental health (Seligman, 2011).

The program aims to increase mental fitness and resilience for every student who in the best of circumstances has a personal tutor who identifies strengths and sets and overseas academic and personal goals. Students are also introduced to activities which are scientifically proven to increase levels of wellbeing and performance. Positive education could more completely be described as bringing together the science of Positive Psychology with best-practice teaching to encourage students to flourish. Students flourishing is simply viewed as both 'feeling good' and 'doing good' (Huppert & So, 2013). Feeling good reflects a wide range of emotions and experiences such as happiness with the present and hopeful for the future. Doing good strives to equip students with capability to help them to face both the challenges and opportunities which life offers. A focus on wellbeing within education is beneficial and supports students' achievement. Howell (2009) found that students who were flourishing reported superior grades, higher self-control and positive attendance rates.

Creating a culture of wellbeing will develop a positive approach where members of the school community see great purpose in their life, their work and the goals of the school as well as greater self-awareness. It will engender more meaningful and satisfying learning and personal relationships enhancing both student and teacher capability, resilience and their potential to cope with the demands of school life. Positive interventions from leaders increase wellbeing, enhancing engagement and a perception of value from the school, its purpose and its vision. It will also encourage positive relations with others, personal growth and role purpose.

Being positive will inform success. According to Fredrickson (2001) positive emotions broaden our thoughts and actions; we pay more attention, are more creative, flexible and are open to relationships.

Positive emotions build psychological resources: resilience, coping, physical abilities, emotional intelligence, social skills and self-mastery. Taking this into consideration these attributes will inform positive outcomes and it's reasonable to say that the only true disability in life is a negative attitude, life may not appear to be fair at times, but it has a habit of responding to a positive attitude. Life is your attitude, and we should have attitude with gratitude. Consider the great things you have, the great things within you and the unlimited potential of your future as well as the positive impact you can have on those around you. A final consideration from Aristotle: 'educating the mind without educating the heart is no education at all.'

References

Fredrickson B. L. (2001): The role of positive emotions in positive psychology: The broaden-and-build theory of positive emotions. *American psychologist*, 56, pp. 218-226.

Fredrickson, B. (2009). *Positivity*. London, UK: Crown Publishers.

Frederickson, B. & Losada, M. (2005): Positive Affect and the Complex Dynamics of Human Flourishing. *American Psychologist*, 60(7), pp. 678-686.

Goddard, R. D., Hoy, W. K. & Woolfolk, H. A. (2004): Collective efficacy beliefs: Theoretical developments, empirical evidence and future directions. *Educational Researcher*, 33(3), pp. 3-13.

Gutman, R. (2011): *Smile: The Astonishing Powers of a Simple Act*. New York, NY: TED books.

Howell, A. J. (2009): Flourishing: Achievement-related correlates of students' well-being. *Journal of Positive Psychology*, 4(1), pp. 1-13.

Huppert, F. A. & Johnson, D. M. (2010): A controlled trial of mindfulness training in schools: The importance of practice for an impact on well-being. *The Journal of Positive Psychology*, 5(4), pp. 264-274.

Huppert, F. A. & So, T. T. (2013). Flourishing across Europe: Application of a new conceptual framework for defining well-being. *Social Indicators Research*, 110(3), pp. 837-861.

Keyes, C. L. M. (2002): The Mental Health Continuum: From Languishing to Flourishing in Life. *Journal of Health and Social Behaviour,* 43(2), pp. 207-222.

Murray-Harvey, R. (2010). Relationship influences on students' academic achievement, psychological health and well-being at school. *Educational and Child Psychology,* 27(1), pp. 104-113.

Norrish, J. M., Williams, P., O'Connor, M. & Robinson, J. (2013): An applied framework for positive education. *International Journal of Wellbeing,* 3(2), pp. 147-161.

Seligman, M. E. P. (2011): *Flourish.* London, UK: Nicholas Brealey Publishing.

Chapter 13:

Teacher Wellbeing: Applying your oxygen mask first

Adrian Bethune

I am sure we have all sat down on a plane, excited to be jetting off somewhere hot, somewhere exciting, somewhere different. We've got our passports and boarding passes safely tucked away in our pockets and, finally, we can sit back and relax. Our holiday is about to begin. But before the pilot takes off, there's the safety briefing. Make a note of the exits. Check. Lifejackets under your seats. Check. Put your oxygen mask on first, before helping the children with theirs. Wait, what? Yes, if the oxygen masks drop down from above, adults must place their masks on first and then, and *only* then, do they help children place their oxygen masks on. This has always jarred with me. Maybe it jars with the instincts of all teachers (and parents). So often we put children first, and *then* attend to our own needs. But the reason for ignoring our instincts on this occasion is very simple and very important: if you don't put your oxygen mask on first, you may not be able to help your children. You may even become a casualty and who will help your children then?

Teaching crisis

I wasn't sure whether to use the phrase 'teaching crisis' in a book about positive education. I mean, it just sounds so negative and depressing.

But, one thing I have learned to develop is my ability for realistic optimism – understand the reality of the situation and then look for what positive action you can feasibly take to improve it. So, let's start with the reality. There is a teaching crisis in the UK. I'm sure there are teaching crises elsewhere too, but I will focus on the UK as that is where I teach. According to Dr. Emma Kell's (2018) research for her book, *How to Survive in Teaching*, 60% of the almost 4000 teachers she surveyed said they would **not** recommend teaching to a close friend or relative. 82% said they had experienced anxiety as a direct result of the job. 54% said they had experienced depression as a direct result of teaching. 29% said they would be leaving the profession within the next two years. The reality is that, in the UK, almost one third of teachers quit the profession within the first five years of qualifying (Weale, 2016). All of this suggests to me that many of our teachers are running out of oxygen!

Why teacher wellbeing matters

As the oxygen mask analogy implies, if teachers are not taking care of themselves, this will inevitably be having a knock-on effect for our children too. Evidence shows that when teachers burn out, not only do they not teach as well but they cannot care for their pupils as well and so pupil wellbeing and attainment falls (Black, 2001). But the opposite of this is true, also. Studies demonstrate that when teacher wellbeing is high, there is a positive relationship with increased pupil attainment. One report into teacher wellbeing entitled 'Staff Wellbeing is Key to School Success' describes the virtuous circle that forms when schools get teacher wellbeing right: 'there is a two-way relationship between teacher wellbeing and pupil performance ... increases in teacher wellbeing can lead to improvements in the performance of pupils, so increases in pupil performance may lead to increased wellbeing in teachers.'

Teacher wellbeing also matters because we are significant role models in our children's lives. It is important that we set a good example. If we want our children to lead happy, fulfilling lives then we, as teachers, must do our best to model how to do that. Child development psychologist, Professor Alison Gopnik says that, 'children actually learn more from the unconscious details of what caregivers do than from any of the conscious manipulations'. This does not mean we should be inauthentic and pretend we are flourishing when, deep down, we are not. Teachers are human too and we can show our children the full extent of our humanity. Being a good role model for wellbeing simply means we start to care for and nurture ourselves as much as we care for and nurture our pupils.

However, to focus on the impact that teacher wellbeing is having on children is to fall in the trap of not putting ourselves first. Everyone's wellbeing matters, including teachers. And happiness and wellbeing matter in and of themselves. Throughout time, philosophers, religious teachers and world leaders have argued that happiness is our sole reason for being. Aristotle once said, 'happiness is the meaning and purpose of life. The whole aim and end of human existence.' His Holiness the Dalai Lama says, 'the purpose of our lives is to be happy.' And British philosopher, David Hume, said, 'the great end of all human industry is the attainment of happiness. For this were the arts invented, sciences cultivated, laws ordained, and societies modelled.' Teachers must begin to prioritise their happiness and wellbeing not just because it will help their pupils but because to learn how to flourish in life is the sole purpose for living. The question now raised is, how can we do this?

Practical ways teachers can nourish themselves

Louis Cozlino (2013) cites evidence for the main reasons teachers burn out. A lack of resources and adequate facilities, unreasonable time demands, high-stakes testing and accountability, excessive paperwork and a lack of autonomy are all key factors, he argues. When you look at this list it would be easy to assume that many of these areas are out of teachers' control and, to a large extent, they are. But that does not mean that teachers are powerless in the face of their challenges. In fact, there are many practical things teachers can do to improve their situation, look after their wellbeing and even flourish. But it does require action and it will take courage. To quote Aristotle again, 'happiness depends on ourselves.' We cannot wait for the 'system' to change, or for our schools to take better care of us. We need to take control and we need to do it now. Below I suggest five ways in which teachers can begin to nourish themselves more. Think of each of them as a deep inhalation of oxygen from your mask.

1. Tribal staffrooms

Humans are an innately tribal and social species. Our evolution and survival as a race has depended on our ability to relate to other humans. Time and time again, in research relating to what contributes to happiness and wellbeing, strong personal relationships always come right at the top. This same research shows that we tend to be happier when we are around other people, regardless of whether we view ourselves as more introverted or extroverted. 'Relationships are themselves a crucial part of psychological wealth, without which you cannot be truly rich,' according to positive psychologists, Ed Diener and Robert Biswas-Diener. But teachers often work in separate classrooms, in isolation from each other. Only coming together briefly at various parts of the day. Teachers need to feel part of a team and part of a tribe. So, why not set up a staff social committee in your staffroom? Arrange regular nights out: comedy nights, trips to the pub, meals out, ten-pin bowling. The activity you choose is less important than the act of getting staff together, away from school and socialising. Encourage all staff to take at least 30 minutes for their lunch break and come together to eat. You could also try setting up a wellbeing committee whose purpose is to find ways to make your working life more conducive to wellbeing – look at ways to work more flexibly, cut-back on unnecessary paperwork and meetings, embrace effective marking strategies that reduce workload. The bottom line is to connect with your colleagues and look at how you can make things better, share successes, vent frustrations, socialise and laugh. Laugh often!

Reset to green

Psychologist, Dr. Rick Hanson, believes the different operating systems of our brain have either a red or green setting (Hanson, 2013). When our brains are on red, we are essentially in fight or flight mode. It means we've sensed a threat, our bodies flood with the stress hormone cortisol and we remain hyper-vigilant until the threat has passed. Except teachers can feel under threat for most of the day. Doing multiple things at once, racing from here to there, processing lots of information and stimulation and working long hours are all examples of things that keep us stuck in 'red' mode. But when our brains are on 'green', they prevent, repair and recover from depleting and harmful bursts of stressful activity. Our green brains release endorphins and nitric oxide which kills bacteria, relieves pain and reduces inflammation. So, Hanson's advice for teachers is to, many times a day, reset to green. Recall someone who loves you. Recall someone you love. Imagine their smiling faces, remind yourself of their support. Look out of the window at a natural setting. Take a few deep breaths in, and exhale at length which is naturally calming. When you reset to green, stay with the experience for 10-20 seconds. Imagine the increasing sense of calm filling you up from your core. Resetting to green several times throughout the day creates a buffer between you and any stressors. Each reset is like a deep inhalation from your oxygen mask.

Laughter

It is impossible to feel stressed whilst laughing. Laughter serves many purposes but one of its main functions is to counteract the negative effects of anxiety and stress. 'Humour helps people handle stress within relationships and communicate difficult information by lightening the mood', according to Louis Cozolino. Apparently, we're 30 times more likely to laugh when with other people than when we're alone. This is because laughter is contagious. Even if we haven't heard the joke, just hearing other people laugh means we're likely to laugh and join in too. So, laughter helps with social cohesion and fostering tribal communities. Us teachers are lucky that we get to work with children every day. Yes, it is stressful, but it also gives us many opportunities to laugh during the day. One of my funniest moments in class happened when I was guiding my class through a listening meditation. It was summer, so we had the doors and windows open. I was asking my class to notice sounds nearby and far away. I asked them if they could hear the sounds of birds outside, or the distant sound of traffic. I asked them to notice if the sounds were pleasant or unpleasant. At that exact moment, a child accidentally broke wind extremely loudly. Cue rapturous laughter than lasted for several minutes! Do not let your funny classroom moments go by unnoticed. Savour them and join in with the laughter.

Perspective

Given our brains' innate negativity bias, it would be very easy for us to dwell on the depleting and depressing aspects of our jobs and the teaching crisis. The lack of resources, the hyper-accountability, the never-ending paperwork. But, is there another way we can perceive our problems? In his book *Man's Search for Meaning*, Victor Frankl, a holocaust survivor, writes these immortal words: 'Everything can be taken from a man but one thing: the last of human freedoms – to choose one's attitude in any given set of circumstances.' This reminds us that we have a choice in how we **perceive** our situation. This is not to diminish the bullying, stress and shame that many teachers experience on a regular basis. The point is to realise that we are not powerless, even if the situation seems largely out of our control. Can we find meaning in our suffering, as teachers? One of my reasons for remaining in the classroom, despite numerous thoughts about leaving due to stress, is to be there for my children, to teach them the skills of wellbeing and to help change the system from the inside out. What is your purpose for being a teacher? Let that purpose guide you and give you strength in times of need. Allow your sense of purpose to keep your perspective wide and know that there is always a solution to every problem.

Courage

Ultimately, it takes courage to believe that our education systems across the world can change for the better and it certainly takes courage to bring about positive change. You may feel that you're a lone wolf in your school. When you mention mindfulness interventions or positive psychology, you may experience the eye-rolls of colleagues and the smirks and whispers of cynics. It takes real courage to dare to be different. But our children depend on 'maverick' teachers to ensure a bright, hopeful and happy future for them. Bring to mind your maverick role models who dared to believe in a better future for humanity, and who have tirelessly worked to bring about positive change: Martin Luther King, Anne Frank, the Dalai Lama, Eleanor Roosevelt, Malala Yousafzai, Ghandi to name a few. Your role models do not have to be perfect. Every great person has their flaws and you do not need to be the perfect teacher in order to bring about change. The positive education movement is not about perfection. It is about creating an education system that is fair, meaningful, and that allows teachers and pupils to be the best they can be. As we work towards this goal, and we find ourselves doubting our mission, simply ask, 'what have we got to lose?' By being bold and courageous, we set our children the example of what it means and takes to positively change the world. There is no better teaching than that.

Further reading

Bajorek, Z., Gulliford, J. & Taskila, T. (2014): *Healthy teachers, higher marks? Establishing a link between teacher health and wellbeing, and student outcomes.* London, UK: The Work

Black, S. (2001): Morale matters: When teachers feel good about their work, research shows, student achievement rises. *American School Board Journal,* 188(1), pp. 40-43.

Briner, R. & Dewberry, C. (2007): 'Staff wellbeing is key to school success: a research study into the links between staff wellbeing and school performance'. London, UK: Worklife Support.

Cozolino, L. (2013): *The Social Neuroscience of Education: Optimizing Attachment and Learning in the Classroom.* New York, NY: W. W. Norton & Company.

Diener, E. & Biswas-Diener, R. (2008): *Happiness: Unlocking the Mysteries of Psychological Wealth.* Oxford, UK: Wiley-Blackwell.

Frankl, V. E. (1946): *Man's Search for Meaning.* Boston, MA: Beacon Press

Gopnik, A. (2016): *The Gardener and the Carpenter: What the New Science of Child Development Tells Us About the Relationship Between Parents and Children.* London, UK: The Bodley Head.

Kell, E. (2018): *How to Survive in Teaching: Without Imploding, Exploding or Walking Away.* London, UK: Bloomsbury Education.

Weale, S. (2016): 'Almost a third of teachers quit state sector within five years of qualifying'. The Guardian. Available at: www.theguardian.com/education/2016/oct/24/almost-third-of-teachers-quit-within-five-years-of-qualifying-figures

www.teachappy.co.uk/blog/rick-hanson – view my interview with Rick Hanson, discussing how we can rewire our negativity bias and what teachers can do when faced with a teaching crisis.

Chapter 14:
Child-Centered School Markers and Resources for the Positive Environment

Leonid Ilyushin & Anastasia Azbel

Schools – a place for transformation

Any school can be seen as the time and the place for transformation of natural makings into personal achievements and meanings of the student. We call a good school the one where this transformation makes teachers, children and parents happier than before. We do not have a universal instrument or device that can 'measure happiness'. But this does not mean that it is impossible to describe a good school in detail. In this chapter we will offer a list of school environment markers, oriented towards optimism and cooperation for all participants in the learning process. The basis of the list that we propose is the practice of several effective Russian schools with which we have been cooperating and which we have been observing for several years.

The school educational process is based on the willingness that a student provides a teacher (or a school generally) with three of his/her resources: personal time 'here and now'; attention and involvement; reflection and readiness to choose educational activities. The school uses these resources continuously, but not always effectively. This is due to the fact that the school's educational environment combines two opposing aspects that affect the state and attitude towards the school on the part of the student. On the one hand, this is 'school tiredness' – a steady pupil's desire to avoid active cognitive and research behavior in relation to educational tasks, no matter whom they are put by. School tiredness (Ilyushun & Azbel, 2016) appears due to several key factors: monotony of lessons, stress caused by external control and testing, and overloading with homework. On the other hand, the student's educational behavior is influenced by his or her inner motivation for so called innovative educational behavior (Ilyushun & Azbel, 2016) – the effective solution of problems in the field of one's own development throughout life. Such behavior is formed in conditions of the person's conscious choice of his or her position in the stream of life-long education, of which the time of school education is a part. Innovative educational behavior is manifested in the 'prism of motives', which the student demonstrates: the desire to understand what exactly it is necessary to learn; the desire to understand why he or she is taught in this way; desire to constantly apply his or her knowledge and skills in the practice of their own lives.

Returning to the very first thesis of this chapter, we want to emphasize that overcoming 'school tiredness' and choosing 'innovative educational behavior' by the student does not happen by accident but depends on the specific conditions that the school provides day by day and year by year. These conditions can be named, proceeding from deficiencies of the school environment, which are eliminated by these conditions. Our observations and system analysis show that there are four such deficiencies. Each of them can be overcome due to active, systematic usage of certain methods and formats of interaction in school practice.

Challenges of school life	Positive practices as resources
Lack of joy and pleasure in the learning process.	School walls; humour; meetings with interesting people; lesson as a joint project for both the teacher and the pupils.

Challenges of school life	Positive practices as resources
Deficiency of understanding the meaning of education and the role of certain training activities.	Research practice; group and individual projects; board games; science-slam and debates festivals.
Deficiency of the sensation of 'flow' (Chikzentmihayi) in the school environment.	Translation of documents from 'official' to 'children's' language; work with the student's personal strategies; practice of involvement; reduction of exaggerated pathos and imitation in the life of the school.
Deficiency of mutual sympathy and respect between adults and children.	Open discussions between children and adults; practice of feedback in learning; a system of formative assessment; providing help for pupils with overcoming anxiety and fear.

In general, we can argue that the 'positivity field' in the school grows if 'right' factors are supported and narrowed if the 'left' are stronger.

Demotivating factors	Motivating factors
Sarcasm and irony	Humour
Overloading with the school work	Flow
Useless slogans and imitation	Meaning
Edification	Respect and Empathy
Fear	Responsibility

Summarizing what was said above, we want to suggest that those who develop a positive learning environment should follow the general principle: 'We have the right to say if we like or not how the pupil learns, only if we allow him/her to estimate how we teach them.'

Next, we will offer several practical steps to develop innovative educational behavior in a school that supports the values of a positive educational environment.

Meetings with professionals

It is important to create situations where kids will be able to discuss issues related to their education and career vision in a dialogue with those who are interesting to them. Of course, there will not be a direct transfer of someone else's experience into the student's own life, but the very situation of the interested discussion will create an important internal setting for finding solutions in one's own life.

When formulating the goal and principles of the project 'meetings with professionals', we were infused by exceptionally valuable supporters such thinkers, scientists and businessmen as Erik Erikson (Theory of the Stages of Human Life), Stephen Covey (Theory of The 7 skills of Highly Effective People), Ayn Rand (*Atlas Shrugged*), Richard Dawkins (*The Selfish Gene*), Victor Frankl (*Man's Search for Meaning: A Psychologist in a Concentration Camp*), Steve Jobs, Richard Branson, Mstislav Rostropovich, and many others.

Our own experience, as well as the analysis of many texts, concepts, practical descriptions of the organization of meetings of schoolchildren with adult professionals led us to a simple but fundamentally important set of methods of interaction at such meetings:

The method of unmistakable attempts

Involving the student in a sequence of actions, events, experiences, the result of which is a new, more profound knowledge of his/her capabilities and intentions. Such a result cannot be 'erroneous' by definition, because any attempt, being made in dialogue and interaction with an adult, gives the experience of realizing one's self.

The method of constructing a dream

A dream is an emotionally colored image of a positive future. The method is aimed to add up, describe the most attractive image of our own future (the dream) from information about our opportunities and abilities; plans and forecasts; representations of the required external resources and assistance.

The method of risk area searching

Even the simplest and the most understandable project, has its own risk areas. They are associated with the dynamics of external conditions and internal human resources. The method consists in a careful analysis of both. This can be done by means of self-diagnosis or a dialogue with an expert. The main thing is that the search for a risk zone does not become an end but is one of the conditions for the student to build his/ her personal career-counseling program.

The method of target audit

The method is based on applying system analysis and evaluation to each of the SMART-target parameters: Specific, Measurable, Achievable, Relevant, Time-bound. In other words, the student, using the previous three methods, analyzes the context, measurability, attainability, significance and time resource of his/her personal goal.

The main themes of the dialogues between schoolchildren and adults would reasonably make such categories as the life path (route, trajectory, direction, movement, development); educational and professional choice (broad, free, responsible, difficult, unambiguous, compelled); assistance in self-determination (assistance, empathy, provision of resources, sharing of responsibilities, pooling of efforts).

Meetings with professionals will also broaden the horizons of schoolchildren in several areas:

- Vertical and horizontal career
- Labor market
- Freelancer/employee
- Part-time
- Irregular working hours
- Civil service
- Salary, income, fee, rate
- Qualification
- Professional limitations and responsibilities
- Creation of projects
- Managing the processes of one's life
- Negotiations for cooperation

- Divergent thinking
- Active and effective rest
- Ability to solve professional cases
- Self-presentation skills

How is the communication between schoolchildren and adult professionals built in such a practice?

We assume that success and happiness are subjective notions, and each person learns to build his/her life in the frame of wellbeing every single day. There are eight areas of life, the development of which must be monitored daily to be successful and happy:

1. Mastery: The field of permanent education, self-realization and personal growth; knowledge of yourself and the world around you.

2. Spirituality and creativity: Projects and deeds, not framed only by money or similar benefits; something for the wellbeing of the soul and joy of the mind.

3. Health, physical activity and sports: The most important categories of personal mobility.

4. Brightness of life, emotions and rest: Positive emotional events that can be remembered for years, something that supports in a difficult moment and brings joy. It is also an opportunity to change activities.

5. Family, friends and comfort: The closest social circle that trusts you, and that is trust by you.

6. Relationships: Active communication and good relations with the social network of friends and acquaintances give points of growth and create a bank of social connections for the ideas and plans execution.

7. Career and business: Work, projects, the main source of income (unlike creativity creates monetary obligations).

8. Finance: The ability to manage revenues, forcing money and ideas to work for you.

There are a lot of exercises for self-analysis and development of these life spheres. Among those, one that works effectively is the 'Balance Wheel'. You may ask your pupils to draw a circle and divide it into eight segments. Than to divide each radius from 0 in the center to 10 on the rim of the circle and name each of eight segments according to the list above (1-8). Ask your pupils to assess their satisfaction in each sphere from 0 to 10, where 0 is a complete dissatisfaction, and 10 is the maximum satisfaction with the situation they are in the moment. Let them paint each sector according to the level it has got and look at the final figure. Does it resemble a wheel? Than the picture is more equal, the more in balance are all life areas. The higher the score appears, the greater the level of overall wellbeing is likely to be.

School walls are not just borders; they are the 'window' into the world of education

School walls as an information and text surface are of great importance for the formation of the pupil's attitude to the school and his life in it. We conducted a study of schools that try to make their walls not only neat and beautiful, but also helping schoolchildren learn, cope with difficulties, believe in themselves and rejoice at how the school talks about it with him. If we summarize the text solutions that have a positive impact on the development of innovative educational behavior and help overcome 'school tiredness', we should talk about the following criteria.

Meaning

Any statement on the school walls must be checked for meaning. It is worth asking questions to each text: why is this text here? Is the information clear? How will this text change over time? Is it trustworthy? What exactly does this text help and what does it prevent? How can it help a student who reads it for the first time, on the tenth or hundredth time?

Emotionality of the text

For a school that wants to develop a practice of personality-oriented approach and pedagogical support, it is important to realize the possibility to regulate the emotional background that can broadcast the school space itself by using certain texts. Humor, friendly style of school text, ease and depth of phrases help make the text not only understandable, but also interesting for the student. A very important factor in the emotionality of the text is the participation of schoolchildren in deciding where exactly and what certain text will be in the school corridor.

Texts style

Publicistic or conversational styles are perceived by students better than formal, business and academic. School texts are usually read quickly and should be understood by anyone who can read and/or recognize other semiotic fields.

Visualization of the text

There are techniques that help to keep interest in the information that the school places on the walls. Info-graphics, the use of QR codes, pictograms, bright, interesting fonts and the general design of the text make it possible to make the text multilayered, oriented to different types of children's perception of information.

Text quality: literacy and vocabulary, etc

All texts located in the extra-curricular space of schools should be carefully checked not only from a substantive point of view, but also spelling, grammatical and lexical.

Texts dynamics and updating

Texts can be either permanent or temporary, and the percentage of temporary texts should be higher, since such texts attracts the attention of schoolchildren, makes school walls interesting and always 'new'. It is the school that determines the dynamics of updating texts. For example, quotations, motivators on the walls are useful only if they are changed periodically, because otherwise they lose their relevance, freshness and begin to perform an exclusively edifying function.

Interactivity of the text

This characteristic of the text helps to involve the student in a mental dialogue, to motivate him/her to solve curious questions, puzzles and thus make his/her spare time more useful and interesting. Presence of such 'interactive-text-places' in schools allows to support the proactive attitude of pupils to the learning-space in which they are. Interactive text or an interactive surface invites both teenagers and younger children to play and express themselves. Teachers who want to develop a person-centered approach in creating school spaces need to be prepared for the fact that in the interaction between the child and, for example, an open writing desk in the corridor, very complex processes of socialization and understanding of the boundaries of self-expression may occur.

Smart games on school TV screens

It's hard to imagine a modern school without wall-mounted video panels. Basically, they are used to show information about the schedule and news of the school. We propose to include them in the general intellectual design of the walls and organize with their help the practice of developing intelligence, scientific intuition and divergent thinking. It may look like this: An image (text or photo) appears on the full screen, while at the bottom of the screen – a short version of the question is displayed (for example: 'Author?', 'Word?', 'Sign?', 'Location?', 'Name?'). There is also a small 'window with a countdown of seconds from 10 to 0.

After the end of the countdown, the correct answer appears and is hold on the screen for five seconds. Then a new 'riddle' opens and so on. Thus, anyone who finds him/herself opposite the LCD panel can try to remember, find, guess the right answer. No further instructions are required. After one or two riddles, any child will understand what they are driving him/her to do. Very likely there will organize the groups of pupils, who would be eager to compete for the higher speed of intellectual reaction and purview. There will be informal records in the length of a 'winning series' of questions from one participant, the speed of articulating the right answer, etc. This can be a bright addition to the everyday intellectual school environment.

It is important to stress that participation in this voluntary intellectual competition develops schoolchildren, broadens their horizons, and rewards them emotionally. The developing effect is supported by the involvement in the process of solving puzzles and by the facts, names, words that will remain in the pupils' long-term memory due to the probability of repeating the same block in a few days.

Directions for making a block of photo-puzzles

- Famous paintings without the author's name (in ten seconds you need to remember it or try to guess).
- A separate fragment of the picture, which should be a step to the name of the whole painting.
- Musical notation (a fragment of a well-known passage, a theme), along which it is necessary to name the author/composition.
- Actual world records in different sports with incomplete time/result indication.
- Information from the field of sports facts (e.g. standard weight of boxing gloves, football, or basketball, pole length, the maximum speed of a shuttlecock in badminton, etc.) that are to be guessed.
- Interesting, smart quotes of great people with one missing word, that should be named with the guidance of the logic and general knowledge.
- A quatrain from a poem, the author of which should be called.
- Foreign words, phrases, which need to be translated.
- Physical formulas with a missed part (sign), which must be named.
- The values of the basic physical constants.
- Tasks for a quick verbal counting.
- Difficult words with a missing letter(s).
- Geographical facts and names (the population of the country, the capital, the continent on which it is located, or the approximate length of a famous river).
- The facts from the area of high technology and modern science in the 'true/false' format (e.g. carbon nanofiber thickness of 0.5mm withstands tensile weight of 100kg – yes/no?)

The school as an object of research, developing applied curiosity

Nobody doubts that in school there can be a lot of interesting things. But can the school itself – the building, premises, engineering solutions, be interesting to the students? We are sure that the study of the school is a very useful educational practice. Firstly, it teaches pupils to understand something that is not always visible at first sight. Secondly, it teaches them to better understand how the school is organized, to respect its complexity, dynamics and the beauty (as we are sure) of the organization of internal processes. Finally, it teaches the student to put questions not only to the teacher, but also to other adults who work in the school.

A modern school building and a school organization can be the basis for creating a lot of very interesting and useful cases for studying and research. School canteen, cellar, schoolyard, financial office – all these are very interesting objects, if you introduce them to the pupils correctly. The cases, based on school objects and places can be solved for a whole year or even several years, especially if you include them in studying of the main school subjects.

The solution of the 'school case' consists of several stages:

- A detailed acquaintance with the school place, about which the students collect information. What is happening there? Who leads the work in this place? What equipment is placed there? What physical, chemical, social processes can be seen in this place?
- Making an 'information map' for different places of the school.
- Solving an interesting problem, using mathematical calculations related to the processes that take place in this place of the school.
- Preparing a video report, excursion, presentation about 'secrets' and bright facts related to the place that was observed.

At the end, we want to return once again to the main idea of this chapter – to develop a positive attitude of students towards extracurricular aspects of school life, we need to follow sustainable principles of such development. These principles should be simple and understandable to all school life actors.

- Responsibility without fear.
- Communicate without conflict.
- Achievement without stress.
- Pleasure without dependence.
- Motivation without enforcement.

References

Csikszentmihalyi, M. (1990): *Flow: the psychology of optimal experience.* New York, NY: Harper & Row.

Ilyushin L. S. & Azbel A. A. (2017): The modern Russian teacher: Studying awareness with the use of the semi-structured interview. *Psychology in Russia: State of the Art,* 10(1), pp. 49-66.

Chapter 15:
Leading Positive Education in a School

Sam Burrows

In June 2014 I received my first days of professional development in the area of positive education from Dr. Paula Robinson of the Positive Psychology Institute of Sydney, Australia. It was enlightening as the key concepts delivered aligned themselves with everything that I believed was essential with education. Avondale Grammar School, a co-educational, international school in Singapore where I was teaching, was known for its quality education coupled with its welcoming, nurturing teaching methodology so I was excited at the potential to build on what the school already had in place and to be part of the continued growth of the school as it began its journey into embedding positive education into the school community. Early on in my reading about positive education I adopted the motto of Geelong Grammar School 'Learn it, Live it, teach it and Embed it' as my mantra as it has underpinned the successful and continued implementation of positive education at their school and many others. Through my role as Positive Education Coordinator of Avondale Grammar School, I was given the opportunity to lead and facilitate Positive Education within the school and in this chapter, I will discuss what are the key ideas, practices and research that I believe are needed to implement and lead positive education within a school community to drive effective organisational change:

- Evaluation of current programs and best practice
- Whole school approach
- Strong leadership
- Training of staff internally and externally
- Embedding of positive education principles into the school community and culture
- Implicit and explicit teaching of wellbeing linked to the curriculum

Evaluation of current programs and best practice

First and foremost, there is the need to evaluate the current programs that are being used to deliver wellbeing within the school. Evaluation will provide evidence on the current positive effects of the school's program for the wellbeing of the school community.

The following four conditions are essential components and need to be evident for a successful program and would form the basis for the evaluation of the program:

- Is the program and interventions being implemented scientifically informed?
- Does the program have a wellbeing theory as its basis or is it trying to develop its own model?
- Is the school evaluating the efficiency of the program against the vision, mission and values of the school?
- How often is the school evaluating the program and interventions?

Is the program and interventions being implemented scientifically informed?

Peterson introduced the idea of positive psychology being applied in 'enabling institutions', his concept of enabling institutions was that the virtues of character should be within all members of the institution not just individuals, so the collective would all play their part in contributing to the improvement within the institution (Peterson, 2006). It is from this that schools have adopted the ideals of positive education to not just educate their students in academics but also to adopt all the common elements of a positive education program with an emphasis on character strengths. If teachers are to adopt a character education approach, then a theoretically informed and evidence-based character framework is required (White and Waters, 2015). 'Positive Education programs in schools appear in three forms: empirically validated and scientifically informed wellbeing intervention programs that have impact on wellbeing; scientifically-informed proactive strategies to the whole school mental health programs in schools; and specific virtues or values and character-based education lessons based in philosophy or values-based learning (White and Murray, 2015, p. 14). With the increasing development of the concepts of positive education across the world has also come evaluations of the effectiveness of trends, perspectives and policy within these areas. 'Topics that roughly align with positive education are very active areas of research by top academics across multiple domains, including psychology, education, public policy, and health, amongst others.' – Kern & Kaufman (2017, p. 32). It is essential for future development that programs, policies and strategies are scrutinized and what works well and what can be improved upon is clearly communicated scientifically.

Does the program have a wellbeing theory as it's basis or is it trying to develop its own model?

There is not a single wellbeing framework that is used by all but one of the most commonly used models for positive education programs that you will find in schools, which are embedding a whole school approach, is the model of PERMA (Seligman, 2011). PERMA was the first model of wellbeing that I was introduced to and has been adopted or adapted by many schools worldwide. It is defined as Positive Emotion, Engagement, Relationships, Meaning and Accomplishments. Positive emotions are seen as a wide range of emotions that are linked to positive outcomes in life. Engagement is seen as when people are truly engaged in an activity which can lead to a state of flow. Relationships are seen to be important to build positive emotions. Meaning is also known as purpose and gives a reason of why we live our life and accomplishments are seen to be the things we achieve through activating the other elements of the PERMA model. These five elements are commonly further explored through further concepts such as resilience, grit, flow, flourishing, mindfulness, mindset, gratitude and character strengths. Each one of those concepts is important in their own right and collectively when taught allow students a range of strategies to enhance their own personal wellbeing.

Schools across the world that have adopted a strengths-based approach have applied a range of different programs that have been published or have developed their own. St. Peters College of Adelaide in Australia have developed their own program. This focus has assisted the implementation and inclusion of character strengths in six student-focused programs and three strengths-based approaches with staff (Murray and White, 2015). Both St. Peters and Geelong Grammar of Australia have used the PERMA model (Seligman, 2011) in developing the key components of their Positive Education Programs. In 2011, St Peter's, strengthened its pastoral care model to embrace wellbeing as a goal in its new strategic direction, organized around the PERMA model, White and Murray (2015). Geelong Grammar have also been a key developer of their own Model for Positive Education which is presented as a framework for cultivating whole-school flourishing. The six domains of the model – positive relationships, positive emotions, positive health, positive engagement, positive accomplishment, and positive purpose – are proposed as core elements. Character strengths are introduced as the underpinning and supportive framework. The domains are an extension and adaptation of Professor Seligman's PERMA model with the most notable difference being the inclusion of positive health (Norrish, 2015).

Is the school evaluating the efficiency of the program against the vision, mission and values of the school?

Leaders within a school must align their schools vision, mission and operational goals to build a clear framework so that they can create a positive environment for the school community to flourish. This can be achieved by evaluating the efficiency of the school's program on a regular basis. Improvement in students' wellbeing starts by developing school culture to support wellbeing. Schools with effective practice review their school culture as part of their desire to improve wellbeing outcomes for all students in their school. Schools that have developed an agreed set of values to underpin the actions in their school have worked closely with the school community to do this. The process will take time but will be worthwhile as it will mean that the community understands, owns, and supports the culture of the school.

Planning for wellbeing should be a conscious action. The positive culture and values will be embedded in the school, integrated into everything school leaders and teachers do – from strategic planning; development of policies; school systems; relationships throughout the community and into the classroom. Schools successfully embedding wellbeing will have a clear vision of what they want for their students. They will have specific wellbeing goals in their strategic plans, with targets to work towards.

How often is the school evaluating the program and interventions?

Schools should be evaluating their wellbeing program on a regular basis as it is imperative that the program is sustainable, so school communities need to provide time for this to take place and to document the evaluation that takes place. Evaluation should take place yearly at a minimum especially when first implementing positive education. It is essential that the school provides data to the community that outlines results of evaluations. The monitoring and documenting of progress is crucial to providing justification of the program and for continuation of future and sustained implementation of positive education within the school community.

Whole school approach

There is the need for collective buy-in from whole the school community. Within a school community there are three key stakeholders who need to be functioning collectively for the whole school to adopt and implement positive education successfully; they are: staff, students and parents. If strong leadership is evident within the school, then the buy-in from staff should be present. It is important to evaluate whether positive education is being incorporated into the school by staff through the strategic intents, policies, curriculum, pastoral care, and psychological services. Finally, staff should be evaluated by the principles of Positive Education and whether they model the behaviours in their actions and interactions with other staff, parents and students by 'Learn it, Live it, teach it and Embed it'.

Student buy-in should be evaluated against the previously mentioned wellbeing model of PERMA (Seligman, 2011). This model contains the following five elements: Positive Emotions, Engagements, Relationships, Meaning and Accomplishments.

Parent buy-in can be evaluated by how relevant and successful they see the program is against the stated aims of the school. If parents, see that the wellbeing of their children is flourishing, and optimal functioning can be achieved then it would be seen to be that the program is achieving its aims. If the implementation of whole school wellbeing to students, staff, and parents is successful they should have been given access to positive psychology theory and applications and united approach to wellbeing should be evident. This requires the partnership of staff, students and parents working together.

Schools need to commit to positive education if they are to derive any benefits from the program. Learning needs to be embedded, ongoing and part of a holistic approach to wellbeing. Staff training, space in the curriculum and regular assessments of the program are examples of enabling factors that need to be employed and represent school-wide best practice.

Strong leadership

Schools who have successfully implemented a whole school approach have had strong leadership within their school community. At each level of administration, strong leadership needs to be provided and a collective approach given by staff who have been trained in positive education. There needs to be clear evidence that a framework and strategy is being integrated by the school's leaders, so the school community is scientifically informed of the wellbeing approach for staff and students.

In my role as Positive Education Coordinator at Avondale Grammar School I was given the following key responsibilities:

- Lead and promote Positive Education across the school.
- Create a 'Positive Education Implementation Plan'.
- Lead the development of a whole school curriculum content map for positive education to be integrated across all subjects.
- Teach positive education classes to middle school students.

Communicate the Positive Education program to the school community through regular contributions to the school newsletter and website outlining the learning taking place around wellbeing explicitly and implicitly around the school.

Lead the school in positive education days of interest including: 'World Happiness Day', 'Random Acts of Kindness Week' and 'Mindfulness in May'.

Leaders should help develop a culture of wellbeing based on shared values and positive relationships throughout the school community. They will manage the change in expectations, taking the school community with them. Their actions should be based on the firm foundation of the shared values. Leaders in schools should give staff and students opportunities to discuss the values and develop a shared understanding of them. Communication around the school should remind people about what is valued. Students should have a clear understanding of the importance of the values to the quality of their school experiences. Leaders should have high expectations that the focus on positive relationships in the values will guide interactions among the whole school community. Leaders in schools should make sure the school values are a key part of day-to-day practice. The values should guide the culture of the school and strongly influenced the aspirations of teachers and students. School values will align well with practices and be used to guide planning. They should be evident in everyday activities and learning, at school events and through the development of a positive environment for everyone.

Schools should recognise and celebrate students who act out the school values. Schools expect their student leaders to model the values. This careful and deliberate embedding of values will mean that schools have caring relationships with the whole school community.

Effective leaders should deliberately use a range of processes to review the relevance of the school values and to find out whether they are understood and used day-to-day.

Training of staff internally and externally

Staff need to be educated in the benefits of positive education if they are to be able to help contribute to a positive environment within the school community. They will need to learn about the science of wellbeing and flourishing during training courses and regular training sessions. Training should be designed to have a meaningful impact on the wellbeing of both educators and their students, allowing them to flourish both inside and outside the classroom. Training courses should allow participants to explore the key concepts and skills of positive education in a practical way, with all content being supported by empirical research. The training of staff can be either done internally or externally. Training taken internally usually allows a greater amount of staff to be trained at once and allows the opportunity for staff to reflect together on current practice and opportunities for improvement. Training taken externally allows staff to learn about positive education in an independent setting and thus not distracted by the day to day operations of staff if taken on-site. The school community needs to be realistic about creating a timeline for implementation of any new program, based on the opportunities provided for staff training, building support systems and establishing a collaborative approach from the whole school community.

It has been noted that one of key influences of program success is related to how engaged the program facilitator was with the program content, so it is essential that they have had the training opportunities to develop their understanding. Having a supportive school infrastructure in which to develop Positive Education is fundamental to the success of such a program. Ongoing training and upskilling of staff is essential as staff should be given regular opportunities to 'learn' about positive psychology and be encouraged to 'live' its principles by modelling appropriate behaviours in their interactions with each other and with students. (Bott, 2017).

Embedding of positive education principles into the school community and culture

'Complementary school-wide processes help embed a culture for wellbeing across the school community.' – Norrish et al (2013)

Every schools culture and community are unique to itself. These can be enhanced by successfully embedding the principles of positive education. This can be achieved through several different aspects and levels. Staff participating in training programs to learn about positive education and how to apply it to the school community and their own personal lives is usually the first step. Leaders should recognise the importance for students to experience a range of academic, sporting and cultural opportunities. These opportunities will help develop student leadership, social skills and individual strengths and interests so that each student can 'Learn it, Live it, Teach it and Embed it'.

'Learn it refers to the sharing of opportunities as a whole-school community to understand and engage with the science of wellbeing. Live it is enacting evidence-based wellbeing practices in an individual's unique way in their own lives. Teach it is providing students with dedicated time to discover and explore each of the key domains of wellbeing. Embed it is adopting long-term, school-wide policies and practices which support and nurture wellbeing within individuals and within the community. It is noted that this framework is designed for schools that have already made the decision and commitment to implement Pos Ed as a whole-school approach, and it is critical to recognise that each process should be considered relative to their unique context and culture.' – Hoare et al (2017, p. 60-61)

The challenge for leaders within the school community is to support their staff in embedding and sustaining positive education while understanding and working within the process of change that will inevitably be taken throughout the process. The school community needs to create opportunities for staff to collaborate, develop and maintain commitment to the school through a whole school approach by planning strategies that will sustain and maintain the program over time.

Implicit and explicit teaching of wellbeing linked to the curriculum

Wellbeing is seen as an essential part of modern life today and it is from this construct that the term positive education has grown in prominence in the early part of the 21st century. In the education sector

233

the understanding that wellbeing should be taught alongside with academic subjects rather than learnt through personal experiences has increased through the evolving use of current best practice and research undertaken by educators and psychologists. The concept of positive education has grown from research in the field of positive psychology and originally from the work of Seligman.

'We conclude that, were it possible, wellbeing should be taught in school on three grounds: as an antidote to depression, as a vehicle for increasing life satisfaction, and as an aid to better learning and more creative thinking. Because most young people attend school, schools provide the opportunity to reach them and enhance their wellbeing on a wide scale.'
– Seligman (2009, p. 295)

Schools that have good wellbeing practices recognise the importance of explicit teaching to achieve desired outcomes for students. School leaders will promote teaching practices that enabled students in each classroom and other learning groups to work as caring, inclusive and cohesive learning communities. Wellbeing values should be consistently actioned in the curriculum, in relationships, and through celebrations. Values should be taught explicitly and modelled by the whole school community. Leaders in schools need to understand that the school's curriculum should give a range of opportunities to build on students' strengths, interests and aspirations, including ways to monitor student progress and wellbeing and to frequently review for relevance and adjust as needed. If positive education is embedded successfully students should see it applied into every course they take and receive direct instruction through a time tabled lesson into the key principles of positive education. This can be achieved by looking into the scope and sequence of each curriculum subject and then creating a school wide curriculum content map which clearly outlines the opportunities of integration of positive education into each subject.

In conclusion, leading and facilitating positive education within a whole school approach is a gratifying experience as you get to oversee and share in growth at all levels of the school community as you help implement the key ideas, practices and research that I believe are needed to implement and lead positive education within a school community to drive effective organisational change.

Further reading

Broadbent, C. & Boyle, M. (2014): Promoting positive education, resilience and student wellbeing through values education. *The European Journal of Social & Behavioural Sciences*, 8(1), pp. 1308-1317.

Chisholm, N. (2013): Why positive education? *TLN Journal*, 20(3), pp. 38-39.

Compton, W. C. & Hoffman, E. (1990): *Positive Psychology: The Science of Happiness and Flourishing.* 2nd ed. Belmont, CA: Wadsworth Cengage Learning, 2013.

Duckworth, A. L., Peterson, C., Matthews, M. D. & Kelly, D. R. (2007): Grit: Perseverance and Passion for Long-Term Goals. *Journal of Personality and Social Psychology*, 92(6), pp. 1087-1101.

Fan, S. (2016): What is Next in Educational Research? In J. Fielding-Wells (Ed.). Singapore: Springer Science and Business.

Frydenberg, E., Martin, A. J. & Collie, R. J. (2017): Social and emotional learning in Australia and the Asia-Pacific: perspectives, programs and approaches. *Social and emotional learning in Australia and the Asia-Pacific.* New York, NY: Springer.

Galloway, R. & Reynolds, B. (2015): Positive Psychology in the Elementary Classroom: The Influence of Strengths-Based Approaches on Children's Self-Efficacy. *Open Journal of Social Sciences*, 3, pp. 16-23.

Heng, T. T. (2011): Teaching happiness and well-being in schools: learning to ride elephants. New York, NY: Continuum International Publishing Company.

Hoare, E., Bott, D. & Robinson, J. (2017): Learn it, Live it, Teach it, Embed it: Implementing a whole school approach to foster positive mental health and wellbeing through Positive Education. *International Journal of Wellbeing*, 7(3), pp. 56-71.

Knoop, H. H. (2012): *Well-Being and Cultures Perspectives from Positive Psychology.* In A. D. Fave & SpringerLink (Eds.), Well-Being and Culture: Perspectives from Positive Psychology. Dordrecht, Netherlands: Springer.

Kern, M. L & Kaufman, S. B. (2017): The State of Positive Education: *A review of History, Policy, Practice, and Research.* World Government Summit in collaboration with IPEN.

Norrish, J. M. (2015): *Positive education: the Geelong Grammar School Journey.* Oxford, UK: Oxford University Press.

Norrish, J. M., Williams, P., O'Connor, M. & Robinson, J. (2013): An applied framework for positive education. *International Journal of Wellbeing,* 3(2), pp. 147-161.

Park, N. & Peterson, C. (2008): Positive psychology and character strengths: application to strengths-based school counseling. Report. *Professional School Counseling,* 12(2), p. 85.

Park, N. & Peterson, C. (2009): Character Strengths: Research and Practice. *Journal of College and Character,* 10(4).

Peterson, C. (2006): A Primer in Positive Psychology. Oxford, UK: Oxford University Press.

Quinlan, D., Swain, N. & Vella-Brodrick, D. (2012): Character Strengths Interventions: Building on What We Know for Improved Outcomes. *Journal of Happiness Studies,* 13(6), pp. 1145-1163.

Ruch, W., Weber, M., Park, N. & Peterson, C. (2014): Character Strengths in Children and Adolescents. *European Journal of Psychological Assessment,* 30(1), pp. 57-64.

Seligman, M. E. P. (2006): *Learned optimism: how to change your mind and your life.* New York, NY: Vintage Books.

Seligman, M. E. P., Steen, T. A., Park, N. & Peterson, C. (2005): Positive psychology progress: empirical validation of interventions. (Author Abstract). *The American Psychologist,* 60(5), p. 410.

Seligman, M. P., Ernst, R., Gillham, J., Reivich, K. & Linkins, M. (2009): Positive education: positive psychology and classroom interventions. *Oxford Review of Education,* 35(3), pp. 293-311.

Sin, N. L. & Lyubomirsky, S. (2009): Enhancing well-being and alleviating depressive symptoms with positive psychology interventions: a practice-friendly meta-analysis. *Journal of Clinical Psychology*, 65(5), pp. 467-487.

Wagner, L. & Ruch, W. (2015): Good character at school: positive classroom behavior mediates the link between character strengths and school achievement. *Frontiers in psychology*, 6, p. 610.

Waters, L. (2015): Why positive education? *TLN Journal*, 22(3), pp. 16-18.

White, M. A., Murray, A. S. & Seligman, M. E. P. (2015): Evidence-based approaches in positive education: implementing a strategic framework for well-being in schools. New York, NY: Springer.

White, M. A. & Waters, L. E. (2014): A case study of 'The Good School:' Examples of the use of Peterson's strengths-based approach with students. *The Journal of Positive Psychology*, p. 1-8.

Chapter 16:
Teaching Wellbeing: The Wellington College Experience

Ian Morris

Section 1: The journey

In 2005, I was asked to take over the running of PSHE (Personal, Social and Health Education) at Wellington College in Berkshire, UK. Wellington is an independent British boarding school that is academically, as well as socio-economically, selective because it sets entrance exams and charges fees. In 2005, the school was predominantly a boys' school with about 700 pupils, with only a small number of girls in the sixth form (less than 10% of the pupil body as a whole). In 2006, the school went co-educational and now, over a decade later, the school is moving towards a 50/50 gender split in a pupil body of over 1000.

PSHE is something of a Cinderella subject in UK schools. The Department for Education and successive Secretaries of State for Education have stressed the importance of school pupils supplementing an academic or vocational curriculum with what might loosely be termed 'life skills' and schools are expected to demonstrate when inspected how they provide such things as sex and relationship and drug education. However, there is little or no formal training in the teaching of PSHE in the UK and many teachers feel ill-equipped to sit in a classroom with young people and cover lessons on what may be deeply personal subject matter, or indeed, subject matter that the teacher has little or no direct personal experience of. For this reason, PSHE is often taught by people who are ill-prepared and under-resourced for the job. This is a tragedy, as the importance of learning about how to live a good human life should be lost on nobody, as is the significance of balancing out a curriculum that is all too often skewed towards the academic.

Coupled with this, is the lack of coherent or suitable philosophy behind much PSHE. It is not uncommon to find PSHE curricula that are driven along by what has been termed 'juvenoia'[1]: essentially the fear that when adults' backs are turned, that children are getting up to no good and that we must do everything in our power to stop this from happening. As a result, PSHE can often find itself running a deficit model of human nature which focuses on all the difficulties of life, rather than exploring how young people might develop their capabilities.

I came into this world in 2005. I followed the government guidance on PSHE curricula and created a programme that focused on issues such as smoking, sex (from a disaster perspective), drug abuse, depression and anxiety, self-harm, eating disorders and so on. To my surprise, the boys I was teaching had little or no interest in these matters and it wasn't until a couple of months later that I realised the reasons why. The main reason is that most of the issues traditionally covered in PSHE – the human disasters – don't affect most people. For example, statistically speaking, smoking, drinking and drug use are minority activities amongst British teenagers,[2] so it is little wonder that most of my pupils felt unaffected by those issues. Secondly, who wants to sit in a room to find out about how life can go wrong? Whilst, of course, it is important for adults to signpost the potential dangers of life, by focusing only on the deficit model we are unwittingly sending out a very negative message about our beliefs about young people and as often as not, disengaging them in the process.

---

1   Specifically by David Finkelhor of the Crimes Against Children Research Center, University of New Hampshire.
2   The UK Office for National Statistics report for 2016 shows that 3% of 11-15 year olds are regular smokers, 10% are regular drinkers and 10% regular drug users.

Something had to change

In January 2006, a new headteacher began his tenure at Wellington and the first visiting speaker he invited in was an academic from The Institute of Wellbeing at the University of Cambridge. As I listened to him speak about the science of human flourishing, I was gripped and immediately knew that this was the approach that our lessons had to take. I was sympathetic to his pitch: as a teacher of philosophy, I spend much of my time teaching Aristotle's Virtue Theory, a theory which had always appealed to me. The 'new' science of human flourishing seemed to cohere with Aristotle and I began work on a new curriculum that was to focus on how we might bring about our flourishing, as opposed to how we might avoid disasters which might never even befall us.

We began teaching the curriculum in September 2006, amidst a bit of media fanfare. It had been decided to put out a press release announcing that we were teaching happiness lessons and there was much interest in this. My first ever wellbeing lesson (they were never called happiness lessons at Wellington) had film crews from three different channels in the room, all jostling for camera angles whilst I was trying to teach mindfulness meditation. A lot of the reporting was supportive or even enthusiastic and some was critical. The criticism seemed to stem from our use of the word 'happiness' and this strikes right at the heart of a very important philosophical issue which I will pick up in Section 2. Because of the coverage, I was contacted by several people who were already working in the fields of wellbeing, positive psychology and later on, character education, and these contacts proved invaluable in helping me to shape the framework of the course in the years that followed.

Section 2: The framework

As mentioned above, a number of commentators were very critical of a school embarking upon the teaching of happiness. The main argument seemed to pivot on the point that happiness cannot be taught: that it is an ephemeral human feeling that is either present or not. Some suspected a more sinister issue: that we were somehow brainwashing our pupils into uncritical positivity and failing to educate them properly about the real vicissitudes of human life.

Of course, it depends on your view of what happiness actually is as to whether or not you believe it can be taught. Hedonism holds that happiness consists in a preponderance of pleasure over pain. This view does seem to make happiness slightly more ephemeral and less teachable: more reliant on circumstance than skill. The objections to hedonism as giving a comprehensive understanding of happiness are well-rehearsed[3] and in my view it would be a grave mistake to base wellbeing education on hedonism[4]. On the other hand, eudaimonism, following Aristotle, argues that happiness or wellbeing results from a life well-lived, through the careful and deliberate acquisition of virtue over time and the similarly careful elimination of vice. The distinction between hedonism and eudaimonism is neatly encapsulated by Julia Annas in her book *Intelligent Virtue*:

'In eudaimonist thinking, happiness is … a matter of how you live your life, how you deal with the material of your life. Happiness is not a matter of the stuff you have, or whether you are beautiful, healthy, powerful or rich. A happy life is not one in which you just have these things – after all, plenty of people have all these things but in no way live happily. A happy life is one in which you deal well with these things that you have – and cope well with illness, poverty, and loss of status, if these things happen to you. Accounts of happiness in this way of thinking are telling us how to live our lives, not urging us either to keep or change the circumstances of our lives.'[5]

For Annas, and others in the eudaemonist world, because happiness stems from the *skillful* and *deliberate* living of a life, it follows that there are certain skills that can be taught that may increase the chances of living life well. The Well-being programme at Wellington is based upon this insight: that wellbeing is founded upon certain skills and over the course of the four-year, 60 hours, taught course, we aim to impart some of those skills to our pupils.

---

3   See for example, *Virtues and Vices on Positive Psychology* by Kristjan Kristjansson, p36.
4   I have argued this point more fully elsewhere. See *Learning to Ride Elephants*, chapter 1.
5   Annas, J. (2011): *Intelligent Virtue*. Oxford, UK: Oxford University Press. P. 129.

The course is structured around six themes which are visited and revisited over the course of the four years. The six themes are[6]:

Physical health: The physical building blocks of wellbeing such as sleep, diet and exercise as well as understanding how the emotion system functions, how the brain works when you learn and how to think intelligently about and manage stress.

Relationships: How to build strong relationships with others through listening, empathy and conflict resolution through to thinking about how to develop ethical skill.

Resilience: Learning how to cope with change, challenge and adversity, how to build self-efficacy and the theory of mindsets.

Engagement: Learning how to get stuck in and stay stuck in to worthwhile activities through understanding flow states and resilience under pressure.

The world: Living sustainably in a consumer culture. Being critical of advertising messages to consume, thinking about the impact of consumption upon the planet and learning how to campaign for change in a positive way.

Meaning and purpose: Thinking about how a human life unfolds and the stages of adult development we may go through and considering the importance of identifying a sense of meaning and purpose for our lives.

We have tried to make the course as practical as possible so that pupils frequently encounter something in the lessons which they know directly benefits their everyday lives. This is supplemented by asking pupils to complete a homework assignment where they must try out something practical from the lesson and write an assessment of how effective it was: this could be anything from adjusting diet (e.g. eating a good breakfast) through to challenging unhelpful beliefs or practicing an act of kindness.

---

6   This is a very brief overview. For more detail, visit www.wellbeing.wellingtoncollege.org.uk which hosts all of the lessons and teaching materials, or consult *Learning to Ride Elephants* (Second Edition) by myself, which explains the theoretical underpinnings of the course and contains ideas for how they might be taught.

One of the main pieces of feedback we receive from pupils is that they find the lessons *useful*. This perception of usefulness continues into our Year 12 programme which focuses on living an ethical life and is much more conceptual. One lesson on transactional analysis landed particularly well with our pupils as they could identify so readily with the game 'one-up: one-down.' We also try to vary the content of the lessons from traditional teaching methods through to game playing and outdoor activities. Our lesson on self-efficacy for example, involves taking pupils outside to try slacklining: a fearsomely difficult activity akin to tightrope walking, which many of them find perplexingly addictive. Our lesson on flow[7] begins with pupils arriving to the classroom to find a range of toys and games and being given half an hour to play (which they love). They remember the lesson and more importantly, the concepts it conveys, for a long time afterwards.

Section 3: What we have learned so far

The Wellbeing Programme has been on our curriculum at Wellington since 2006. Over that time, we have learned five main lessons that may be useful to colleagues embarking upon structuring a similar programme of study.

Be prepared to take your time

The creation of an effective wellbeing programme is not something that can be accomplished in a summer holiday. Good teaching resources take time to create, time to test and time to bed in. It took us about five years to arrive at a programme we were content with and even now, 12 years on, we are still re-writing and tinkering. If possible, start teaching the programme to one or two year groups (in the UK, you might start with pupils at the beginning of two Key Stages, e.g. Years 7 and 10) and roll the programme out over time as those pupils go through the school. You would need a skeleton plan beforehand, but the donkey work of resource production can take a bit of a backseat and you can also learn about what works as you go. It will also take time to assemble a team of colleagues who are skilled enough to teach the subject.

---

7   The magical state described by Mihaly Csikszentmihalyi where our competence is perfectly suited to the task at hand and we become completely absorbed in what we are doing.

Collaborate and research widely

There is already a lot of good practice in the field, some of which has been produced by generously funded organisations who disseminate their materials for free.[8] There is also a lot of very good writing in this area from a range of disciplines covering the theoretical underpinnings[9] to practical books giving step by step guides to planning lessons.[10] As well as drawing from sources outside your school, draw from sources within your school. Work with your best teachers to develop the materials and get regular feedback from the pupils on the effectiveness of the lessons.

Be guided by philosophical principles

It is important to identify the philosophical position that your programme starts from. Once we had identified that we were following an Aristotelian/eudaemonic model, this helped to inform all our lessons and gave us a set of criteria to test our lessons against. This is especially important in immunising yourself against some of the hysteria that can erupt concerning the 'crises' facing our young people. At the time of writing, it is social media. At the time of reading, it may well be something else. If you have a philosophical position, this gives you a lens and a filter to view the issue through. For example, the problems which arise with misuse of social media, when viewed through the lens of virtue and vice can be understood as ancient human problems which are explored at least as early as Plato in the story of the Ring of Gyges. This then enables you to tackle the human universals, rather than get bogged down in the contemporary peripherals.

Don't just rely on off-the-shelf

There are some very good wellbeing programmes available, but they will always need to be tailored to the particular needs not only of the pupils

---

8   For example, The Jubilee Centre for Character and Virtue at the University of Birmingham UK. They have a wide range of teaching resources available for free at www.jubileecentre. ac.uk

9   For example, *Intelligent Virtue* by Julia Annas, *The Happiness Hypothesis* by Jonathan Haidt and Exploring Happiness by Sissela Bok.

10 For example, Ilona Boniwell and Lucy Ryan's book *Personal well-being lessons for secondary schools* or Karen Reivich and Andrew Shatté's excellent book on teaching resilience, *The Resilience Factor.*

in your school, but also of the teachers that you work with too. Ideally, you would have a team of teachers you can collaborate with to produce teaching materials that best suit your school.

It's never finished

Be prepared to re-write the course as your awareness of what has the most impact increases. Our programme has been through two major re-writes since its inception and even now individual lessons get adjusted. Take informal feedback from your pupils as you go along. In my experience they are very good at giving constructive feedback when you give them a genuine opportunity to do so. Our course has been shaped significantly by comments and suggestions from pupils over the years and it is better for it.

Summary

Being part of devising and structuring a wellbeing programme for a school has been the most professionally rewarding experience of my career. The ideas that I have encountered and now incorporated into our course have had a profound impact on me not only as a teacher, but in my personal life too. But it has been a long road and, at times, a difficult one. It has been vital therefore, to have a philosophical position which informs everything that we do on the programme, because during those times when the work is hard, there is a reassuring confidence in knowing that the work is part of a larger movement.

Chapter 17:

Leadership: Growing flourishing teachers

Katy Granville-Chapman

Many teachers in the UK are not flourishing and this is a major issue not only for the wellbeing, recruitment and retention of our teachers, but also for the quality of education we are able to provide British children. In an NASUWT survey of 3500 teachers, 84% of respondents said their job impacted negatively on their health; 76% were 'seriously considering' leaving the profession.

The UK has been described as having a recruitment and retention crisis in teaching and whilst workload is the most frequently cited reason for leaving the profession, Lynch et al (2016) argue that overall job satisfaction, plus the extent to which teachers feel supported and valued by management are the greatest motivating factors for intention to leave.

This chapter, therefore, argues that the primary goal of school leadership is to encourage and grow flourishing teachers. Professor Elaine Fox says that to flourish means 'living at the top of your range, enjoying a life filled with goodness, growth and creativity, and, when things go wrong, a strong resilience to get over the hump'. There has been a lot of research into flourishing recently, reflecting the increasing interest in the topic in a range of fields. The research has included cross-sectional, longitudinal and experimental studies. These studies have shown high levels of flourishing to be related to a variety of positive outcomes, such as effective learning, productivity and creativity, good relationships, pro-social behaviour, and good health and life expectancy: all of which are certainly worthy goals of school leadership.

Teacher flourishing plays a significant role in improving pupils' outcomes

Teacher flourishing has also been shown to have a significant role in improving pupils' outcomes. Briner and Dewberry (2007) for example, conducted a study of 24,100 teachers in 246 primary schools and 182 secondary schools in the UK. They considered three dimensions of positive and negative aspects of wellbeing: feeling valued and cared for; feeling overloaded; and job stimulation and enjoyment. They found that there was a significant relationship between these aspects of teacher wellbeing and statutory assessments (SATs) Key Stage 4 in secondary schools. They also found a significant relationship with the 'value-added' measure in primary and secondary schools.

How can leaders grow flourishing teachers?

A particularly useful model for leaders who want to grow flourishing teachers is Su, Tay and Diener's (2014) 'Core Dimensions of Psychological Wellbeing', which combines and develops ten of the most prominent theories of wellbeing, flourishing and thriving from psychology into seven dimensions:

1. Subjective wellbeing (SWB), covering high life-satisfaction and positive feelings.
2. Positive, supportive and enriching relationships.
3. Engagement and interest in daily activities.
4. Meaning and purpose in life.
5. A sense of mastery and accomplishment.
6. Feelings of autonomy and control.
7. Optimism.

Let's now consider how relevant these dimensions are to the flourishing of teachers, and whether they could be influenced by school leaders. While, for clarity, I will address each dimension separately, no single element of wellbeing should be considered in isolation since enrichment of one dimension can enhance others.

Dimension 1: Subjective wellbeing

Subjective wellbeing (SWB) comprises an emotional element (the presence of positive emotions and the absence of negative emotions) and an evaluative element (life satisfaction). SWB is like an internal measure of the extent to which other aspects of psychological wellbeing or needs are being fulfilled. The experience of wellness can also enhance other aspects of psychological wellbeing. Furthermore, feelings of wellbeing can affect behaviours directly through emotions, or indirectly through improving psychological capital from which to draw. Numerous reviews also support the value of positive emotion across a variety of life outcomes.

Leaders, and indeed teachers, can have a significant direct impact on their teams' and pupils' SWB, not least through a process of emotional contagion, or the transfer of emotions from one person to another. Vijayalakshmi and Bhattacharyya (2012) analysed and critiqued empirical and theoretical studies of emotional contagion through a literature review. They conclude that the impact of this transfer of emotions can influence work effectiveness.

Another series of studies (Bono and Ilies, 2006) found that leaders' positive emotional expressions were linked to ratings of charisma in a natural work setting, and that positive emotional expressions of leaders were linked to mood states of simulated followers. This suggests that mood contagion might be one of the psychological mechanisms through which leaders influence followers. They also employed a trained actor and influenced leaders' positive emotional expressions to isolate the effects of positive emotions from the potential non-emotional features of leadership (such as vision or other inspirational processes). This study found a positive relationship between leader emotions and follower mood. Mood is very difficult to measure objectively and accurately, but there are indications that both leaders' positive emotional expressions and the mood of followers' impact ratings of leader effectiveness. This means that it is worth leaders considering what kind of emotions they are transferring to their teams and whether these emotions could be more positive.

Dimension 2: Positive, supportive and enriching relationships

Social relationships are fundamental to a flourishing life. One review, covering from 2002 to 2012 found, more than 18,000 articles on social relationships and health, with positive relationships being linked to a lower risk of depression and psychopathology, better physical health, lower risk of mortality, healthier behaviours, and other positive outcomes (Tay, Tan, Diener & Gonzalez, 2012).

Professor Paul Gilbert (2013) says we have evolved to function best when we are loving, affiliative and caring and when we feel loved and valued. The human functions Gilbert is referring to are:

- The functioning of our pre-frontal cortex, which is involved in working memory, creativity and problem solving.
- Stress hormone regulation (for example, cortisol secretion, which triggers the 'fight or flight response').
- Immune and cardiovascular systems.

Thus, both leaders and followers benefit physically and mentally when leaders are compassionate and focus on the wellbeing of their team members; an added benefit is that performance also improves.

Trust is important in cultivating positive relationships

Trust also seems to be particularly important in cultivating positive relationships. Tschannen-Moran & Gareis (2015) say that trust in leaders and among academic staff is associated with the qualitative nature of professional relationships in schools and the impacts of those relationships on, for example, teachers' practices and student achievement.

Relationships and behaviours characterised by benevolence, honesty, openness, competence, and reliability can cultivate trust between principals and teachers, and the presence of genuine trust can thereby facilitate other factors associated with student learning.

Dimension 3: Engagement and interest in daily activities

Research into engagement can be found across several disparate areas. In positive psychology, for example, measures have focused on flow, or a high level of psychological engagement that involves deep concentration, absorption, and focus. Leaders can contribute to engagement through aiming to give team members autonomy over as much of their work as practical; match tasks to each team member's skill set and skill level; allow teachers the chance to immerse themselves in activities without distractions; ensure that their work is meaningful to them.

Dimension 4: Meaning and purpose in life

Steger (2012) defined a sense of meaning as having direction in life, connecting to something greater than yourself, feeling that your life is valuable and worthwhile, and that there is a purpose to what you do. Meaning has been linked to better physical health, reduced mortality risk, and higher life satisfaction. Ensuring that teachers feel that their work is valuable and purposeful is a key role of school leaders and can be achieved in a number of ways: through finding out in a group discussion what motivated your team to join the teaching profession; what your team believe the purpose of education is; and what kind of young people they'd like to see leaving their schools having benefited from your education. It is then worth following these discussions with consideration, as a team, how to prioritize your work so that you are focused on areas that will provide the greatest impact to the lives of the pupils you teach. This will also build connection between team members and strengthen relationships, which are also fundamental in meaning.

The removal of as many tasks as possible that teachers do not perceive to be meaningful and purposeful can have a significant impact on teachers' wellbeing and their ability to educate students effectively. An overreliance on data, rather than a focus on cultivating meaningful relationships with pupils is one area that leaders can look to address; as well as reducing low-impact administrative burdens that prevent teachers coming to the classroom energized and ready to connect with their pupils.

Coaching is another helpful way a leader can improve purpose and meaning in teachers' work. Coaching helps those being coached to connect with their values; and then to take decisions and act in accordance with their values. This is done through a process of asking questions to find out what is most important to them and how they think they can achieve the things that matters most to them. The coach also needs to hold the permanent belief that the person you are coaching is both capable and intrinsically valuable.

By learning to ask the right questions, a coach can enable people to take responsibility and action; to develop independence of thought and purpose; to become more motivated; to improve performance; to cope more effectively in adversity and become more resilient; and to think and make decisions more independently (Passmore and Brown, 2009).

It is interesting to note that research is supporting the value of coaching. One example is a meta-analysis of 107 papers (Theeboom, Beersma and van Vianen, 2013), which found the impact of coaching on the following areas was significantly positive:

Outcome	Effect size
Performance/Skills	0.60
Wellbeing	0.46
Coping	0.43
Goal-attainment	0.74
Work/Career attitudes	0.54

Dimension 5: A sense of mastery and accomplishment

Self-Determination Theory proposes that competence is a core basic human need. Objective accomplishment, or competence, is influenced by circumstances, opportunities, and personal ambitions. Subjectively, accomplishment involves a feeling of working toward and reaching goals, mastery, and efficacy to complete tasks.

The extent to which a leader can impact a person's objective and subjective sense of accomplishment is a debated theme in the literature, but giving recognition and gratitude are almost universally accepted to boost the wellbeing of the person receiving and giving thanks (Emmons, 2010). The next dimension, autonomy, is also something that leaders can influence, ties in here as it is thought to improve both accomplishment and a sense of mastery.

Dimension 6: Feelings of autonomy and control

Teacher autonomy is a common theme that emerges when considering teacher motivation, job satisfaction, stress (burnout), professionalism and empowerment. A significant amount of research has revealed the importance of autonomy for teachers' effectiveness and their happiness. Pearson and Moomaw (2005) argue that autonomy is emerging as a central variable when examining educational reform initiatives and some researchers argue that granting autonomy and empowering teachers is an effective place to begin in solving the problems of today's schools (Short & Rhinehart, 1992).

In a survey into the effects of teacher empowerment on motivation, job satisfaction and stress, Davis and Wilson (2000) surveyed 660 elementary teachers and 44 principals. Their findings showed a significant positive correlation between Principals' Empowering Behaviours (PEB) and teacher motivation, particularly when teachers were able to choose to do tasks that they perceived would have a positive impact on pupils.

Dimension 7: Optimism

Rasmussen and colleagues (2009) demonstrated that optimism is a key predictor for physical health and general wellbeing. Warren Bennis, in *The Leadership Advantage*, argues that optimism is also one of the key qualities people need from their leaders to achieve positive results.

Bennis says: 'every exemplary leader that I have met has what seems to be an unwarranted degree of optimism and that helps generate the energy and commitment necessary to achieve results.' Optimism can be incorrectly perceived as a negative trait and has been falsely linked to a lack of realism.

Time and again, however, it's been shown that teams won't follow leaders who lose faith when things don't go to plan and that people are much happier following leaders who are able to remain committed to a vision and keep their belief in the team's ability to succeed, even in the face of adversity.

Seligman (1998) says that optimism is defined by how a person interprets events. Optimists perceive positive events to be permanent and they give themselves credit for them. They don't, however, give permanence to negative events. Rather, when things go wrong, they believe this will only be a temporary setback and they don't blame themselves for this if it is out of their control. This type of explanatory style is good for leaders who want to improve flourishing because:

- It means leaders believe they have the ability to change things when they go wrong, and they are motivated to make the necessary changes.
- Leaders are more resilient when they face adversity, so they are more likely to see setbacks as temporary and will therefore seek solutions energetically, rather than give up hope.
- A leader's behaviour is contagious as it has an emotional component. Team members will copy the behaviour of the leader, whether this is optimistic or not. When they see a leader motivated to continue when they hit a roadblock, the team members are more likely to follow suit.

Summary

Flourishing should be the primary goal for school leaders and this chapter has explored seven areas in which leaders could contribute to teachers' flourishing:

1. Subjective wellbeing (SWB): Through emotional contagion, leaders can have a significant impact on the SWB of their teams, so it is worth being mindful of your mood as a leader and whether you can bring more positive energy to your team.

2. Positive relationships: Through being compassionate, trustworthy and prioritising positive relationships, leaders can have a great impact on their team's wellbeing and its performance.

3. Engagement and interest in daily activities: Can you focus on your team members' strengths and give them more autonomy to improve their level of flow?

4. Meaning and purpose in life: focusing on teachers' values and allowing them to work on meaningful activities that they believe are making a positive difference to the pupils they work with. Individual coaching and group exercises to establish what the team believes would have the most impact on their pupils' education can be very beneficial

5. A sense of mastery and accomplishment: Giving recognition and gratitude for teachers' contributions and successes has been shown to improve both the giver and receiver.

6. Feelings of autonomy and control: The more autonomy a leader can give teachers to make decisions the teacher believes will most help their pupils to progress the greater the success the teacher is likely to have with their pupils and the happier they'll be.

7. Optimism: When leaders have an optimistic explanatory style and persist energetically in the face of adversity, teams will mimic their behaviour and everyone is more likely to flourish.

Human relationships tie all these dimensions together and the most important thing a leader can do is to genuinely care, and want the very best, for their team members.

I served for seven years in the British Army where I witnessed the remarkable impact that both great and poor leadership could have on the lives of those being led. The impact of leadership on flourishing was demonstrated to me even more starkly on operational tours. Every day, soldiers faced unknown threats of IEDs, ambushes and the dangers of living in a war zone; one day a rocket even flew through the roof of the dining tent and landed in an ammunition compound, meaning even the camp wasn't safe. My time in Iraq, however, showed me that in the most demanding environment a leader who cares about their soldiers could still enable their teams to flourish and experience high levels of wellbeing.

Part of my role now is running leadership courses for our school's leadership & coaching institute and our teaching school partnership. Schools might seem a less dramatic setting, but I still frequently hear about the extraordinary impact that caring, and indeed, uncaring leaders can have on teachers' and therefore pupils' lives. Leadership is about wanting the very best for your team, whether you're in a war zone, the staffroom or the classroom. And when leaders in schools give this unconditional care, they enable teachers to flourish and to give the best possible education to our young people.

Further reading

Bennis, W. (1999): The Leadership Advantage. *Leader to Leader*, 12, pp. 18-23.

Bono, J. E. & Ilies, R. (2006): Charisma, positive emotions and mood contagion. *The Leadership Quarterly*, 17(4), pp. 317-334.

Briner, R. & Dewberry, C. (2007): *Staff Wellbeing Is Key to School Success: A Research Study into the Links Between Staff Well-being and School Performance*. London, UK: Work Life Support.

Davis, J. & Wilson, S. M. (2000): Principals' Efforts to Empower Teachers: Effects on Teacher Motivation and Job Satisfaction and Stress. *The Clearing House: A Journal of Educational Strategies, Issues and Ideas*, 73(6), pp. 349-353.

Emmons, R. (2010): Why Gratitude is Good. Greater Good Magazine.

Fox, E. (2013): *Rainy Brain, Sunny Brain: How to retrain your brain to overcome pessimism and achieve a more positive outlook*. London, UK: Arrow Books.

Gilbert, P. (2013): *The compassionate mind*. London, UK: Constable.

Lynch, S., Worth, J., Bamford, S. & Wespieser, K. (2016): Engaging teachers: NFER Analysis of Teacher Retention. Slough, England National Foundation for Educational Research.

Passmore, J. & Brown, A. (2009): Coaching non-adult students for enhanced examination performance: a longitudinal study. *Coaching: An International Journal of Theory, Research and Practice*, 2(1), pp. 54-64.

Passmore, J. (2010): Foreword. In Passmore, J (Ed.) Leadership Coaching. London, UK: Kogan Page.

Pearson, L. C & Moomaw, W. (2005): The Relationship between Teacher Autonomy and Stress, Work Satisfaction, Empowerment, and Professionalism. *Educational Research Quarterly*, 29, pp. 38-54.

Rasmussen H. N., Scheier M. F. & Greenhouse J. B. (2009): Optimism and physical health: a meta-analytic review. *Annals of Behavioral Medicine*, 37(3), pp. 239-56.

Seligman, M. E. P. (1998): *Learned Optimism*. New York, NY: Pocket Books.

Short, P. M. & Rinehart, J. S. (1992): School participant empowerment scale: Assessment of level of empowerment within the school environment. *Educational and Psychological Measurement*, 52, pp. 951-961.

Steger, M. F. (2012): *Meaning in Life. The Oxford handbook of positive psychology.* In Lopez, S. J. & Snyder, C. R. (Ed's), Oxford, UK: OUP.

Su, R., Tay, L. & Diener, E. (2014): The Development and Validation of the Comprehensive Inventory of Thriving (CIT) and the Brief Inventory of Thriving (BIT). Applied Psychology Health and Well Being, 6(3), pp. 251-279.

Tay, L., Tan, K., Diener, E. & Gonzalez, E. (2012): Social relations, health behaviors, and health outcomes: A survey and synthesis. *Applied Psychology: Health and Well Being*, 5(1), pp. 28-78.

Theeboom, T., Beersma, B. & van Vianen, A. (2013): Does coaching work? A meta-analysis on the effects of coaching on individual level outcomes in an organizational context. *The Journal of Positive Psychology*, 9(1), pp. 1-18.

Tschannen-Moran, M. (2003): Fostering organizational citizenship in schools: Transformational leadership and trust. In Hoy, W. K. & Miskel, C. G. (Eds.) *Studies in Leading Organizing Schools*, (pp. 157-179). Greenwich, CT: Informational Age Publishing.

Tschannen-Moran, M. (2004): *Trust matters: Leadership for successful schools.* San Francisco, CA: Jossey-Bass.

Tschannen-Moran, M., Christopher, R. & Gareis, C. R. (2015): Principals, Trust, and Cultivating Vibrant Schools. *Societies.* 5(2), pp. 256-276.

Vijayalakshmi, V. & Bhattacharyya, S. (2012): Emotional Contagion and its Relevance to Individual Behavior and Organizational Processes: A Position Paper. *Journal of Business Psychology.* 27, p. 363.

Chapter 18:
A Window and a Mirror: The story of wellbeing in Dubai schools

Dr. Abdulla Al Karam

You may have heard this old story about John Lennon: when he was at school, his teacher asked the students in his class what they wanted to be when they grew up. They replied in turn 'a doctor' or 'a lawyer' or 'a chef', among other professions. When it came John's time to speak, he said, 'I want to be happy.'

'No, John,' the teacher said, 'you don't understand the question.'

'No,' John replied, 'you don't understand life.'

This story neatly illustrates our belief that education is not about what we put in, but what we bring out; that the purpose of our education is not simply to do well, but also to be well. At KHDA, we consider education as an experience to enable students to flourish in a rapidly changing world; to exist in harmony with each other and with themselves, and contribute to the good in the world they live in.

Dubai's private education sector is unique: imagine all the various education systems around the world, imagine the differences in pedagogical approaches, and imagine the differences in parental expectations – in teacher training and in student outcomes. Now imagine them co-existing in Dubai. With 194 schools offering 17 different curricula to 280,000 students from 182 different nationalities, it would be easy to focus on the sector's disparity rather than its diversity; on its challenges rather than its successes.

As a government regulator that oversees a private education sector, KHDA is responsible for the growth and quality of private schools, but not what schools teach, how they teach or who is teaching. One of the first questions we asked ourselves when we were established in 2007 was, 'what then, is the role of a government regulator if it does not regulate curriculum, pedagogy, assessment or teacher development?'

Turning on the lights

We looked around us and saw the equivalent of a neighbourhood on a dark night, with all the residents locked in their houses, unable to see out. We then imagined what that neighbourhood would look like on a bright summer's day, with the people stepping out from their houses to appreciate the environment around them, to gather on the street and meet each other and talk. The answer to our question then, was simple: our role as the government regulator of a private sector was to illuminate, and to convene.

In our first year, we learned from international best practice, consulted with local educators and policy makers, and helped to switch the lights on to Dubai's education sector. We put in place a number of tools and policies to increase transparency and quality of education. School inspections, begun in 2008, have given us a shared language for talking about the quality of our schools. Currently, 66% of all school students receive an education rated 'good' or better, more than double the proportion ten years ago. The data that illuminates the private schools sector gives us a global and granular view, enabling us to harness the strengths of each school and, through positive engagement and collaboration, channel those strengths to improve all schools.

Our vision for education in Dubai did not come ready-made: it has changed and shifted as we have matured as an organisation, as we have engaged with and learned from our community, and as we have responded to the world around us.

What Works

Working in education, we often find ourselves in conversations that are deficit-based; that focus on challenges and obstacles. That these conversations have merit is less important than how they make people feel – dejected, powerless, and incapable of making meaningful change.

We realised that if we truly wanted to improve education, we had a choice: we could dwell on the difficulties, or we could highlight the positives; we could make decisions for others, or we could give them the torch to make those decisions for themselves; we could focus on finding solutions to problems, or we could make more of the successes.

During this time, we became aware of David Cooperrider and his work on Appreciate Inquiry, based on the simple concept that if we focus on positivity, we will create yet more positivity. The choice we had before us then, is referred colloquially as a 'no-brainer'.

By 2012, we could rely on data from five years of school inspections to give us a deep understanding of Dubai's schools and their strengths. And so, using our authority to convene, we consulted principals from Dubai's private schools and together came up with the idea of 'What Works'.

Three times a year, teachers from across Dubai's schools come together to run and attend workshops and share the best of what they do in their classrooms. Since the first What Works was held in September 2012, more than 14,000 teachers have attended upwards of 800 workshops at 30 events.

The real value of What Works has been not just in the connections made and learning shared on the day of the events, but in the culture change it has affected. The value of positivity; of concentrating on what's working, has strengthened the working practices of educators across Dubai and the learning outcomes of students. Teachers from different schools regularly visit each other to give and learn. What Works has created a compassionate ecosystem of schools, teachers, parents and students that recognises and values the role each plays in improving education in Dubai.

What Works introduced concepts like 'positive change' and 'collaboration' into our shared experience of education in Dubai; it was a window that showed us how positivity could transform our sector. Yet that window was not enough. We understood that if we truly wanted to inspire and create lasting change, we would need a mirror as well.

Big change is coming

The more we looked for positivity around us, the more we found it, and the more we attracted those with a similar mindset. We gravitated to the ideas and people that spoke of hope and passion and positive change, who were led by the generosity of their hearts rather than the pragmatism of their strategies. One of these people was Nic Marks, a happiness researcher and a fellow of New Economics Foundation in the UK. In his role with NEF, Nic had developed the 5 Ways of Wellbeing – evidence-based approaches to improve people's happiness. In his role with his organisation Happiness Works, he had created the Happiness at Work survey, a tool to give organisations a deeper understanding of their team's happiness. These would both play a pivotal role in KHDA's journey.

Measuring happiness

At this time, our main method of understanding what our team thought and how they felt about their work was through the annual Employee Satisfaction survey, and later, the Employee Engagement survey. The first implied that 'satisfaction' was the responsibility of the organisation, while the second shifted the responsibility of 'engagement' to the employee. Neither of these reflected how we viewed ourselves as individuals or as an organisation, nor were they an accurate measure of what we wanted to know most about – our people's happiness.

Through the 'Happiness Survey', we introduced our people to the concept of happiness as an organisational objective and gained the insights that would enable us to embed it into our everyday work. The survey measured the sense of pride our people took in their organisation; the purpose and meaning they gained from and gave to their work; their personal and professional resources and how much these enabled them to do their work; their sense of control; their freedom to be themselves; and their relationships with others, to name a few. Each team member received a report of their own results, as well as that of the organisation overall

– indicating that happiness depended not only what the organisation could do for its people, but also what our people could do for themselves. The first survey we completed in May 2014 with a participation rate of 87%. It gave us a score of 6.1, putting us in the top 35% of organisations worldwide, and left plenty of room for improvement.

The 5 Ways of Wellbeing – Take Notice, Connect, Be Active, Give and Keep Learning – transformed our view of happiness from an abstract concept into an achievable state. They became the blueprint for our processes, our policies, and our culture. We looked at the strengths of our organisation – our people's relationships with each other, their sense of control over their own work, their freedom to be creative, the feedback they received from others around them, and aligned those with the 5 Ways. Then we looked at the policies that were stifling those strengths and got rid of them. Processes that were designed to serve the organisation were replaced with those that served our people.

We understood the futility of using a head count to determine the size of our organisation and the impact of our work. It was not the heads, but the hearts of KHDA that would make positive change. It was the team members who approached their work with purpose, passion and positivity who would change the face of KHDA and of education in Dubai.

The death of HR

Our human resources function – responsible for recruitment, retention and performance management – became obsolete. Instead, we created teams made up of people from throughout the organisation to develop and implement new ways of recruiting people, of retaining them, and of rewarding them.

The first victim of our happiness journey was the ubiquitous CV. Our new scouting team concluded that what a person had achieved in the past was less important than what they could achieve in the future; that their CV could give you an idea of their experience, but nothing of their empathy. We developed an app through which we channeled all our recruitment. Instead of job interviews, candidates were asked to attend an 'Open Week', during which they worked together to try to solve 'tensions' in our work. Those who showed that they worked well in a team, that they treated others with kindness and respect, and that they were resourceful and creative in finding solutions were invited to the 'Living@KHDA' programme, a three-month immersive experience during which they worked with different teams on different projects, gaining an understanding of the organisation, and often finding new skills and talents they were unaware they had.

The second victim to fall was the job description. Our existing employees wanted the opportunity to keep learning and try something new, with many asking to transfer to another department, to start projects not directly related to their job titles or departments, or to split their work between two or three departments. The lack of set criteria of duties enabled our people to be more creative and to take more control over their happiness at work. If they wanted, they could even leave their job – without having to leave KHDA.

The third casualty of our improved wellbeing was the annual performance review – the dreaded document that employees completed once a year, scarcely referred to, yet depended on to grow and progress within the organisation. As we were increasingly working on cross-functional projects, line managers were no longer best placed to judge how well their team members had 'performed.' We could not rely on old processes to drive new ways of working: if our team members were judged and not appreciated, if performance criteria were forced upon them and not determined by them, as long as 'performance' only mattered once a year, there would be little incentive for them to go out of their comfort zones and learn how much they were truly capable of giving.

Two new peer-recognition platforms were introduced – again, by a team made up of people from different parts of KHDA. The first of these was Pearls – an online platform through which colleagues can openly post their appreciation of each other's work. Pearls are linked to the character attributes we most appreciate in our people – positivity, curiosity, creativity, reliability and approachability – and each carries a monetary value, payable at the end of each quarter.

From Pearls grew the idea of 'Awesome Achievers.' To determine who had learned and grown most as an individual, and who had given the best of themselves to the organisation, colleagues nominated themselves, their teams, and each other. This programme gave us the gift of reflection – thinking about what we were truly capable of achieving, taking notice of the achievements of others, and using that as inspiration for our own growth and development. Taken together, Pearls and Awesome Achievers now form the basis of performance management, which incidentally values not performance, but personal growth and giving, and which does not manage it but enables it.

5 Ways of Wellbeing

These structural improvements helped to transform the culture of KHDA. Over time, our people became more open to new ideas, more welcoming of change, and more likely to initiate change themselves. To enable our colleagues to 'Keep Learning,' we began hosting talks at KHDA, given by local and international visitors. A library was set up to encourage our people to spend more time reading. A personal development fund was established to give colleagues the freedom to attend training and learning programmes of their choice.

We were encouraged to 'Give' by participating in charitable activities throughout our community – at hospitals, at special needs centres, at mosques and at animal rescue centres – and by making more time to help each other during our working day. We established a programme with an orphanage in Banda Aceh, Indonesia that enabled teams to travel and spend a week working with the children and their carers. These trips were funded partly by KHDA, and partly by fundraising activities we held throughout the year. We learned to 'Take Notice' by beginning our meetings with mindfulness exercises and by practicing an 'attitude of gratitude', sharing the small things that we were grateful for throughout the day.

Our office environment, meanwhile, made it easier for us to 'Connect'. We replaced standard-issue carpets and cubicles with sofas, mobile desks, beanbags and green spaces. Rather than an 'open-door' policy, we established a 'no-door' policy, with communal areas taking the place of private offices.

In the KHDA lobby, people mingle freely and have conversations over coffee, often entertained by someone playing on the baby grand piano, or by our parrot screeching his welcome as customers arrive. Guests are indistinguishable from employees; board members are no different from new joiners.

To help us 'Be Active' we integrated a fully functioning gym into our workspace. A 300m running track around the perimeter of the office served as the warm-up for daily fitness sessions before and after work. A boxing ring helped us to release stress, while a yoga room with daily classes helped us to channel it more positively.

KHDA regularly began participating in races and obstacle races such as the Desert Warrior Challenge and the Spartan Race. Our first participation in this type of event included a team of ten colleagues – all committed to exercise and fitness. In our most recent race, we entered a team of 70, made up of people who had never previously considered taking part in such an endeavour, and who found new joy within themselves for having done it.

Our working practices, too, nurtured greater happiness in our people. Mothers with young children were able to spend less time at work and more time at home; an on-site nursery allowed parents to stay near their children while they were at the office; flexible hours and working from home were options available to our team, depending on the type of work they did.

All these changes helped to establish a culture of change at KHDA, a culture of collaboration and creativity, and above all, a culture of trust. 92% of our people completed the most recent Happiness Survey, scoring an overall 7.6, putting us in the top 10% of organisations worldwide. While there was still plenty of room for improvement, the practices we had put in place were clearly working.

Now that we were happier with what we saw in the mirror, we turned our attention again to the window. We began to engage our community of school leaders, teachers, parents and students more deeply in the conversation around happiness.

At that time, What Works dedicated two events to happiness, bringing in internationally renowned speakers and practitioners to inspire and inform principals and teachers. We partnered with the International Positive Education Network to set up a regional office in Dubai, tasked with raising awareness and cultivating more positive education practices in schools. We invited the Institute of Positive Education at Geelong Grammar School to give positive education workshops to teachers. Conferences, meetings, and other events became a platform through which we could talk about the benefits of happiness for individuals, for the education sector and for Dubai.

The momentum of change

We were caught up in this momentum of change, encouraged by the support of our people and the success of our initiatives. Yet this change did not exist in a vacuum: it was the outcome of living in a young city that thrived on innovation and change; a city with bold leadership that welcomed disruption; a city whose success was determined not by the height of its buildings, but by the happiness of its people. In 2015, the UAE was the first country in the world to appoint a Minister of State for Happiness and Wellbeing. Happiness initiatives were introduced throughout government and the private sector. Happiness was no longer an abstract concept; it was a national objective.

We saw the goal ahead of us, we felt the momentum of our city behind us, and we took inspiration from the people working beside us. We began to introduce more initiatives for parents, students, teachers and principals to enable them to integrate more wellbeing into their practices, and to live happier lives.

For students

Inspired by the Sorrell Foundation's National Saturday Club, we launched the Dubai Saturday Clubs in 2016. Designed to build students' empathy, creativity, collaboration and communication skills, Dubai Saturday Clubs was a service-driven programme that brought students from different schools across Dubai together with social entrepreneurs to design and create meaningful projects that benefited the community – all while having fun and building friendships with each other.

The Hatta Wellbeing Campus – located two hours from Dubai – provided students with the opportunity to trade their indoor classroom for an outdoor one, enabling them to get closer to nature, to learn about sustainability and to practice mindfulness. We have recently launched a programme for teachers at the Hatta Wellbeing Campus, helping them rejuvenate and recharge in a new environment, and providing them with physical and mental space to engage and connect with each other.

For teachers

Too often the media narrative around teachers and teaching is negative, pointing to an overregulated system that breeds stress, resentment, and poor learning outcomes. Yet we knew from the teachers we met every day that this wasn't the complete picture. Across Dubai were thousands of teachers who loved what they did, who got a deep sense of fulfilment from their work and who enriched their students' lives. But when we looked around to find positive stories about teachers like these, we found a near barren landscape.

Inspired by Humans of New York, a that which tells the stories of ordinary New Yorkers through photographs and quotes, we started our own version for teachers of Dubai on World Teachers' Day in October 2015. Using social media, Teachers of Dubai tells the stories of teachers in their own words, helping to bring the community together in support of teachers and teaching. More than 500 teachers from across Dubai's schools have shared their stories on Teachers of Dubai so far.

Through comments and replies, we've seen wonderful interaction from our local community – from parents thanking their children's teachers; to other teachers showing appreciation for their colleagues; to ex-students expressing their gratitude for their teachers' role in their education. Some teachers who have been featured on Teachers of Dubai have told us that they felt like celebrities the day their stories were published, such was the support and love they received from students, parents and other teachers. By spreading the positive stories of teaching in Dubai and the around the world, we could encourage appreciation of teachers, instill a greater sense of pride in current teachers, and inspire a generation of future teachers.

In April 2017, we started the Teach Together initiative. During Teach Together, I became a teacher's assistant – photocopying, mopping up spills, handing out materials – so that I could better understand teachers' experience of their work, and so that KHDA could co-create policies and wellbeing initiatives for teachers that are founded on empathy.

During my Teach Together experience, I gained new skills in cooking, painting and swimming, and I also gained insights into what great teachers have in common. Interestingly, these were not skills, nor knowledge, nor experience. Great teachers brought empathy, love and joy to their classrooms. Children were happy in class and eager to learn and showed the same kindness to each other as the teacher showed to them. As the old adage goes, 'students don't care how much you know, until they know how much you care.'

For teachers to care, they must love what they do, and for them to love what they do, they must have a strong sense of wellbeing. In fact, we cannot hope to improve students' wellbeing without also considering the wellbeing of teachers. Studies conducted in the UK and elsewhere have found a clear correlation between teacher wellbeing and student outcomes. Yet, it's also important to remember that we are not focusing on teachers' happiness and wellbeing simply because of their influence on our children, but because teachers are people too. Teachers are also parents, they are our friends, they are our neighbours, and all of them are important members of our community. We believe that the wellbeing of teachers is important because we believe that the wellbeing of people is important.

For principals

School principals have taken part in the Lighthouse initiative since 2014. Taking on a different shape every year, Lighthouse brings school principals together to work on projects and build collaborative relationships. The latest iteration of Lighthouse involved principals becoming students again, experiencing what their students experience every day, with a view to increasing empathy and enabling more wellbeing. Because of her experience of being a student, one principal realised how much discomfort school ties caused children in the summer months and decided to remove them from the uniform. We were inspired to see the quality and quantity of changes principals made when they focused on the child – rather than the curriculum – to improve wellbeing.

For parents

Since 2017, KHDA has been hosting regular positive parenting workshops for mothers and fathers who want to learn more about how they can bring out the best from within their children and help them to flourish, both at school and in life. Run by local and international practitioners, these workshops have featured topics such as dealing positively with problem behaviours, identifying children's character strengths, building hope and pride in young children, and improving children's wellbeing through better nutrition. The response to these workshops has been phenomenal – parents are sharing their learning on social media, telling their friends and helping to spread the messages of positivity and wellbeing. More than 700 parents have attended the workshops in the last 12 months, a number we expect to increase in the next 12.

Positive education takes hold

Our engagement with our community, and their engagement with each other, is crucial if we hope to improve wellbeing in Dubai and together build a future in which we will all flourish. We've been humbled and heartened to see schools and teachers begin to make – and continue to make – real and meaningful changes to bring wellbeing into the heart of their curriculum and their pedagogy.

One new school in Dubai – committed to the tenets of positive education – provides intensive training to each of its teachers before they start work. As well as an in-house positive education team responsible for embedding positive education into the school, the school has set up a wellbeing department with trained counsellors. It teaches positive education implicitly and explicitly, and regularly invites parents to attend positive education workshops.

Another school has renovated a classroom into a mindfulness and wellbeing room, adding smart tablets loaded with guided meditation routines, a gratitude tree for students to display what they are thankful for, a sensory room with a range of stimuli and a positive affirmation space to maintain good mental health.

We are aware of several schools that have incorporated mindfulness into the curriculum, as well as reassessed their student discipline policies to focus not on punishment, but on empathy and kindness. Many schools have appointed non-teaching Heads of Positive Education at primary and secondary school levels to adapt the curriculum towards wellbeing and support more wellbeing for students and teachers.

Approximately 30% of Dubai private schools now have dedicated full-time staff that focus on positive education and wellbeing – a figure echoing the 30% of students who attended good or better-quality schools ten years ago. As a community, we are at the beginning of our positive education journey. As we progress, we must be mindful to not confuse inputs with outcomes, and we must be diligent in providing our community with the data it needs to form evidence-based policies that truly improve wellbeing.

School of Hearts

In 2015 and 2016 we partnered with American research firm WestEd to develop School of Hearts, an opt-in survey designed to measure the wellbeing of late primary and middle school students in Dubai. 69,000 students, parents and teachers from 98 schools answered questions on physical wellbeing, relationships with adults, and relationships with others, with 96% of parents telling us that their children enjoyed school, and 95% of teachers stating that they enjoyed working at their school. School of Hearts was our first attempt to measure student wellbeing in Dubai, and paved the way for a more comprehensive, holistic measurement tool – the Dubai Student Wellbeing Census.

Dubai Student Wellbeing Census

Partnering with the Department of Education and Child Development of the Government of South Australia – which had many years of experience of conducting a similar census in their own schools and other school systems around the world – we embarked on a five-year project to measure, improve and switch the light on student wellbeing in Dubai. Conducted for the first time in November 2017, the Dubai Student Wellbeing Census was completed by 65,000 middle school students across 168 schools, answering questions about their happiness, their relationships at home and at school, and their lifestyle, among others.

Each participating school received an individualised report, and teachers attended workshops designed to help them interpret the data, as well as use them to formulate plans to improve their students' wellbeing over the next 12 months.

The results of the Census told us that 84% of students are happy most of the time, that 77% of them feel safe at school, and that 76% enjoy close relationships with friends at their school. It also told us that three main contributing factors to wellbeing are a good breakfast, a good night's sleep, and good relationships with adults. These results make it clear that wellbeing is not just the responsibility of schools, or of parents, or of teachers, or of regulators, but of all of us working together so that our children can thrive and be happy.

The death of management hierarchy

As progressed in our wellbeing and happiness journey, we learned the skill of looking out of the window and into the mirror at the same time. The 5 Ways of Wellbeing were now embedded into our processes and our culture, and our people had risen to the challenge of taking control of their own work and wellbeing. Again we looked at the strengths of our team and scrutinised our systems and processes to ensure they were still fit for purpose. They were not.

Our people were taking initiative and starting projects they felt were important; they were working in roles outside of their job description and established skill set; they were forming teams based not on shared functions but on shared passions; they were relying not on their line managers for support, but on each other. It was clear that the time had come for management hierarchy to go.

In 2017, we started implementing a new self-management system based on Holacracy, a corporate governance framework developed by Holacracy One in the United States and implemented in several organisations in the US and Europe. Our work is organised in circles, roles and accountabilities. Each circle serves a purpose aligned to the purpose of the organisation, and each role has accountabilities aligned to the purpose of the circle. Holacracy is based on making progress, not building consensus; on autonomy, not approvals; on self-development, not promotions.

Doing away with management hierarchy may sound like a dramatic step for a government organisation to make, yet the changes we had made up to that point prepared us to be adaptable and flexible in our practices and mindset, to be open to new experiences and to be prepared to see them fail.

Education never stops moving, and continuous improvement demands continuous innovation. It is what we expect of our schools, and it is what we expect of ourselves. We look back at the progress we have made personally and professionally in the last ten years, and we look ahead with wonder and excitement at the progress we will make in the next ten.

Ten years into the future, in just two years

We are currently involved in 10x – a Dubai Future Foundation initiative to take Dubai ten years into the future – in just two years. Our contribution to 10x is *Rahhal*. Meaning traveller in Arabic, the message of Rahhal is simple: the world is a classroom, and all learning counts. Rahhal is a fully customisable platform that will help turn anyone, and any organisation, into a learning provider, and turn all of us into lifelong learners. It will be a conduit that harnesses the community's knowledge and skills and channels it to each individual learner. And the best part? All learning on the platform will be given the stamp of approval by Dubai government.

Rahhal provides a creative and innovative alternative to mainstream education – an alternative that brings out the best from within the community and recognises learning wherever it occurs. It is a platform that helps to integrate learning with life, and life with learning.

By providing a supportive regulatory environment, *Rahhal* will enhance learning opportunities for all members of the community, whether they are children or adults. It will support learners with special education needs as well as those with special gifts and talents; it will diversify the choices for parents who wish to supplement their children's education; and it will provide adults with a flexible, modular form of learning that can be used to further their careers, enrich their lives and enable them to flourish. United by a grand vision and a common purpose, we are currently working with parents, schools, government bodies and private organisations to bring Rahhal to life.

A simple answer to a simple question

Our vision for education in Dubai, for our organisation, and for ourselves, is simple: to not only do well, but to be well; to be in harmony with nature, with each other, and with ourselves; to keep looking out of the window and into the mirror; to learn from and give inspiration to others; and to live in a world where the only meaningful answer to the question: 'what do you want to be when you grow up' is 'happy'.

Lightning Source UK Ltd.
Milton Keynes UK
UKHW02f0052020918
328164UK00006B/141/P

9 781911 382782